GHOSTS & GALLOWS

TRUE STORIES OF CRIME & THE PARANORMAL

PAUL ADAMS

For my father, Arthur P. Adams (1919-2004),
of whom my memories are of nothing but kindness.

First published 2012

The History Press
The Mill, Brimscombe Port
Stroud, Gloucestershire, GL5 2QG
www.thehistorypress.co.uk

British Library Cataloguing in Publication Data.
A catalogue record for this book is available from the British Library.

ISBN 978 0 7524 6339 1

Typesetting and origination by The History Press
Printed in Great Britain

GHOSTS & GALLOWS

TRUE STORIES OF CRIME & THE PARANORMAL

CONTENTS

ACKNOWLEDGEMENTS

I would like to thank and acknowledge the help of a number of people, who, either through supplying information, assisting with and allowing the reproduction of illustrations, or by their general encouragement and support, have made the writing of this book not only possible, but for someone embarking on their first extended solo work, more of an enjoyable experience and less like the 'Loneliness of the Long Distance Runner'. I am indebted to Richard Lee Van den Daele, Steve Fielding, Eddie Brazil, Rob Nicholson, Peter Underwood, Charles Beck, Phil Baker, Tony Broughall, Richard Clarke, Keith Stokes, Veronica Keen, Rita Goold, Bob Cracknell, Andy York, Donald Whannel, Chris Hobbs, Keith Brannen, Stephen Butt, Glynis Baxter at St Edmundsbury Borough Council, Andrew Leah, Paul Heslop, John Mooney, the Governors of HMP Walton, HMP Manchester and HMP Hull, the Metropolitan Police Crime Museum, Mark Slater at Manchester City Council, the staff at the National Archives, the staff at Leagrave Public Library and St Albans Central Library, Janice Fleckney, Jane Santana, Matilda Richards at The History Press, and especially to Aban, Idris, Isa and Sakina, for their patience and inspiration.

INTRODUCTION

Around lunchtime on 10 October 1977, Detective Chief Inspector Tony Fletcher, head of the Fingerprint Bureau of the Greater Manchester Police, received a call to attend a crime scene at a section of disused allotments near Princess Road in the Chorlton district of Manchester, where the naked body of a young woman had been found by two local men. When Fletcher, an experienced police officer, arrived, his initial thought was that a maniac had exhumed and violated a body from the adjacent Southern Cemetery; it was only when a search of the immediate area recovered items of female clothing: a skirt, cardigan, boots and underwear, that it became clear a horrific crime had taken place. Fletcher fingerprinted the body and the following day visited the home of Alan Royle, who had reported his common-law wife Jean Royle, also known as Jean Jordan, as missing. From a fingerprint match found in the house, as well as Royle's description of his wife's clothing, the identity was established. Results from a post-mortem examination quickly confirmed to the Greater Manchester Police that a brutal serial killer – who had already murdered five women in the west of Yorkshire over the preceding two years – had now finally crossed the Pennines: Jean Jordan had become the sixth victim of the infamous 'Yorkshire Ripper'. Seven months later, DCI Fletcher was called to the grounds of the Manchester Royal Infirmary, where he fingerprinted the body of another woman whose injuries, and the circumstances in which she had been found, made it immediately clear that the murderer had claimed another – his ninth – victim. It would not be until twenty months later that the killer, who ultimately went on to claim a further four lives, would be brought to justice, and the case is one we will return to in due course.

As well as the numerous crime scenes, some gruesome, many others mundane, at which Fletcher was called upon to carry out fingerprint work during the course of his professional police career, there were other more specific and at times quite bizarre assignments, such as the fingerprinting of Harold, an orang-utan (known to his keepers as 'Harold the Bastard') at Belle Vue Zooological Gardens, as well as Asru, an Egyptian mummy which makes up part of the collection held at the archaeology department of the Manchester Museum. Despite their unusualness, perhaps the most *outré* task ever to come his way took place sixteen years before his involvement with the Ripper inquiry, when Fletcher was approached by a Manchester ghost hunter with a request to attempt to obtain the fingerprints of a phantom . . .

The Manchester Psychical Research Society was a small paranormal group particularly active in the late 1950s and early '60s – a time when ghost hunting was looked on in the UK as an interesting hobby carried out by an eccentric minority rather than the full-scale entertainment industry that cable and satellite television has attempted to make it in the past ten years. Under the Honorary Presidency of George A. Knowlson BA of Rishton, Bradford – a retired headmaster with an interest in the supernormal – the society met on Tuesday evenings at the Milton Hall in Deansgate, Manchester for lectures and discussions on the many aspects of psychic phenomena and spiritualism. The organisation's Investigation Officer and leading light was David Cohen, a machine operator in his early fifties. By day Cohen stitched raincoats in a Manchester factory, while his nights, weekends and holidays were given over almost exclusively to a determined and enthusiastic study of poltergeists, mediums and hauntings.

In the spring of 1959, Cohen had been asked to visit an unassuming house in the Fallowfield district of South Manchester. The owner, a recently widowed woman with a teenage son and a younger daughter, claimed their terraced house was haunted by the ghost of an old man named Nicholas, who appeared to the young boy in his bedroom at night and, in what must be a first where the paranormal is concerned, played Ravel's *Bolero* on the youth's own violin. Over the course of several months the mother had heard the sound of music (always the same piece) coming from the adjacent bedroom, and on every occasion when she had gotten out of bed and looked into the room, her son was apparently asleep with the violin closed away in its case. Distressed by what was happening, the woman had eventually tackled the teenager about the bizarre music and he had calmly explained the reason behind the nocturnal concerts. Relieved that she was not suffering a breakdown, and in the hope that the ghostly musician could be persuaded to leave, the lady contacted the Manchester Psychical Research Society and its Investigation Officer quickly swung into action.

Cohen and other members of the society began holding séances in the living room of the Fallowfield house in an attempt to establish contact with 'Nicholas'. These experiments continued regularly for a period of two years and, by the beginning of 1961, had successfully progressed to the point that during blackout phases of the séance meetings, a pair of hands apparently began to materialise and interact with the sitters. It is at this point that Cohen approached Tony Fletcher, then recently appointed to the Greater Manchester Police's Fingerprint Bureau, and the case changed from a *Blithe Spirit*-type scenario into something far more interesting.

During the 1930s, materialised 'spirit' hands which had appeared at séances given by an American medium known as 'Margery' had left impressions in specially prepared wax that were later discovered to be fake; the fingerprints, rather than belonging to a spirit control, were in fact those of the family dentist who was very much alive. Mindful of the 'Margery' exposure, Cohen wished to recruit the services of a professional fingerprint expert who would attend one of his Fallowfield séances in order to take the prints of the materialised Nicholas, which would then be compared with the hands of all the sitters in the room. If either the mother or her son were playing tricks, then the test would quickly show who the violin-playing spectre really was. On the other hand, literally, there was a hope that what would be produced was physical evidence of a genuine materialisation.

Unfortunately for Cohen, Fletcher declined to co-operate (a decision he later admitted he regretted) as he didn't believe in ghosts and felt becoming involved in the affair would make him appear foolish. However, Sergeant Rowland Mason, a colleague of Fletcher's and a well-respected member of the Bureau, was less sceptical and eventually agreed to take part, albeit in a private capacity. Mason visited the house accompanied by David Cohen and attended two séances, which were held on Friday evenings. He quickly became mystified by his experiences. In the darkened room the table, around which the woman, her son, Cohen and the policeman were sitting, rose into the air and practically touched the ceiling; a tambourine marked with luminous paint began moving about the room, constantly changing its direction and travelling at such a speed that it seemed impossible that anyone present could be faking the effect, while the table itself shook violently and loud knocks sounded across its surface. The highlight of the second sitting was the manifestation of what purported to be the hands of Nicholas himself, which in the blackness touched Mason on the shoulders and arms. These hands have been described by David Cohen as being 'dry and scaly' and having lace cuffs over the wrists, although Mason at that time was only able to feel their touch and could not confirm the appearance.

At a third séance, the policeman decided to try and catch the ghost's fingerprints by surreptitiously dusting the tambourine prior to the commencement of the sitting. Alone in the living room, he managed to wipe the instrument clean, dust it with mercury powder and replace it on the sideboard without anyone apparently noticing. Soon after the blackout séance had begun, Mason was shocked to suddenly have the duster with which he had wiped the edges of the tambourine – and had left lying on the sideboard – thrown into his face. A recording of Ravel's *Bolero* was played on a portable tape machine and, as before, there were levitations and knocks on the table and the tambourine flew wildly about the room. When the lights came on, Rowland quickly seized the tambourine and dusted it with fingerprint powder. To his astonishment, the instrument was as clean as he had left it at the beginning of the sitting. On a fourth visit, he openly dusted the tambourine before the commencement of the séance and again it was found to be clean at the end of the evening, despite having been seen to rise from the sideboard and circle the room. At this séance, 'Nicholas' was asked by David Cohen whether he would consent to have his fingerprints taken and, through a series of knocks on the table, replied in the affirmative.

At the next séance, Mason brought a chemically charged pad and sensitized paper to the house and placed it on the séance table in front of him. During the course of the sitting, Mason was able to catch hold of what appeared to be a dry human hand in the darkness and, with his own free hand, guided it first to the fingerprint pad and then to the specially prepared paper. Despite the blackout, the policeman was confident that he had managed to bring about what appeared to be the first professional fingerprinting of a paranormal entity. The next morning, Mason brought the paper to the Bureau and showed it to his colleagues. Instead of a set of fingerprints, they were able to see a strange set of marks which resembled three parallel scratches, each about one inch in length. 'They could have been made by a bird's claw; they could equally have been made by three fingernails scratching the paper,' was how Tony Fletcher, who inspected the marks personally, later described them.

The final stage of this unofficial police investigation into the musical ghost was an attempt to capture a photograph of Nicholas himself using a camera loaded with infra-red film. For this, an experienced police photographer named John Cheetham agreed to visit Fallowfield. He attended a preliminary séance where he reported similar experiences to Rowland Mason – the table knocked and levitated, the tambourine danced about the room and Cheetham and his wife, who accompanied him, were touched on several occasions by what appeared to be two hands in the darkness. It was agreed that the following week, the photographer would set up a camera on a tripod aimed and focused at an armchair in a corner of the séance room and, during the course of the sitting, Nicholas would be invited to sit in the chair and the camera would be operated using a cable-release.

The séance took place and at the prescribed point in the proceedings, Cheetham took his infra-red photograph. The resulting print, which was developed at the police laboratory the following morning in front of an expectant crowd of Scenes of Crime officers, showed only an empty chair with a large cushion resting against the back. Nicholas had failed to appear, or had he? Although a simulacrum is the most likely explanation, several of the policemen, including Tony Fletcher, thought that they could see the outline 'of a very old man, bearded and turned to the right, rather like the head of the old king on a coin' amongst the creases in the chair cushion. If the photographer had been able to take his infra-red picture while either the tambourine was in flight or Rowland Mason was fingerprinting the 'spirit' hands, perhaps something far more interesting would have appeared, but ultimately Cheetham joined the ranks of a number of investigators who have been unsuccessful in effectively bringing infra-red technology into the séance room.

At this point the case of Nicholas the musical ghost, including the unofficial involvement of the Greater Manchester Police, was published in a national newspaper, effectively bringing the investigation to an end. The presence of the policemen, despite the fact that no official police time had been used, came to the attention of the Chief Superintendent of the Greater Manchester CID who requested both men to make written reports, which were completed and filed. Whether Cohen and his team succeeded in 'laying' the ghost is unclear, as the Manchester researcher was soon moving on to other things. The case remains a mystery to this day.

As we will see during the course of this book, tales of ghosts and gallows have been with us since time immemorial, as the perpetual human fascination with the strange world of the paranormal is matched only by humankind's continuing inability to escape from a self-induced and continuous campaign of violence and murder. The involvement of the Manchester Police in David Cohen's case of the eerie Fallowfield hands is an interesting fusion of the two, but for the psychical researcher and ghost hunter, the organised and serious investigation of hauntings and psychic phenomena is in itself a unique and specialised form of detective work involving a complex mixture – and understanding of – human psychology, investigative reporting and scientific experimentation.

It is interesting to compare the views of respected personalities involved in both fields – criminal investigation and paranormal investigation – as they are both remarkably similar. Peter Underwood, President of the famous Ghost

Club for over thirty years and one of Britain's most experienced paranormal researchers, has described in his 1986 book *The Ghost Hunter's Guide* the ghost hunter as someone who seeks 'to discover and record as objectively as possible what people have experienced or believe they have experienced and seek by experimentation to establish scientifically or demolish the reported phenomena'. Writing in his *Memories of Murder*, published the same year as Underwood's comments, Tony Fletcher felt the best piece of advice he could offer to a young policeman was to remain open-minded:

> [w]hether, as in the case of Asru the mummy, he needs to be looking into the past or, because of the need for computerization, the future must be comprehended or, as in the case of the ghost Nicholas, the unknown must be respected, he should always try to look at things with a fresh and open mind.

Both the psychical researcher and the policeman, despite the politics, media scrutiny and entertainment exploitation of their individual professions, are continually involved in a diligent and patient search for the truth.

This book is a collection of accounts of British murders that have some connection with the world of the unseen: psychic detection, prophetic dreams, mediumship, as well as ghosts and hauntings associated with both murderers and their victims. In order to establish the relevance and introduce particular aspects of the various cases under discussion – both criminal and paranormal – I have, out of necessity, made mention of and included material from other sources, such as various international cases of murder and psychic phenomena, which I feel are pertinent to the discussions at hand. I also have a personal interest in the history of psychical research and the development of organised paranormal investigation, with the result that some aspects of this fascinating and engaging subject have found their way into the cases that you are about to encounter.

Paul Adams
Luton, Bedfordshire
2012

CHAPTER 1

THE HILL OF CHRISTIE SPECTRE

SERGEANT DAVIES, 1754

Early one morning at the beginning of June 1750, a young shepherd, Alexander MacPherson, left his master's sheiling hut at Glen Clunie, a remote spot in the Cairngorm Mountains over forty miles north-east of Dundee, and set out across the lonely but familiar hillside in the general direction of Dubrach. The landscape was wild and uninhabited but MacPherson made his way with practiced ease around the treacherous mountain bogs and windswept rocks. As he approached an expanse of moorland tract known locally as the Hill of Christie, the Highlander slowed his pace and quickly took stock of the locality before moving forward again, this time seeking out a particular spot amongst the peat moss.

After a short time of searching, MacPherson located a steep bank and began pulling with his staff at a bundle clearly visible under an overhang. Part of the object quickly revealed itself to be a human head, practically decayed down to a skull, but with lengths of mouse-coloured hair still attached and tied back with a faded black ribbon; the rest of the corpse, still wearing a pair of brown brogues and partly covered by strips of faded and weather-beaten material, had also been reduced to a skeleton, which the shepherd now drew out from under the sphagnum. Unsettling as this discovery no doubt was, MacPherson was prepared for it, as he later testified that he had been given specific instructions on where to find the body of this unfortunate person who had been missing, presumed dead, for nearly nine months. The young shepherd had, so he later declared, been given his information by the ghost of the very man whose ravaged remains now lay scattered at his feet. It was a supernatural encounter that was ultimately to make its way without precedent four years later to the High Court of Justiciary at Edinburgh.

MacPherson's grim discovery on the lonely Highland moor was played out in the immediate aftermath of the 'Forty-Five', the last great Jacobite uprising which saw the Young Pretender, Charles Edward Stuart, attempt to reclaim the British throne for the House of Stuart, then in exile in France. On 16 April 1745, a weary Jacobite army, already in retreat, was routed by William, Duke of Cumberland at Culloden. Over 1,500 of Stuart's men were killed and in the weeks that followed, amid Cumberland's brutal repercussions as defeated Jacobites were hunted down and brought to trial, the Bonnie Prince became a fugitive before finally escaping on a French frigate to the Continent.

The Hanoverian government was quick to put in place measures to quell any future revolt and to stamp out the last embers of the rebellion as those of Stuart's fighters who had escaped imprisonment or execution melted back into the Highlands. Parliament passed the Heritable Jurisdictions Act of 1746 that stripped the Scottish lords of much of their power, while the Proscription Act of the same year was a powerful measure to destroy the clan system by outlawing traditional Highland dress – anyone caught wearing tartan faced a prison sentence of up to six months and transportation for a second offence. Garrisons were established in districts where Stuart sympathisers were suspected of remaining active and these supplied troops to smaller outposts in rural locations who carried out regular patrols, constantly on the lookout for signs of underground rebellion or resistance to the new laws.

One such station was located at Dubrach, a small upland farmstead in the clachen of Inverey in Braemar (the last place in eastern Scotland where Gaelic was still spoken in the 1930s) and two miles from where Alexander MacPherson lodged with his employers, the MacHardie family. In June 1749, a picket of eight footsoldiers from Lieutenant-General Guise's regiment stationed at Aberdeen took up a billet at this lonely post, while a second detachment from the same company occupied a similar position at the Spittal of Glen Shee, around eight miles away. Patrols from both stations kept the immediate countryside under close observation and met regularly twice a week at a location equidistant from their respective headquarters to exchange information. An un-named corporal officiated at Glen Shee while at Dubrach, Guise's men were under the command of Sergeant Arthur Davies, a newly married man whose wife was the widow of the former paymaster of the regiment.

Davies was to spend little short of four months at his billet but during this time, despite being an obvious hate figure for the Highlanders around him, managed to garner a certain amount of respect from the locals through a tactful and somewhat moderate approach in enforcing the laws of the land.

Writing about the case for his *Twelve Scots Trials* (1913), William Roughead describes Davies as a likeable man 'of a genial disposition, a keen and indefatigable sportsman, fearless, thrifty, and particular in his dress.' Despite these welcome characteristics, they were ultimately to prove disastrous. Additionally, the Englishman's individual approach to policing the district, namely going out alone in advance of his men on both the outward and return leg of patrols to shoot game, and his habit of carrying two purses, one of green silk holding fifteen and a half guineas in gold and a second of leather containing an unspecified amount of silver 'for current expenses', became well known and were factors that lead to tragedy.

On 28 September 1749, Sergeant Davies rose early and made ready to carry out a routine midweek patrol of the district. As was the norm, the Dubrach soldiers were to meet up with their counterparts from Glen Shee and Davies set out in advance of his regular company of men dressed in his usual blue surtout coat, striped silk vest, breeches and brown stockings, and carrying his money purses and a long-barrelled musket, which had been given to him as a gift by a fellow officer. An hour after sunrise the sergeant reached Glen Clunie, where he had cause to stop and briefly detain John Growar, a kilted Highlander who, despite over three years of Proscription, was wearing a tartan coat. Luckily for Growar, he was sent on his way with a reprimand rather than being handed over to Davies' company of footsoldiers, four of whom were following at a distance. The sergeant's leniency was most likely due to his desire to spend the day 'pursuing his sport' rather than escorting a prisoner to the stockade, and, after dismissing the Scotsman, he continued on his way; the Dubrach soldiers glimpsed him briefly on the skyline as they made their way to the rendezvous, and at one point heard him fire a shot.

Later that afternoon, the Glen Shee company, having met up with the Dubrach soldiers, were returning to their billet when they came across Arthur Davies at a hollow known as the Water of Benow. The sergeant informed them that he intended to walk up onto the Hill of Christie to try and bring home a deer for his evening meal, and, despite the Glen Shee corporal's reservations on him venturing out alone at such a distance from the station, Arthur Davies, confident of being able to protect himself, parted company with the patrol and the group of soldiers turned for home. They were the last of Guise's regiment to see him alive.

The following morning it quickly became clear that Sergeant Davies had not returned from his hunting expedition and was in fact missing. The soldiers from Dubrach set out to retrace the route he had taken the previous day but despite a combined search, neither they nor the Glen Shee company could find any trace or indication of what might have taken place. On the following afternoon, a Saturday, a runner was sent to Braemar Castle and a search party mustered, which marched to Dubrach the same day. For the next four days the entire district was scoured, with the local populace being coerced into assisting with the search. However, a week to the day that the Englishman had gone missing, and with no trace as to his whereabouts, the manhunt was abandoned and the search party returned to Braemar.

Despite the rumour spread by the local Highlanders around Inverey that Sergeant Davies had simply deserted, his wife was convinced from the outset that he had been robbed and left for dead somewhere out on the wild and lonely hillsides. As well as the money purses he was known to habitually carry, Davies wore two gold rings, a silver fob watch and had a dozen silver buttons on his waistcoat, which would, she insisted, have been temptation enough for someone to waylay him on his return home to the station. His position in the army was a solid one and his fellow officers conceded that his future career within the service was assured – it was widely accepted that he would receive a promotion to Sergeant-Major at the first vacancy and, as a person, Davies was well-liked and respected throughout the entire company. This, together with the security of his marriage and the great affections of his wife soon convinced the regiment, and the district as a whole, that Sergeant Davies had in fact met a murderer – or murderers – out on the wild expanse of the Hill of Christie, although it was to be over nine months before both the regiment and his wife were to learn with certainty that she had indeed become a widow for a second time.

One night in the early summer of the following year, Alexander MacPherson awoke in his shepherding hut at Glen Clunie to find the figure of a man standing at the foot of his bed. The person, dressed in a blue coat, was solid and lifelike, and the young Highlander automatically assumed it was a brother of Donald Farquharson, his employer, who was sending word for him to attend to some matter on the farm. The figure moved silently out of the door of the hut and MacPherson rose and followed. Outside, the figure made its supernatural nature clear by announcing that he was in fact Sergeant Davies, late of Lieutenant-General Guise's regiment, and confirmed the now commonly held belief that he had been murdered the previous year. The apparition spoke in Gaelic, the only language that the Highlander was familiar with, and directed him to go to a particular spot on the Hill of Christie, where he would find the soldier's body, with the additional request that MacPherson arrange with Donald Farquharson a decent burial. The young shepherd had the courage to reply to the ghost and asked who had carried out the murder, but the figure was either unresponsive or unable to do so and immediately faded away.

Alexander MacPherson returned to his bed, telling no one of his experience. The following day he did visit the Hill of Christie, as instructed, where he recovered the sergeant's skeletal remains, which lay within a few yards of where the apparition said he would find them, and at a spot not far from where Davies had stopped and reprimanded John Growar for his tartan coat on the day of his murder. Despite this evidential outcome to his extraordinary experience, MacPherson in fact did nothing else, returning instead to Dubrach, where he kept his encounter with the spectre to himself.

A full week later, at the same time and place, the ghost of the murdered soldier appeared to the shepherd again. This time the apparition was naked but its message was the same, that MacPherson return to the lonely hillside and bury the Englishman's body. MacPherson repeated the question as to the identity of the killer and on this occasion the apparition complied, naming two local men, Duncan Clerk and Alexander MacDonald, both of dubious character, as his slayers. Having spoken, the figure of Sergeant Davies vanished and was seen no more.

Following this second visitation MacPherson spoke with two local men about his strange experience and the subsequent discovery of the bones of the murdered soldier. Both these Highlanders, the aforementioned John Growar and another, John Shaw, were unwilling to become involved and advised the shepherd to either do nothing or, if he felt inclined to carry out the apparition's bidding, to undertake the burial in secret. Fearing reprisals should it become common knowledge that the killing had been carried out by local men, on no account should he allow the military authorities to discover either the whereabouts of the body or the identity of the killers.

Taking their advice, MacPherson sent word to Donald Farquharson and the two men met. The elder Scotsman at first dismissed the Highlander's story as fantasy, but, on being told that the bones had been discovered exactly as the apparition had directed, reluctantly agreed to accompany the shepherd out to the Hill of Christie to view the remains. The two men made the trip onto the desolate hillside where the bones lay just as MacPherson had described them, now scattered about over the peat moss by the wind but still discernable as parts of a human skeleton, complete with the tattered remnants of the sergeant's blue overcoat and striped vest, and a pair of waterlogged leather brogues from which the silver buckles had been cut. Feeling it unwise to remove the remains to the local kirk for fear of discovery, and in the absence of any direct instructions from the apparition itself as to where its mortal remains should be interred, both men agreed to bury the body at the location where the killers had concealed it. A shallow grave was dug with a spade that MacPherson had brought for the purpose and the bones of the unquiet soldier were finally laid to rest without ceremony.

Despite the Highlanders' common reticence about disclosing both the location of Sergeant Davies' remains and the alleged identity of his killers, at some point after this clandestine burial, word that the Englishman's body had indeed been found on the Hill of Christie became common knowledge in the locality, most likely through the indiscretion of John Growar, with the result that over a period of time a body of evidence, albeit circumstantial, began to grow in support of the spirit's claim that both Duncan Clerk and Alexander MacDonald were involved in the murder. The locals also became aware that the two men had been named as the killers by the ghost of the murdered man.

Not long after, a local girl, Isobel Ego, who had been sent to fetch horses from the hillside, returned to Dubrach carrying a silver-laced hat. Her mother, convinced it belonged to the murdered Englishman and might summon both the garrison soldiers and the unquiet spirit of its owner in equal measure, took the hat and hid it under a stone by the side of a nearby burn. The hat was subsequently found by local children who took it to the village, where several people either saw it or temporarily had it in their possession. They included Donald Downie, a miller at Inverey, and James Small, who was employed as a managing agent on the Strowan estate, and it was he who passed it to John Cook, the barrack-master at Braemar Castle, who recognised its significance and held the item in safekeeping. John Growar evidently told about his conversation with Alexander MacPherson, as the dead sergeant's rifle was also subsequently recovered by a relative from the hillside.

John Cook at the Braemar garrison may well have been the person who finally began investigations into the rumours concerning Clerk and MacDonald, but four years were to elapse before the suspects were arrested and formally charged with the murder of Sergeant Davies. During the winter of 1753, James Small, the factor of Strowan, carried out enquiries in the district for the Sheriff-Substitute and was able to amass a collection of interesting evidence. Since the Englishman's death, Duncan Clerk, a reputed sheep-stealer who also went by the name of Duncan Terig, had married local girl Elizabeth Downie, whose gold wedding ring with a heart-shaped design was remarkably similar to one that had been on the hand of the murdered soldier, although Elizabeth was adamant that the ring had been given to her by her mother. Clerk had also become the employer of Alexander MacPherson. He apparently gave the shepherd a promissory note for £20 as an incentive to keep whatever he knew of the murder to himself, but Clerk later refused to honour it.

As a prelude to James Small's investigations, Clerk and MacDonald had been arrested in the September of 1753 and, charged with the murder of Arthur Davies, were being held at Braemar Castle (now itself a reputedly haunted building where, amongst other eerie happenings, the cries of a ghostly baby have been heard and the apparition of John Farquharson, the Black Colonel of Inverey, has been reported over the years). Towards the end of January, the prisoners were examined by the Lords Commissioners of Justiciary and the trial began in Edinburgh on Monday, 10 June 1754. A jury of Edinburgh tradesmen was sworn in and the presiding judge was Lord Justice-Clerk Alva assisted by Lords Drummore, Strichen, Elchies and Kilkerran. A panel comprising the Lord Advocate, William Grant, together with 'His Majesties Solicitors' Patrick Haldane and Alexander Home conducted the prosecution, while the two Scotsmen were defended by Alexander Lockhart and Robert Macintosh.

Lockhart and Macintosh were confident and stated in their opening remarks on the first day that they would be able to satisfy the jury as to the complete innocence of the Highlanders – the men had business in the area at the time Sergeant Davies went missing; being engaged as foresters they had a legitimate reason to be armed and would be able to prove that after they had departed from the Hill of Christie that day, the Englishman was with his company alive and well. Despite this, it soon became clear that the prosecution was able to present a compelling and seemingly unassailable raft of evidence to the contrary: Jean Ghent, the murdered man's widow, confirmed that the hat and rifle found on the hillside belonged to her husband and that she had implored Duncan Clerk, who was on friendly terms with her and her husband, and therefore knew his habit of carrying money on his person, to assist the search party once he had gone missing; Donald Farquharson testified to burying the bones where he had found them in the company of Alexander MacPherson, and also stated that he had seen a ring identical to that worn by Davies on the hand of Duncan Clerk's wife; Peter M'Nab, a neighbour of Clerk's, together with Elspeth Macara, a servant, also stated they had seen the same ring on a number of occasions, while James MacDonald of Allanquoich claimed that Alexander Downie, Clerk's father-in-law, had confessed to him that her knew his daughter's husband was the murderer.

Other witnesses said they saw the two men depart for the Hill of Christie on the morning that Davies went missing, each armed with a rifle, but their explanation was that they were intending to spend the day hunting deer, and that Alexander MacDonald subsequently was seen carrying a penknife very similar to one known to belong to the murdered man.

Alexander MacPherson also took the stand, describing the supernatural encounter which had led both to the discovery of Arthur Davies' skeleton and the names of the alleged murderers from the lips of the very man's own ghost.

As compelling and astonishing as the sum of this information no doubt was, the Crown's most powerful piece of testimony came from Angus Cameron, a Highlander from Rannoch. In the autumn of 1749, Cameron, together with a companion of the same name, was in hiding from the authorities on suspicion of inciting a local uprising in the region and had spent the night of 27/28 September in a hideout on a hillside at Glen Bruar. The following day, in anticipation of a meeting with a group of fellow political fugitives from Lochaber, they took up refuge in a hollow on the Hill of Galcharn and, around midday, while waiting for their co-conspirators to arrive, saw two men approaching from a distance. From their vantage point, Angus Cameron recognised one of these men as Duncan Clerk, a person whom he knew by sight. Both Highlanders were armed and passed by close to where Cameron and his compatriot were hiding, before moving on without being aware that they had been observed.

Later on that day, towards sunset, while still sheltering on the hillside, Angus and Duncan Cameron observed a figure in a blue coat carrying a rifle 'about a gun-shot off' on a rise opposite. Soon after, walking up the hill towards him, came into view the two men they had spied upon earlier in the day. The three figures met on the brow of the hill and after a short time Angus Cameron saw one of the Highlanders strike out at the blue-coated figure, who recoiled and made to move away, upon which the two men raised their rifles and as one shot the man dead. Shocked by what they had seen, the watchers 'deemed it prudent to beat a retreat' and, scrambling away from the hollow unobserved, they left the area. It was not until the summer of 1750 that Angus Cameron became aware of the mystery surrounding the disappearance of Arthur Davies and quickly realised that he and his companion had in fact witnessed his murder. By the time he was empanelled to testify at the trial in Edinburgh, Duncan Cameron had been executed, leaving Angus to explain that he had kept the facts of the matter to himself as he feared reprisals by the military authorities.

Lockhart and Macintosh attempted to prove that Clerk and MacDonald had been elsewhere on the day of the killing, and railed against the wealth of circumstantial evidence and the eyewitness testimony of Angus Cameron. At six o'clock on the evening of 12 June, the jury unanimously found Duncan Clerk and Alexander MacDonald not guilt of the murder of Sergeant Arthur Davies and the two men were dismissed from the court. The defence council, it seems, found that they were able to turn one piece of the Crown's evidence against the prosecutors, namely the supernatural testimony of Alexander MacPherson. It is easy to see how, for when the shepherd was cross-examined and asked specifically what language the ghost addressed him, the Highlander responded, 'As good Gaelic as I ever heard in Lochabar', prompting Alexander Lockhart to wisely respond, 'Pretty well for the ghost of an English sergeant'.

Sir Walter Scott (1771-1832), who published an account of the Davies case for the nationalist Bannatyne Club, included mention of the trial again in his *Letters on Demonology and Witchcraft* (1830), in which he felt that 'although there were other strong presumptions against the prisoners, the story of the apparition threw an air of ridicule on the whole evidence for the prosecution', something that the jury clearly agreed with. Sir Walter was of the opinion that MacPherson, having found the remains of the Englishman during the course of his normal business on the hillside, and knowing of the local suspicion regarding Clerk and MacDonald, invented the story of the spectre in order to avoid being branded as an informer. 'To have informed . . . might have cost MacPherson his life; and it is far from being impossible that he had recourse to the story of the ghost, knowing well that his superstitious countrymen would pardon his communicating the commission intrusted to him by a being from the other world,' adding, '. . . we know too little of the other world to judge whether all languages may not be alike familiar to those who belong to it.'

Scott may well have been correct as at this distance of time it is difficult to cast new light on this interesting case. However, during the trial, support was given to MacPherson's account by Isobel MacHardie, the wife of his employer, who stated that she also saw the apparition on the occasion of its second visit. Awoken during the night, she was aware of a naked figure which entered 'in a bowing posture' through the doorway of the hut and moved across towards Alexander MacPherson's bedside. The vision was enough to make the woman through 'either modesty or fear' pull the bedclothes over her head, and as such she was unable to say what happened next.

Despite the trial's unsatisfactory outcome, no further reports of the ghost of Sergeant Davies have been forthcoming since those times, although it is conceivable that, somewhere out in the wild landscape around Inverey, his bones still lie in an unmarked grave, now over 250 years old.

CHAPTER 2

THE RED BARN MURDER

WILLIAM CORDER AND MARIA MARTEN, 1828

Far more well known than the Hill of Christie phantom is the case of William Corder, who entered the annals of English criminal history nearly eighty years after the death of Arthur Davies for his perpetration of the notorious Red Barn murder, described as 'one of the best known and most curious murders in history'. This is the first instance in this book of a prophetic dream being linked with the apprehension and subsequent execution of a convicted murderer, and the immortalisation of Corder's crime through the medium of melodrama in Victorian Britain was assisted in no short measure by this specific association with the supernatural – a subject which by its own unique nature has always leant itself to exploitation – while the murder site, a long-vanished farm building in the isolated hamlet of Polstead, Suffolk, some fifteen miles west of Ipswich, has become as unique a location in the annals of both ghostlore and criminology as Borley Rectory or Rillington Place[1].

In the opening decades of the nineteenth century, Polstead, the 'place of pools', consisted in the main of around twenty or so cottages situated on the northern slopes of the River Box. The parish as a whole contained only 900 persons and the two ponds which gave the village its name were located between the village's chief landmark, the twelfth-century church of St Mary, and the Cock Inn adjacent to the green at the top of the hill. Only one of these ponds survives today but a number of the buildings and locations which feature prominently in the Corder case are extant. The manor of Polstead was held at this time by Mrs Mary Ann Cook who lived at Polstead Hall, a sixteenth-century house sited next to the church in what, up to the 1940s, was still a deer park. Mary Cook was a major local landowner and in the 1820s had two tenant farmers, William Chaplin and John Corder.

Corder was a forthright, God-fearing man who worked a substantial farm of 300 acres in Polstead and the surrounding area. He was the father of eight children, of whom two died at a young age, leaving four sons – the eldest John, then Thomas, William and James – and two daughters, the eldest of whom, Mary, was married to a miller named Boreham and lived not far from the village. The Corder family resided in a substantial timbered farmhouse known as Street Farm, which still stands today relatively unaltered from those times and not far from St Mary's Church. John Corder senior was a hardworking and at times difficult man and whatever affection he had for his children was directed mainly at Thomas, who was widely expected to inherit the running of the farm in the event of his father's death.

William Corder, who was born in 1803 and whose short life was to end immortalised in tragedy, had a strained relationship with his father, who, for reasons that are now unclear, bore him much resentment and disfavour. Writing about the case in the mid-1960s, Donald McCormick has described how William was belittled by the elder man, who 'made a point of holding him up to ridicule on every possible occasion, insisting that if any of his children committed any misdeed, however slight, William was to be punished as an example to them all'. The young man countered this with a simmering resentment of his own and found solace in the affections of his mother, which grew in proportion to the disdain that John Corder viewed his second youngest son. William grew to be a short, unprepossessing man who walked with a characteristic stooping gait. Despite being unpopular at the village school, where he was known as 'Foxey' Corder, he was intelligent and had a lively imagination, which found expression in creative writing.

Following local schooling, William was sent at the age of thirteen as a boarder to a private academy at Hadleigh, near the Essex coast. After three years he left with a favourable report, but any personal hope of directing his talents into a career in journalism or teaching was swiftly crushed by John Corder, who forbade any such plan and instead set his son to work with his brothers on the family farm. Instead of enjoying an equal status with his siblings, William was unfairly employed as little more than a farmhand, 'with the meagrest perquisites of the small crofter', and it seems likely that an unhappy realisation of this fact, coupled with the continued indifference and hostility of his father, created conditions which were to eventually lead to murder. William is known to have committed several acts of theft and other frauds against John Corder and others, but although it is true that he could be devious and cunning by turn, the reality of these times would appear to be far removed from the 'wicked squire' persona with which he would be posthumously cast in stage plays and 'penny dreadfuls'.

Corder's relationship with his father eventually deteriorated to the point that around the beginning of 1825 he was dismissed from Street Farm and sent to London to enlist in the Merchant Navy. Several reasons have been given for this, ranging from heavy drinking and womanising to continued acts of thievery, but Corder was lucky enough to be prevented from going to sea due to poor eyesight and, unwilling to return to the drudgery of village life in Polstead, stayed on in the capital, where he spent what little money John Corder had given him to assist his seafaring in a heady explosion of drinking, gambling and whoring. It was during this period that William fell in with three unsavoury people who were to significantly shape future events – prostitute Hannah Fandango, Samuel 'Beauty' Smith, a habitual thief, and Thomas Wainewright, a painter turned murderer who in later years has been compared to the Frenchman Pierre Lacenaire, another man of letters who subsequently became a killer.

Hannah Fandango, of Creole descent on her mother's side and the daughter of an English sea captain, was a former actress with expensive tastes who had left a boarding school at the age of fourteen in order to seek fame and fortune on the London stage. By turn she had descended from acting to being the mistress of a number of wealthy playboys as well as working as a smuggler and common prostitute, and it was as one of her many clients that William Corder first encountered this alluring but totally unscrupulous woman, who quickly infatuated the young country boy with her looks and talents. As a receiver of contraband goods, Hannah maintained a small cottage about a mile from Polstead, a remarkable coincidence that helped convince Corder he had in fact found the perfect match, with the result that John Corder's meagre allowance was quickly spent and the farmer soon found himself looking around for another source of income in order to secure her affections.

At this time Corder still maintained hopes of beginning a career in journalism and it was to this end that the devious Hannah made introductions to her 'manager' Samuel Smith, in reality a card-sharp and pimp who, as part of the same smuggling ring, was an occasional visitor to Polstead where William Corder may have already heard of him by reputation – he is known to have been involved in the theft of livestock in the district and had served prison sentences for these and other offences.

It was through the efforts of both 'Beauty' Smith and Hannah Fandango that Corder also came to the attention of Thomas Wainewright, an enigmatic figure later immortalised by no less than Charles Dickens as 'Slinkton' in his 1859 short story *Hunted Down*. By the time he was introduced to Corder, who he later described as 'a stooping youth with Napoleonic gestures and a sense of drama', the thirty-one-year-old artist and sometime critic had already made attempts to support his extravagant lifestyle by defrauding the trustees who controlled his stocks and shares, and would later gravitate to murder in order to pay off his creditors and continue his affluent lifestyle. Corder obviously hoped that Wainewright would assist in developing his literary career but in fact the elder man, who published articles and criticisms intermittently under the pseudonym of Janus Weathercock, was of little help in this respect, despite being on friendly terms with several notable writers and artists such as the poet Sir Wentworth Dilke, essayist Charles Lamb and mystic William Blake, and appears to have mentored William more successfully in the art of forgery than journalism. The association was a brief one and, following on from their time together in London, both would become notorious in the history of criminology for their later activities, Corder for his murderous connections with the sinister Red Barn and Wainewright as a compulsive poisoner who 'became fascinated with murder for its own sake'.

A short while after he met William Corder, Thomas Wainewright was suspected of killing his grandfather with strychnine and, in 1830, his mother-in-law also died suddenly. The proceeds of both these crimes went mostly in paying off his mounting debts but by the end of the same year Wainewright had resorted to poisoning his sister-in-law, Helen Abercromby, carefully insuring her life for £18,000 beforehand. He later claimed he had carried out the killing because he was offended by the thickness of the woman's ankles. When the insurance company refused to pay, Wainewright fled to France, where he committed another insurance murder before returning secretly to England in 1837, but was recognised by a Bow Street Runner in a hotel in Covent Garden and arrested. Put on trial for forgery rather than murder, Wainewright was sentenced to transportation to Tasmania, where he died at the age of fifty-eight in 1852, 'a vain and garrulous man who never ceased to boast of his past acquaintances with the great', which included the young farmer from Polstead.

Corder's tempestuous relationship with Hannah Fandango ended in April 1825 and, leaving London, he returned to Suffolk, where John Corder allowed his son to continue in the family business. However, William was haunted by his experiences in the low-life dens of the capital and its persistent spectres were later to follow him out into the peaceful English countryside. Seemingly free from the negative influences of the likes of 'Beauty' Smith and Thomas Wainewright, as well as the temptations of Hannah, Corder appeared to live a reformed and respectable life at Street Farm for some time. However, the seeds of destruction were sown when, in the winter of 1825, John Corder died suddenly and almost immediately afterwards two of the Corder boys, James and John, were struck down with tuberculosis, which left them virtual invalids for the rest of their lives. Assisted by William, Thomas Corder took up the role which had been his practically from birth, but with the dominating influence of his father gone, conditions became right for William Corder to see the possibility of rekindling the pleasures of former days. However, in the spring of the following year, Corder was to have the encounter that, in just over two years, would not only send him to the gallows, but would make the tiny hamlet of Polstead forever synonymous around the world with both murder and supernatural prophecy.

Maria Marten was the twenty-five-year-old daughter of Thomas Marten, the Polstead mole-catcher who supplemented a specialist but poorly paid profession by selling vegetables and poultry from his small garden, the cottage of which, like the Corder farmhouse, survives to this day. Despite their having never met before, William Corder knew her well by reputation as, at the age of nineteen, she had born his elder brother Thomas an illegitimate child which had died in infancy and was buried in St Mary's churchyard. Such was the clear favouritism shown by the God-fearing John Corder that the affair, well known through Polstead village gossip, had been both quietly ignored by the family and wrestled with some ease from the old man's conscience, with the result that unlike William, Thomas Corder had not been banished to a life on the high seas for his misdemeanour. Far from being the village saint that later Victorian writers and commentators made out, Maria was in fact a forceful, highly sexed and promiscuous young woman, the course of whose short life of illicit affairs and drama was to ultimately begin and end with tragic associations with the Corder family.

The eldest of four daughters, Maria had been born to Thomas and Grace Marten on 24 July 1801. At the age of seven, and to assist with the family finances, she was put into service in the household of a clergyman at Layham, a nearby village, where she was taught to read and write, and for a number of years enjoyed a good relationship with her employer who unwittingly created the conditions for the girl's later love of the high life by allowing her to wear his daughter's cast-off dresses. By the time she was fifteen Maria's true colours began to show. Dismissed from Layham 'for levity of behaviour and an inordinate love of fine clothes', she returned to Polstead where circumstances dictated – much to her dissatisfaction – the necessity of taking on much of the responsibility for running the Marten household; by this time Grace Marten had died and there were three other children besides her father to look after, a situation that continued for some time until Thomas Marten eventually remarried. Maria's stepmother Ann, a local woman, was young, the equal of Maria in terms of good looks, and the two women found it difficult to get along. Ann Marten was known locally for her 'second sight' whose accuracy was to prove distressingly accurate as the years wore on.

As the Polstead 'village belle', Maria had many male admirers but her years living amongst the finery of the rector's household at Layham had created the desire and a firm belief that she was destined for something better than simple country life. Then came the affair with Thomas Corder, which was followed soon after by another liaison, this time with a relative of the owner of Polstead Hall, Mary Cook. This was Peter Matthews, a wealthy visitor from London with his own estate in Berkshire, who Maria encountered for the first time as he rode through Polstead during the Cherry Fair, an annual fête, and whose introduction to the seductive village beauty was said to have been foretold by a gypsy fortune teller passing by the Marten cottage some years before. Such was the power of the Red Barn murder in Victorian England that, grafted onto the story in later years, was an alleged village tradition that this gypsy was none other than the formidable Hannah Fandango in disguise, filling the impressionable young girl's head with tales of future riches and high living that would be brought to her by a handsome stranger riding a grey horse.

Whatever the truth of such tales, Maria needed little encouragement to keep an appointment with Matthews in a hotel bedroom in Ipswich. It was the beginning of another illicit affair, this time with secret meetings in Suffolk and London, a second pregnancy and the birth of another bastard child, Thomas Henry, who was brought up in the Marten household with support from Peter Matthews, who drew a line under his involvement with Maria by agreeing a quarterly £5 allowance for her and her son. By the time that William Corder returned to Polstead, Maria, whose promiscuity seemingly knew no bounds despite the disapproval of her family and the continued gossip of village locals, was regularly away from the village pursuing further affairs in Bury St Edmunds, Ipswich and sometimes as far as London. Ultimately she was to find another eligible and willing suitor – her last – much closer to home.

There were no witnesses to the first meeting between Maria Marten and William Corder early in 1826 but by the summer of the same year the two clearly were lovers. Much of their early affair was carried out in secret as for their clandestine meetings they chose the one place in the whole of Polstead that villagers were unlikely to visit, or if they did happen to pass by, were certain not to linger near for long. The Red Barn was an old agricultural building with a sinister and possibly haunted reputation located on the Corder estate around half a mile south-east of the village centre and within easy reach of both Street Farm and Maria Marten's cottage. An old Suffolk superstition well known in the area at the time told of the uncanny ability of the evening sunlight to act as a warning against evil by picking out buildings, woods and similar places that held bad luck in a characteristic red glow. One such site noted by the village locals to be afflicted by this particular portent was the Corder barn and as such it was normally given a wide berth by travellers passing along the road between Polstead and Withermarsh Green, where it could be seen silhouetted and eerily illuminated on the hillside. It would seem that the building's ominous title derives mainly from this association, although the roof, despite being mainly of thatch, was also partly covered with red clay tiles.

As their relationship continued, the couple became bolder and less inhibited about being seen together in public, with the result that Corder became a regular visitor to the Marten cottage. With his position in the family business much improved due to the demise of his father, William was in Maria's eyes an eligible catch, not quite as high on the social scale as some of her previous conquests, but worth pursuing due to the future certainty of an inheritance from the Corder farm. For William, the young village girl, despite her penchant for promiscuity, was a far cry from the scheming and tempestuous Hannah Fandango, with the result that for much of their early time together there was genuine affection between the couple. This, however, was to change as fate soon began dealing both Maria and William heavy and ultimately deadly blows.

The first of these was in the late autumn of 1826 when, with alarming predictability, Maria announced to her lover that she was carrying his child. Corder's initial reaction was to conceal the pregnancy from both his own family and Maria's, but as the weeks passed this proved impossible and he was forced to confess to Thomas and Ann Marten that he was the father of Maria's unborn child. In an attempt to mitigate matters, William insisted he would marry Maria at the most opportune moment, more specifically when his financial situation improved, and made the suggestion, to which all agreed, that to hide the birth from the rest of the Corder family and the village as a whole it would be prudent for Maria to go into lodgings until after the baby was born. However, as Corder was making arrangements for this to take place he suffered a personal tragedy. On the morning of 23 February 1827, his younger brother Thomas was killed within sight of Street Farm when hurrying to catch up with a friend, he had attempted to take a shortcut across a frozen pond and died after falling through the ice. His death quickly left William struggling to run the family business almost single-handed.

On 19 March, Maria left for the market town of Sudbury twelve miles away and it was there, in a small house in Plough Lane, that she gave birth to a baby boy in the second week of April; later the same month she and her son returned to Polstead where, both in poor health, they were looked after discretely by Ann Marten. Whatever happiness the couple and the Marten family may have shared in this new parenthood, however, was to be short-lived as the infant grew progressively weaker and died a fortnight after Maria's return; Corder himself may not even have seen the child alive.

Whether he felt genuine grief at the loss or simply considered his son's death to be a partial alleviation of his gradually mounting financial commitments is unclear. In what was no doubt a charged and emotional atmosphere following the bereavement, Corder persuaded all concerned that it would be prudent to conceal the birth and death from becoming common knowledge around the Polstead area and as such the infant's body should be buried secretly and outside of the district. To these ends Maria agreed to accompany the farmer and, under increasing pressure from Thomas and Ann Marten to honour his promises to their daughter, Corder placed the corpse in a wooden box and the two left to bury the child in Sudbury.

What passed between the couple during the course of this unpleasant task is unknown but the grim facts are that the tiny body never reached the town and in fact was buried in an unmarked grave, probably in a field somewhere on the Corder farm on the outskirts of Polstead. Why they chose to do this has never come to light but most likely the decision was Corder's and not Maria's. At this point in time no one would have realised that this tragic young woman had in fact less than a month to live.

Maria Marten was last seen alive on 18 May 1837. Despite a growing tension between the couple, understandable due to the macabre circumstances of the clandestine burial of their child – something that Maria clearly felt unhappy with – and which was undoubtedly not helped by an earlier incident of thievery on Corder's part when he intercepted and spent one of Peter Matthew's maintenance payments for Thomas Henry, Corder began making arrangements for marriage. On the excuse that, according to local rumour, John Balham, the district police constable, was about to serve Maria with an arrest warrant for bastardy (which amounted practically to a charge of prostitution), Corder made the suggestion that they travel to Ipswich to marry by special licence and a date was fixed for Monday 14 May. However, business at Stoke Fair delayed the farmer's return to Polstead and this, coupled with the sudden illness of James Corder at Street Farm, had the result that it was not until the following Friday that William Corder finally arrived at the Marten cottage.

Relief that the man was at last acknowledging his commitments was somewhat tempered by his immediate plans for the trip. Corder was insistent on secrecy and that they should not be seen leaving together. To achieve this the couple would take to the Red Barn a bag containing Maria's clothes; they were to go there separately and, to ensure the success of the plan, Maria was to travel dressed in male clothing. Corder later left with a brown holland bag containing an assortment of clothes: a black silk gown, stockings, a leghorn hat and other items, returning some time afterwards with a suitable disguise for Maria comprising clothes apparently belonging to his brother James. Maria changed into these: a brown coat, striped waistcoat and blue trousers; she wore a man's hat over her hair combs and concealed her earrings with a large silk handkerchief. Around half-past twelve, following a tearful farewell with her parents, the couple left the cottage by separate doors and made their way across the fields towards the distant Red Barn, out of village obscurity and into the annals of both criminal and supernatural history.

The following day Corder returned to Polstead alone. Problems with the marriage licence, so he informed Thomas and Ann Marten, had delayed the union and until these were sorted out Maria had decided to stay on in Ipswich. Over the next few weeks Corder continued to work on at Street Farm, but without Maria. When questioned by the Martens, Corder insisted she was well and busy in Ipswich preparing for their imminent marriage, something that the couple seemed to accept; their daughter had not written personally due to rheumatism in her hand.

During the summer, Corder was spared the increasing concerns and questions of the Marten family by events at Street Farm, which kept him away from the Marten cottage for long periods – both James and John Corder died within days of each other of a combination of tuberculosis and typhus, leaving practically the entire running of the business to William alone. Corder later informed the Martens that, fearing for his health, he had decided to take a holiday and was going to join Maria at a resort on the Isle of Wight, where she had travelled after enjoying a holiday by herself at Yarmouth. Corder borrowed £400 from his mother and left for London, ostensibly en route for the south coast. On 18 October, five months practically to the day that Maria had last been seen in Polstead walking over the fields towards her rendezvous in the Red Barn, Corder wrote to the Martens from the George Inn in Leadenhall Street, informing them that they were now married and that he was travelling to Newport where, after completing the sale of Street Farm, they would be setting up a new business together. It was the last the old mole-catcher and his wife were to hear of William Corder for several months.

We have already noted the belief in local circles for what today would be called psychic abilities on the part of Ann Marten, and, during the winter of 1827, this singular talent began to come to the fore, specifically in connection with the whereabouts of her own stepdaughter. The woman's sleep became restless and she was often heard to cry out in the night, but whatever troubled her either did not make itself fully clear or she was unwilling to reveal its cause.

However, around the beginning of April the following year, on three successive nights, Ann Marten dreamt a vivid and terrible dream that on waking retained such clarity she felt sure it was in fact some supernormal vision. In the lonely Red Barn across the fields she saw Thomas Marten's daughter dead, shot to death and buried beneath the earth floor; such was the intensity of the dream that she could describe, even though she had not set foot inside the building, the layout and exact spot where Maria lay cold and alone in a shallow grave.

Thomas Marten, who had been the most inclined to accept William Corder's various explanations for the absence and continued silence of his daughter, was reminded that Maria's stepbrother had claimed to have seen William striding towards the barn carrying a shovel and a pickaxe on the day they departed for Ipswich, and despite the initial shock at his wife's outburst, was subsequently persuaded to make enquiries. On the pretext that his daughter may have left some clothes belonging to her at the barn, Thomas obtained permission from William Pryke, the Corder's bailiff who had been retained on the estate by Mary Cook, to make an inspection and on the morning of 19 April they went together to look around the building.

The Red Barn was laid out in four principle bays with a central area used for threshing; one bay was allocated as a calf shed while the others were filled with straw, the layout corresponding exactly with the description given by Ann Marten in her dreams. In the bay where she claimed to have seen Maria killed, Marten and Pryke soon found some large stones under which the earth looked as if it had been disturbed at some time in the past. Pushing the handle of a rake and a mole spike down into the earth, Marten 'turned up something that was black, and pieces of something like flesh stuck to the spike'. Locking the barn, Marten and Pryke went to fetch another villager, William Bowtell, and on returning the three men quickly cleared away a large amount of earth, beneath which they found a heavily decomposed human body fixed into the ground with a metal spike. The barn was locked again and the following day Thomas Marten and William Pryke returned accompanied by the local coroner, John Wayman, and Dr Lawton, the village surgeon. The body was fetched up from the grave and laid out on a door; an examination of the clothes subsequently identified the corpse as that of Maria Marten.

William Corder, immediately the prime suspect, was discovered within a few days in London where John Balham, the Polstead policeman, was directed to make enquiries. Assisted by James Lea, a detective from Balham police station, the two men followed a trail which lead eventually to a house in Ealing Lane, Brentford; Corder, about to sit down to breakfast, was arrested by Lea as he stood in his dressing gown timing a boiled egg on the stove with a fob watch. Charged with murder, Corder was taken back to Suffolk where, after an overnight stop at the George Inn at Colchester, he was committed for trial at Bury St Edmunds. On 20 April, Maria Marten was laid to rest in the churchyard of St Mary's at Polstead, not far from the grave of the child she had born to William Corder's brother, Thomas. The funeral was attended by hundreds of sightseers and was a growing indication of the public interest which the murder in the Red Barn, with its supernatural revelation, was soon to generate.

William Corder's trial opened at the Shire Hall, Bury St Edmunds on 7 August 1828. The courtroom was 'crowded to suffocation' as people from all over East Anglia filled the public gallery, eager to be present at the proceedings. At the time of his arrest, Corder had been living a remarkable double life as the honorary headmaster of an Ealing girls' school. A few weeks after he had written from Leadenhall Street to the Corders telling them about his alleged marriage to Maria, the Suffolk farmer had placed a notice in both the *Morning Herald* and the *Sunday Times* advertising for a wife: 'To any female of respectability, who would study for domestic comfort, and is willing to confide her future happiness to one in every way qualified to render the marriage state desirable', Corder advertised himself as a 'private gentleman, aged twenty-four, entirely independent'. He received a hundred replies (some of which were later published as a sensational book of love letters) and from these selected Mary Moore, a young schoolteacher; they were married by special licence at St Andrew's Church, Holborn in December 1827, Corder finally finding at last the teaching vocation denied him several years before by the forceful John Corder – he even bought a pair of spectacles to make himself appear more studious.

The trial lasted two days, much of which was taken up by the testimony of Ann Marten, who recounted in great detail the last hours of her stepdaughter's life and her clandestine arrangement to meet William Corder at the now notorious Red Barn. Throughout her testimony she made no mention of her prophetic dreams, but they were well known outside of the courtroom. Towards the end of the second day Corder took the stand and in an impassioned speech protested his innocence to the last, claiming that Maria had in fact turned a pistol on herself following a quarrel and in a panic he had buried the body and fled to London. The jury, however, were unconvinced and took just thirty-five minutes to find him guilty of murder.

Nearer to our own times there have been various suggestions as to what actually took place in the Red Barn on that fateful May day, even to the point of questioning whether Corder was in fact guilty of the crime; this despite the condemned man's own confession which was published over the weekend in the brief forty-eight hours between him leaving the crowded courtroom and stepping onto the scaffold at Bury Gaol. In the late 1940s, authors Dorothy Gibbs and Herbert Maltby suggested that Ann Marten was the mastermind behind the killing and, due to her own desire to marry William, persuaded the farmer to kill her stepdaughter so they could be together after Thomas Marten had died. When Corder reneged on their agreement and subsequently left for a new life in London, Ann revealed the crime out of spite by pretending to dream about Maria's unquiet ghost and gladly went into the witness box to see him hanged. In 1967, crime writer Donald McCormick issued *The Red Barn Mystery* in which he suggests that after the initial shot and with Maria lying wounded, Corder was assisted in the murder by 'Beauty' Smith, while Suffolk historian Leslie Sheen has put forward the case for Corder's complete innocence with Maria's death being the result of a mock suicide which went wrong and Corder the victim of a miscarriage of justice. However, in the 1990s, writer Peter Haining, who made an extensive investigation into the case, became convinced of Corder's guilt but felt Smith's presence in the later part of the story (he was seen drinking with Corder at Polstead after the farmer's return from London) provided an unsatisfactory conclusion to what actually went on inside the Red Barn on that fateful summer day.

William Corder was hanged outside the walls of Bury Gaol in front of a crowd of several thousand people (estimated but not confirmed to be as high as 20,000) on Monday, 11 August 1828. In the days before the 'long drop' system of Victorian execution pioneered by Horncastle cobbler William Marwood and the later lightning-fast twentieth-century hangings of Albert Pierrepoint, Corder's death was slow and agonising: after Corder had fallen through the drop, executioner John Foxton (under the usual pseudonym of Jack Ketch) was forced to grip the struggling felon by the knees and pull on his legs for two minutes to speed up what was in effect death by strangulation. The body was left hanging on the scaffold for an hour before being cut down and taken by cart to the Shire Hall, where it was briefly put on exhibition and 5,000 people filed past to see it.

Later, to complete a series of gruesome incidents, Corder's body was dissected, his scalp and ears pickled and plaster death masks were made – these sinister relics survive to this day and are on display at Moyse's Hall Museum in Bury St Edmunds, along with a copy of Victorian writer James Curtis' bestselling book on the case, bound in Corder's own tanned skin. Such bizarre trophies were an indication of the phenomenon that the murder in the Red Barn (itself stripped by souvenir hunters and later demolished) would become in Victorian Britain and beyond, with stage plays, 'penny dreadful' novels, ballads and, much later, films and television dramas. Writing about the case in the early 1960s, Colin Wilson was able to state that romanticised versions of the story were still appearing 'in the more lurid of women's journals' of the day.

Ghostly associations with the story of the Red Barn did not end with the dreams of Ann Marten. William Corder's ghost, a shadowy figure dressed in a Victorian frock coat and stove-pipe hat, was allegedly seen walking through Polstead one summer evening in the mid-1920s and there is a tradition that his unquiet spirit returns to the district at intervals, particularly when 18 May, the anniversary of Maria Marten's death, falls on a Friday.

However, it was the Englishman Robert Thurston Hopkins (1884-1958), a ghost hunter who had a penchant for investigating a number of screaming skulls and similar hauntings, who provided some of the most detailed evidence regarding paranormal associations with the Red Barn case, specifically in connection with the death's head of William Corder himself.

Thurston Hopkins was well qualified where the Red Barn mystery was concerned: when Bury Gaol was sold off by the Prisons Commission, his father bought the property and Robert lived at Gyves House as a boy. Thurston Hopkins senior, a man who 'spoke of ghosts as though their existence had always been accepted by all sensible people', was a close friend of Dr Kilner, whose family, many years before, had been bequeathed the Corder relics, including the murderer's articulated skeleton and pickled scalp. This skeleton was used for many years as a teaching aid at the old West Suffolk General Hospital[2] and around the 1870s, Dr Kilner made a display of William Corder's skull by swapping it with a replacement and repairing the original with parts of a third anatomical skull. From this moment on, Kilner seemed to be haunted by some terrible presence and a number of curious and unnerving incidents, reminiscent of events in Robert Bloch's screenplay and later novel *The Skull of the Marquis de Sade* (1976), were related by him to Thurston Hopkins' father. These included being followed by a shadowy figure dressed in an old-fashioned greatcoat and beaver hat, footsteps walking the house, psychic attacks and the materialisation of a disembodied hand on the handle of a bedroom door.

Tiring of these encounters with the unseen, Dr Kilner ultimately presented the death's head to Robert Thurston Hopkins' father, who claimed to have experienced the sinister power of the skull himself: the day he took possession of the relic he slipped and badly twisted his ankle, while the next day his horse was killed when it fell over the edge of a quarry. According to the account that Thurston Hopkins senior often related to his family – by way of a supper-time Christmas ghost story it must be said – he later suffered 'illness, sorrow and financial disaster such as he had never dreamed possible' and finally broke the curse of the haunted skull by bribing a gravedigger to give it a Christian burial (enclosed in a japanned cashbox) in an unnamed churchyard near Bury St Edmunds. An account of the haunting has been given by Peter Underwood in his 1985 book *The Ghost Hunters*.

The Red Barn murder is the first in this volume where strange paranormal forces seemingly sent a murderer to the gallows. It is not, however, the last . . .

NOTES

1. Borley Rectory, a rambling Victorian building in rural Essex, built in 1863 and badly damaged by fire in 1939; demolished in 1944 and long known as the 'most haunted house in England'. It was the subject of a lengthy investigation by Harry Price (see Chapter 7), a well-known and controversial researcher during the inter-war years who wrote two full-length books on the case. For a modern reassessment by the present author in collaboration with Eddie Brazil and Peter Underwood see *The Borley Rectory Companion* (2009). Number 10 Rillington Place, Notting Hill, London, was one of the most notorious murder houses in post-war England, known for the crimes of necrophile serial killer John Reginald Christie and the controversial execution of Timothy John Evans, hanged in March 1950 for the murder of his daughter. Following publication of the book *Ten Rillington Place* (1961) by journalist and broadcaster Ludovic Kennedy and subsequent campaigning, Evans was granted a posthumous free pardon in October 1966, his crime attributed to Christie. For an alternative viewpoint see John Eddowes' *The Two Killers of Rillington Place* (1994).
2. In August 2004, at the request of a descendant, Linda Nessworthy, Corder's skeleton was released by the Royal College of Surgeons and subsequently cremated at the South London Crematorium at Streatham; the ashes were later interred in St Mary's churchyard at Polstead.

CHAPTER 3

AUTUMN OF TERROR

ROBERT LEES AND JACK THE RIPPER, 1888

When the *Leicester Mercury* published an obituary for one of the city's noteworthy sons on 12 January 1931, it contained among a number of statements one particular item that would have caught and held the attention of all but the most casual of readers. According to the unnamed writer, as well as being a former Fleet Street reporter, author and a social worker who conducted King Edward and the Prince of Wales incognito on a tour of a London mission for the poor, Mr Robert James Lees, father of fifteen children and associate of former Prime Minister William Ewart Gladstone, also 'claimed to be the only surviving person who knew the identity of Jack the Ripper, the notorious murderer'. The responsibility of this knowledge was something that had weighed heavily on Mr Lees in his later years, so the newspaper was told by one of his daughters, Miss Eva, who also informed the *Mercury* that she hoped 'to receive a message from my father in the dream-state', a comment that Robert Lees' standing as a 'noted spiritualist' puts into context.

Local readers with a reasonable memory may well have found the information somewhat familiar as just over a year before, another newspaper, the *Illustrated Leicester Chronicle*, had published an interview with Robert Lees himself, in which his singular knowledge about the killer of Whitechapel was given a brief and somewhat throwaway mention. This curious provincial story proved to be surprisingly persistent and three months later it was to be given national prominence. Expanding on the original material, the *Daily Express*, in its editions for 7-9 March 1931, published the contents of 'an astonishing document . . . one of the most remarkable narratives that has ever reached a newspaper office' which went on to describe in three instalments how Robert Lees, a gifted clairvoyant, had used his abilities to assist Scotland Yard in tracking down the East End murderer, who, contrary to popular belief, had been caught and on the findings of a medical committee locked up as an anonymous inmate in an asylum for the criminally insane. The document was described as a testimony dictated by Lees himself, who had placed an embargo on its publication until after his own death.

Not surprisingly, the paranormal aspect of this information proved to be of particular interest to at least two of the many personalities involved in organised psychical research during the inter-war years. Three years after the *Express* articles, Dr Nandor Fodor (1895-1964), a practising New York psychoanalyst and one of the great unsung heroes of twentieth-century supernormal investigation, included Lees in his monumental *Encyclopaedia of Psychic Science* (1934) in which he described the clairvoyant as having 'rendered the greatest service to the English police' in his tracking down and closure of the Ripper case. Fodor was not the only psychical researcher who gave credence to this version of events which had been played out in the dark forbidding streets and alleyways of East End Victorian London. Writing in the fledgling *Fate Magazine* in May 1949, British-born American Hereward Carrington, a veteran of over half a century of paranormal research which included ground-breaking séance room investigations with physical mediums such as Eusapia Palladino and 'Margery' Crandon[1], was confident that 'Dr' Robert Lees, 'at the height of his powers as a "seer"', had led the police to a solution of the Ripper's crimes.

The end of the 1950s and through into the following decade saw the beginning of a modern resurgence of interest in and intensive study of the Whitechapel murders, a phenomenon which continues with great persistence to this day, over 120 years after the brutal events of the autumn of 1888. The catalyst was the simultaneous but unconnected activities of a number of interested writers: in 1959, at the same time as broadcaster Daniel Farson, nephew of *Dracula* author Bram Stoker, was researching the case for a BBC television programme, crime journalist Donald McCormick (who would later carry out a personal investigation of the Red Barn mystery) issued his book *The Identity of Jack the Ripper*, while the following year fellow writer and criminologist Colin Wilson also published a series of articles entitled 'My Search for Jack the Ripper' in the *London Evening Standard*. In 1965, two major Ripper books appeared within a few weeks of one another – *Autumn of Terror* by Tom Cullen and *Jack the Ripper in Fact and Fiction* by Robin Odell – both of which quickly became the benchmark texts for a new generation eager to pull back the veil of many decades in the hope of finally putting a name to not only one of

England's most merciless and sadistic killers but, as Colin Wilson has described him, 'the most notorious killer of all time'.

All of the authors writing in the 1960s presented what has become a reasonably official and generally accepted version of these events. Between 31 August and 8 November 1888, at least five women, all working as prostitutes, were murdered by an assailant armed with a knife within close proximity of each other in the Whitechapel district of East London; with the exception of one victim, the killer mutilated the bodies and removed internal organs after initially strangling them into unconsciousness and cutting their throats.

Earlier in the year two other murders, both unsolved, took place in the same area which some commentators have attributed to the Ripper: in the early hours of the morning of 3 April 1888 (Easter Monday), forty-five-year-old Emma Elizabeth Smith died of peritonitis in the London Hospital in Whitechapel Road after being viciously assaulted (according to her own account) by four men in Osborn Street who pushed a metal rod into her vagina; while just over four months later, on 7 August, thirty-nine-year-old Martha Tabram (or Turner) was found dead, the victim of a frenzied knife attack, on the first-floor landing of a communal stairwell in the George Yard Buildings, a tenement block to the north of Whitechapel High Street. However, what is considered to be the first Ripper murder, the first of the 'canonical five', took place a few streets away at the end of the same month.

Just before 3.40 a.m. on the morning of Friday 31 August, a carter named Charles Cross walked into Buck's Row, a street behind the main thoroughfare of Whitechapel Road, and noticed what he initially took to be a tarpaulin bundle lying in the entrance to Brown's stable yard. It proved to be the body of London-born Mary Anne 'Polly' Nicholls, a prostitute in her early forties; her throat had been cut and the lower part of her abdomen slashed, exposing the intestines. A week later, on 8 September, forty-seven-year-old Annie Chapman was refused a bed at a lodging house in Dorset Street for not having sufficient doss money. Her body was discovered a few hours later just after six in the morning by a resident in the back yard of a house at 29 Hanbury Street off of Brick Lane. The yard, accessed by a narrow passageway from the street, was often frequented by prostitutes and their clients. Annie Chapman had been brutally murdered – the head, practically severed from the neck, was tied in place with a handkerchief and as well as disembowelling his victim, the killer had removed and taken away the uterus. Seventeen people asleep on the premises only yards away heard nothing.

At the end of the same month, on 30 September, two more women were murdered within an hour of each other on what has become known as the night of the 'double event'. Around 1 a.m., Louis Diemschutz, a jewellery hawker, drove his horse and cart into Dutfield's Yard behind a working men's club in Berner Street, Whitechapel, and came across the body of a woman lying in a pool of blood, her throat cut. This was Elisabeth Stride ('Long Liz'), a forty-five-year-old Swedish-born prostitute originally from Torslanda near Gothenburg. The lack of mutilation has given some commentators reason to doubt whether this was actually a Ripper murder but it is highly likely that the sound of Diemschutz's approach interrupted the killer before he could begin his butchery and, hiding in the shadows, he made his escape as the peddler ran into the club to raise the alarm. Forty-five minutes later and half a mile to the west, Police Constable Edward Watkins was passing on his regular beat through Mitre Square when, in a secluded corner opposite Church Passage, the light from his lantern revealed the horrific sight of another dead East End woman, forty-three-year-old Catherine Eddowes who had been, in Watkins' own words, 'cut to pieces'. The Ripper had worked quickly and in only a few minutes (the policeman had passed the same spot a quarter of an hour earlier and seen nothing) had laid open Eddowes' abdomen – this time both the left kidney and the uterus were missing and, as well as gashing open the throat, the killer had viciously slashed and disfigured the face[2].

In between the killing of Annie Chapman and the double slayings of Elisabeth Stride and Catherine Eddowes, a letter sent to the Central News Agency on 17 September and signed 'Catch me if you Can, Jack the Ripper' was the first of several communications (all of which may or may not have been written by the murderer) to give the killer a chillingly anonymous identity and, subsequently, set the benchmark for sadistic slaughter which, in the words of crime writers Joe Gaute and Robin Odell, has become 'a kind of universal standard against which other murders are measured'. For the whole of October, Victorian London held its breath; several weeks passed with no new killings, but in reality it proved to be the eye of the storm. Forty days after the grim events of Dutfield's Yard and Mitre Square, 'Jacky' seemingly concluded his reign of terror with a final killing of almost mind-numbing savagery.

On 9 November 1888, around a quarter to eleven in the morning, Thomas Bowyer, assistant to Mr John McCarthy, a local landlord and candle maker, knocked on the door of 13 Miller's Court, effectively the twelve foot square ground-floor back room of 26 Dorset Street, only yards from the main Commercial Street thoroughfare, to collect twenty-nine shillings-worth of back rent from one of the tenants, twenty-four-year-old Mary Jeanette Kelly, who was several weeks in arrears. Receiving no response, Bowyer reached through a broken windowpane and, pulling back the curtain, peered into the room. As his eyes adjusted to the gloom he was greeted with a scene from a nightmare. With little chance of interruption, Jack the Ripper had subjected the young Irishwoman to a prolonged and ferocious assault lasting over an hour, inflicting appalling injuries and leaving the tiny room looking like an abattoir. Police constables and later Scotland Yard detectives found what was left of Mary Kelly lying on a bed soaked through with blood. Flesh had been stripped from the legs and arms, the abdomen opened and organs removed (the liver was found placed between her feet), both breasts had been sliced off and the heart cut out and taken away. Ashes found in the grate suggested the killer had worked (possibly naked to avoid saturating his outer clothing with blood) by the light of a pile of burning rags in the fireplace.

Over the next fifteen months several more murders, all of women, took place in and around the same area which have been described by some researchers as further Ripper crimes. They included parts of a headless body dredged from the Thames in June 1889, which were subsequently identified as that of a prostitute named Elizabeth Jackson from Turks Row, Chelsea; Alice McKenzie ('Clay Pipe Alice'), found the following month in Castle Alley, Whitechapel with her throat cut and gashes across her abdomen, and twenty-five-year-old Frances Coles, discovered with similar injuries under a railway arch at Swallow Gardens in Whitechapel on 13 February 1891. Most commentators, however, consider the killing of Mary Kelly to be the final Ripper murder, whose brief but unprecedented reign of terror was curtailed either by the killer's suicide or anonymous incarceration in an unknown lunatic asylum. For those both investigating and rediscovering the mystery of Jack the Ripper during the renaissance of the 1960s, the Whitechapel murderer – despite many imaginative theories as to his real identity – was an unidentified man who was never caught.

In the sixty years between the execution of William Corder and the chilling 'autumn of terror' of Jack the Ripper, a significant landmark in the history of the paranormal took place when the small village of Hydesville, twenty miles from Rochester in New York State, became the birthplace of Modern Spiritualism. Two decades after Ann Marten's prophetic dreams of the Red Barn, strange things began to happen in the home of the Fox family.

On 11 December 1847, John D. Fox became the tenant of a small cabin-like house and moved in with his wife and six children. The building itself had in the local area something of a haunted reputation. Nothing of any particular significance happened until March 1848, when curious events started to unfold. The Fox family became disturbed at night by strange rapping noises and knocks sounding within the house itself. These were accompanied by noises suggesting the movement of furniture and later the sound of footsteps. The rapping noises seemed to be centred around three of John Fox's daughters, twelve-year-old Kate, fifteen-year-old Margaret and later their sister Leah, who also became a focus for the disturbances[3]. What today's modern researchers would recognise as being a spontaneous poltergeist outbreak was to be the catalyst that would unlock a doorway to seemingly dormant psychic faculties inherent in mankind.

It became apparent to the Fox family that the alarming noises seemed to have some form of intelligence behind them, something that was confirmed when they began putting questions to whatever was making the sounds. Answers were received in the form of raps and knocks and a gruesome picture began to emerge. Apparently, a thirty-one-year-old man had been murdered in the house five years previously and his remains buried in the cellar of the building. The news of the disturbances quickly spread throughout the area and the family soon became inundated with visitors wanting to hear the rappings for themselves. During the course of a few days, over 300 people came to Hydesville and whatever was causing the disturbances did not disappoint them. The sinister knockings continued and volunteered more information to the effect that the murdered man was a peddler who had been killed for money. Digging took place in the cellar of the house in an attempt to ascertain the truth behind the bizarre affair. The work was temporarily suspended until the summer, when the excavators finally unearthed part of a skeleton. This was too much for the Fox family and they finally vacated the house. Kate Fox moved to her brother's home in Auburn, in New York State, while Margaret went with her sister Leah to Rochester. The remaining parts of the murdered peddler had to wait a further fifty-six years before they were finally unearthed in 1901 when the house itself, then as now considered of immense importance to the Spiritualist movement, was physically moved in its entirety to a new location in Lily Dale, New York.

For the Fox sisters, however, their move away from Hydesville did not end the attention of the forces that were now apparently at work. The rapping noises continued to disturb the three girls and were now accompanied by other phenomena that included the eerie movement of objects. Margaret, Kate and Leah Fox continued to communicate with the noises and through a system of rapping were finally able to establish permanent contact with the spirit 'entities' that were making the sounds, proclaiming a new era of interaction with the departed.

On 14 November 1849, not quite two years since the Fox family had moved into their little Hydesville home, the first Spiritualist meeting took place at the Corinthian Hall in Rochester, New York. Before long the movement began to grow, but its spread was greeted with hostility and was denounced by the establishment. Despite this the circles that had formed around the three Fox girls began to develop and it soon became apparent that

Margaret, Kate and Leah were not the only ones who were able to establish contact with spirits. The Kate Fox circle developed two new mediums, Mrs Tamlin and Mrs Benedict, who went on to become well known in their own right. In other circles sitters discovered that they too had the ability to cause phenomena. On 28 November 1849, Leah Fox became the first professional medium, charging sitters a fee for her services as an intermediary with the spirit world. At this stage the phenomena demonstrated consisted of rapping noises, movement of the table about which the sitters gathered – giving rise to the popular term 'table turning' – and psychic touches experienced by the sitters themselves.

The Fox sisters were public mediums for many years but as time went on their own reputations, as well as those of the many mediums who followed in their footsteps, came under attack as the new movement continued to be derided and dismissed as either hysteria or fraudulence by the scientific fraternity, newspapermen and the public alike. In 1861, Kate Fox became engaged to a New York banker named Charles Livermore and over the course of the next five years gave nearly 400 private séances in Livermore's home. These sittings were significant as in several Kate achieved an alleged materialisation of Livermore's dead first wife Estelle that convinced him of the genuineness of her mediumship. Kate herself travelled widely, visiting England and Russia, where she continued to expand the Spiritualist movement. However, the personal relationships between the three founding sisters of Modern Spiritualism deteriorated over the years, fuelled by Margaret's descent into alcoholism. She managed to turn Kate and Leah against one another and, in 1888, the same year that Jack the Ripper stalked the East End of London, and some forty years after the Hydesville rappings began, made a confession denouncing the movement. A year later, Margaret issued a full retraction, but her actions caused much damage to the Fox sisters' reputations. All three sisters died within three years of one another, Leah first in 1890; Kate followed her on 2 July 1892 and finally Margaret on 8 March 1893. The founders were gone but in their lifetimes they had seen the incredible growth of the movement and this was to go from strength to strength in the years to come.

The spread of Spiritualism outside of its native America was inevitable due to the activities of travelling mediums. In October 1852, Mrs W.R. Haydon was one of the first to arrive in England from Boston. She was a medium in the mould of the Fox sisters who demonstrated rapping phenomena and table turning. The popularity of the latter method of communication, the simplest involving the tilting of a specially built lightweight table to which questions were directed, became immense and quickly exploded into a craze.

Society invitations were extended to include five o'clock tea and table turning. Many mediums followed Mrs Haydon and many diversities of spirit communication began to be represented. P.B. Randolph was a notable trance medium who arrived in 1857.

The early 1850s saw the first experimental organisation for the study and development of English mediumship. This was the Charing Cross Spiritual Circle, which in July 1857 was superseded by the London Spiritualist Union. Several other organisations developed but in time either fell by the wayside or were incorporated into other groups. As well as the London Spiritualist Alliance, inaugurated in 1884, English Spiritualism was consolidated by various other factors. In 1871, Kate Fox settled in England and gave many séances. Mrs Emma Hardinge Britten (1823-1899) was an inspirational speaker and propagandist for the Spiritualist movement who visited England during the course of her extensive travels, as was Mrs Cora L.V. Richmond (1840-1923), who arrived in 1873 and spent several years in the country.

However, the single most important influence in England was the mediumship of Daniel Dunglas Home (1833-1886) whose phenomena galvanised the entire spiritualistic scene in this country and his importance in the history of mediumship cannot be overstated. The New York scholar and theologian Professor George Bush was the first to investigate him, after which Home travelled to England, arriving in April 1855. Many Victorian Spiritualists were converted through experiencing his phenomena first hand and he impressed a number of notable persons of the day as to the genuineness of his abilities. These latter men included the Victorian scientist Sir David Brewster (1781-1868), noted for his work with optics and the inventor of the kaleidoscope, *Vanity Fair* novelist and journalist William Thackeray (1811-1863) and Lord Edward Robert Lytton (1831-1891), later Viceroy and Governor of India. The most famous aspect of Home's mediumship was levitation but he also produced materialisations and the telekinetic movement of objects. His most famous feat of defying gravity was in December 1868 at Ashley House in London, where he is said to have levitated himself out of one first-floor room and entered another by floating in through the windows.

Nearly a century after the psychic feats of Home, the unlikely scenario that the Victorian world of Spiritualism had in fact solved the mystery of Jack the Ripper and that his arrest and imprisonment had been brought about by paranormal means surprisingly refused to go away. In 1970, journalist Fred Archer, former Editor of the Spiritualist newspaper *Psychic News*, published a book entitled *Ghost Detectives* in which he confidently supported the posthumous testament of Robert James Lees nearly forty years before:

that the Whitechapel murders, the 'crime mystery of a century', had been solved by Lees, the 'human bloodhound' who had tracked the sadistic killer. Archer knew members of the Lees family well and they were able to relate some of the 'more sensational aspects of their father's career', events the medium himself had apparently been reluctant to discuss during his lifetime. Despite this close relationship with the source, it was the journalist's belief, as a convinced Spiritualist, that gave the accounts of Robert Lees and Jack the Ripper such credibility. Was it possible then that Archer was right, that Robert Lees did know the identity of the Whitechapel killer, that he was caught and the truth behind his apprehension was and remains a conspiracy of silence?

Robert Lees, born at Hinckley on the outskirts of Leicester on 12 August 1849, was in his late thirties during the 'autumn of terror'. A former journalist on the *Manchester Guardian*, Lees had moved to London with his wife Sarah ten years before and was working on the staff of *Tit-Bits* magazine, a somewhat sensationalist weekly founded by Sir George Newnes in 1881. As with many of the mediums that were to flourish in the new era of Modern Spiritualism, Lees' psychic powers were said to have manifested at an early age. His daughter Eva, one of fifteen children of whom three died in infancy, later claimed that her father was a deep trance medium by the age of twelve and while still a teenager had already given the grieving Queen Victoria a series of séances at Buckingham Palace, channelling for her the spirit of her beloved Prince Albert.

According to Fred Archer, Lees' involvement with the Ripper crimes took place early in September 1888. Alone in his study the medium was 'seized by a clairvoyant vision' which gave him a supernatural insight on a deadly tableau being played out somewhere close by in the Victorian capital. Lees saw remotely a man leading a heavily drunken woman down a dark street, the only illumination being the glare from a nearby gin palace window by which the medium noted the man's dark tweed suit and the light raincoat he carried over one arm. Lees' psychic powers allowed him to follow the couple as both turned into a narrow court and penetrate the blackness as they sought out a dark corner. As the woman drunkenly made to raise her skirt the man stepped forward, simultaneously clapping a hand over her mouth and slashing open her throat with a hidden knife. The killer quickly lowered the body to the ground and, with Lees a horrified voyeur, used the same knife to cut into the prone torso. The mutilations took only a few minutes after which the man wiped the blade on the woman's clothes and, straightening up, he slipped on his overcoat, easily concealing his blood-soaked shirtfront, and casually walked back out into the street at which point, thankfully for the horrified medium, the psychic vision faded away and he found himself alone in the familiar surroundings of his home.

Shocked and sickened by what he had experienced, Lees regained enough composure to realise that he had been a premature witness to a crime that was yet to take place and hurriedly took a cab to Scotland Yard. Unfortunately for the gentle mystic, he was treated with derision by the duty sergeant and dismissed as a harmless crank, although the policeman went as far as to humour his persistence by making a note of when Lees said he saw the murder take place by recalling the time on the bar-room clock through the gin palace window. The following night, 8 September, Annie Chapman was slaughtered in the back yard at Hanbury Street. Accompanied by a manservant, the medium visited the murder site and was overwhelmed to find the same grim street and shadowy courtyard from his vision. Lees suffered a severe nervous breakdown and, debilitated both by the experience and his inability to make the authorities believe his story, he decided to take his family on a short holiday to the Continent, where, for a couple of weeks, he was untroubled by further visions.

On his return home from abroad the unwelcome and supernatural connection with the Whitechapel killer soon returned. While riding with Sarah Lees on a London omnibus, the couple had reached Notting Hill when Lees became aware of a man who had just stepped onboard – 'a man of medium height wearing a dark tweed suit and a light overcoat'. By this time the unknown killer had acquired his famous and chilling title and Lees, who had scanned the newspapers for news of further crimes, was able to confidently whisper across to his wife, 'That man is Jack the Ripper'. When the stranger got off at Marble Arch, Lees instructed his wife to continue home alone and set out to follow him. As the two men walked along Park Lane, Lees saw a policeman and, hurrying over, pointed out the man ahead. Not surprisingly, the constable was in no mood to believe the claims that the Whitechapel killer was in fact only 100 yards away and as Lees began arguing the stranger hailed a cab and was driven out of sight.

That night as he sat working, Robert Lees was again overpowered by a paranormal vision, this time the aftermath of another gruesome murder due to take place very soon. Lees was aware of a heavily mutilated body and saw the face terribly slashed, 'one ear was completely severed, the other remained hanging by a thin shred of flesh'. Again the horrified man went to the police at Whitehall Place and insisted on an interview with a detective involved in the investigation. By this time Scotland Yard had received (on 29 September) a letter dated four days previously addressed to 'Dear Boss' in which the writer, again signing himself 'Jack the Ripper', had threatened on his 'next job' to 'clip the ladys [*sic*] ears off' and send them to the police 'just for jolly'. This time Lees' description of the murdered woman, the head injuries and lacerated ears, made the policeman less likely to dismiss the psychic as a crank. The following night, the time of the 'double event', left the police with two more murders, and the cruel facial injuries inflicted on Catherine Eddowes seemed to confirm some aspects of Lees' statement, although Archer states that an attempt was made to sever the ears of Elisabeth Stride, the first victim of the night, who was (as we have seen) found only with a cut throat. The responsibility of his foreknowledge again affected the psychic to the point that, on reading about the murders in the newspapers, Lees again suffered another nervous collapse.

A month later, Robert Lees was dining with two American friends in the Criterion Restaurant in Piccadilly when a third premonition took place. Certain that the Ripper had struck again, the journalist hurried to Scotland Yard and made a statement only a few hours before Thomas Bowyer twitched back the curtain at Miller's Court and saw the terrible scene that sent him running for the police. According to Fred Archer, it was at this point that the Yard, unable to apprehend the killer and seemingly in internal disarray (Sir Charles Warren, the unpopular Chief of Police, had resigned on the day of Mary Kelly's murder), finally approached Lees with a request that he use his powers to track down Jack the Ripper.

Accompanied by detectives the medium made his way through the streets of the East End, following a psychic trail only he could detect. Lees led the policemen across the capital until finally, at four in the morning, his 'face worn and pallid, his eyes bloodshot', he brought them to a large house in the West End of London and stated that the man that the whole of London sought was at that moment inside. The Scotland Yard inspector was dismayed as he recognised the address as that of a well respected and fashionable society physician, but Lees was adamant that this was the home of Jack the Ripper.

Undecided on whether to proceed further but having come this far, the un-named police inspector asked the medium to describe in detail the hallway that lay beyond the closed front door – if this was seen to be accurate then they would proceed with a thorough investigation of the doctor and his household. Using his powers of remote viewing, Lees immediately spoke of a black oak porter's chair located to the right of the doorway, a stained-glass window over the staircase and, critically, a dog – a large mastiff – asleep at the foot of the stairs. As the vision faded the party approached the house and the inspector rang the bell. It was answered by a maid and as she showed the men through into the vestibule they saw that Lees' description was accurate in every respect – only the dog was absent but when questioned the maidservant told them she had let the animal out into the garden only a few minutes before.

Now sure of his ground and confident as to the accuracy of Robert Lees' psychic powers, the police inspector asked to speak with the mistress of the house and a gruesome story soon began to unfold. The eminent doctor had a sinister split personality given to periodic mood swings of violent and sadistic behaviour. Only through the actions of his wife and the servants had this brutal mania for inflicting pain been kept from becoming public knowledge – she had found him on one occasion torturing a cat in his study and he had to be physically restrained several times from beating his son and causing serious injury. Recently, the doctor's wife had noticed with 'a great dread' that the terrible Whitechapel murders had all occurred on the nights that her husband had been absent from the house.

When confronted, the physician admitted to periods of memory loss during which he was unable to account for his actions. After one such blackout he regained consciousness at home with his shirtfront covered with blood and another time with scratches on his face. Soon a search of the house revealed the dark tweed suit and light overcoat that Lees had seen the murderer wearing in his first vision. Horrified that he may have committed the murders while in some strange altered state, the unnamed doctor begged them to kill him, unable to live with the knowledge that he was 'a monster'. An impromptu 'commission on lunacy' held behind closed doors found the doctor criminally insane and he was sent to a private asylum on the outskirts of London. Robert Lees was quickly sworn to secrecy and it was commonly held that he became a pensioner of the Privy Purse as a reward for his psychic services (both to Queen Victoria and in the Ripper hunt) and for his discretion as to the true identity of Jack the Ripper, a pledge he fully honoured to the day of his death.

In summing up his account, Fred Archer concluded: 'Why the hearing was held in private, and the Ripper's identity kept secret, has never been satisfactorily explained. It has been claimed that he had highly placed connections, which is not too unlikely. It has even been suggested that in his professional capacity he had attended on one or more members of the Royal family, but there is no evidence for this so far as I know'. So ends the crux of the case for Robert Lees and Jack the Ripper.

A secret Royal connection is a now familiar aspect of the Whitechapel case but in fact it was a theory that circulated in Ripper circles almost from the very beginning of the modern renaissance. In 1960, Dr Thomas Eldon Stowell, formerly of St Thomas' Hospital in London, lunched with Colin

Wilson and disclosed that through a personal investigation of the Lees story he was inclined to believe that the mysterious doctor tracked down by the psychic bloodhound was Sir William Gull, Physician in Ordinary to Queen Victoria. During the 1930s, Stowell had known Sir William's daughter Caroline Acland, who told him that on one occasion a detective accompanied by a medium had visited her parents' house at 74 Grosvenor Square in Mayfair and had asked 'some impertinent questions' that had upset Lady Gull. However, Dr Stowell did not believe that Sir William Gull was Jack the Ripper but rather that as a Royal physician he was involved in a conspiracy to shield the real killer and that the Duke of Clarence, Prince Albert Victor, known as 'Eddie' and grandson of Queen Victoria, was actually the murderer. Over fifteen years later this 'Royal Conspiracy' theory achieved its widest audience through English journalist Stephen Knight's 1976 book *Jack the Ripper: The Final Solution* which presents a Masonic plot to cover up a clandestine marriage between Prince Eddie and a working-class girl, Annie Elizabeth Crook, and suggests the murders were carried out by Gull in collaboration with a coachman, John Netley, with the assistance of Sir Robert Anderson, the Assistant Commissioner of Scotland Yard.

In the early 1980s, television researcher Melvin Harris published an article entitled 'The Murders and the Medium' in the part-work magazine *The Unexplained*, which effectively blew the Spiritualist story of Robert Lees and Jack the Ripper out of the water. Through clever research, Harris had established that the posthumous testimony published by the *Daily Mail* and both supported and used by Fred Archer in his *Ghost Detectives* was in fact a plagiarised version, by Fleet Street crime reporter Cyril Morton, of an article which had appeared seven years after the Whitechapel murders in the Chicago *Sunday Times-Herald* on 28 April 1895, itself 'a few facts coloured by fiction' and in reality a piece of sensationalist journalism engineered by a notorious American society of hoaxers known (appropriately enough) as the Whitechapel Club. The original article is easy to discredit due to its plain inconsistencies with the known facts of the case, the most blatant being the Chicago piece citing a total of seventeen victims being killed over a period of several years rather than the generally accepted total of five murders taking place during a period of ten weeks.

Harris was in fact following in the footsteps of criminologist Professor Donald West, who, as Research Officer for the London-based Society for Psychical Research (SPR), had investigated the Lees-Ripper story and in 1949 published a paper in the Society's *Journal* showing up much of the inconsistencies of the previously published versions, including the Chicago article. Several years before (in 1931) another of the Society's representatives,

Mrs Brackenbury, had visited Scotland Yard but had failed to find any documentation confirming Lees' involvement in the events of 1888. In 1963, another psychical researcher, Simeon Edmunds, had written a similar article to West's which appeared in the paranormal-related *Tomorrow* magazine; however, the specialist nature and limited circulations of both this and the SPR publication meant that it was not until Harris' work during the 1980s that the revelations found more or less mainstream exposure.

Melvin Harris later went on to publish an expanded study of Robert Lees' involvement with the Ripper in his *Jack the Ripper: The Bloody Truth* (1987). This also contains demolitions of other Ripper anecdotes and theories, in particular the Freemasonry conspiracy of Stephen Knight. Recently (in 2001) Ripper authors Stewart Evans and Keith Skinner also drove another literary nail in the Lees-Ripper coffin by offering an alternative translation to a phrase contained in a 'Dear Boss' letter received by the police at the time of the murders, which had been used (particularly by Knight) to support the medium's connection with the case, when they suggested that 'You have not caught me yet you see, with all your cunning, with all your *Lees*, with all your blue bottles' should in fact read 'with all your *tecs*', a slang term for detectives[4]. Almost overnight any paranormal connection with the 'autumn of terror' seemed finally to fade away.

Robert Lees was a respected figure both within and outside of the Spiritualist movement (his diaries are preserved at the Spiritualists' National Union headquarters at Stanstead Hall in Essex), a gentle man known for his humanity and social work – in 1893 he established a community project for the poor and homeless, the People's League, which operated out of purpose-built premises in Peckham High Street in South London – and to be willingly a part of what to him and his family would have struck as being a distasteful fraud seems out of character. In reality Lees neither confirmed or denied, publically or in print, any involvement in the Ripper case (even the interview mentioning his involvement that appeared in the *Illustrated Leicester Chronicle* was written by a supporter) and much of his posthumous reputation as one of the greatest of twentieth-century Spiritualists and a worker of paranormal miracles lies in the untiring support of his devoted daughter Eva Lees, who nursed the medium in his final years (his wife died in 1912) and spent the rest of her days, until her own death in 1968, as a propagandist for his life and published works, a total of six books said to have been dictated by spirit communicators with Lees acting as an amanuensis.

When Donald West interviewed Eva Lees in November 1948, he found her 'an elderly but well-preserved lady' who was 'voluble in the extreme'. 'She talked incessantly for over two hours,' he later commented, 'relating the most fantastic stories concerning her father's mediumship'. These included accounts of objects materialising in his presence and spirits appearing in Lees' study who spoke naturally to him like real people, in much the same way that full-form materialisations were often seen and photographed in the presence of Brazilian medium Carmine Mirabelli[5]. Miss Eva claimed to have seen the materialisations herself and in the 1960s told Leicester Spiritualist Barry Jeffrey a similar story, of hearing several spirit voices in her father's room when she knew for a fact that no one had been previously admitted to the house. West was, however, unimpressed and felt that these accounts were nothing more than hysterical fantasies, although there was no doubting her devotion to Lees' memory, who she described as being 'an intensely spiritual man'. That his name was continually associated with what she described as 'garbled newspaper versions of the Ripper story' was something that caused her great personal annoyance.

Interestingly, the Leicester house that Eva Lees lived in for many years following Robert Lees' death, a three-storey villa known as 'Rodona' in Fosse Road South, itself gained something of a haunted reputation in the early 1980s, when several student lodgers (the house by this time had been split into bedsits) claimed to repeatedly hear strange sounds and footsteps coming from the old ground-floor kitchen.

Perhaps the most intriguing aspect of the Lees-Ripper story lies in the one piece of documentary evidence connecting the medium with the murders but which has been used by a number of commentators to effectively dismiss his association with the case. In Lees' diary for the week following the 'double event' of 30 September 1888, he notes three separate visits to the police with offers of help in tracking down the killer; on each occasion he was turned away as 'a fool and lunatic' although on the third visit (to Scotland Yard), probably to humour his persistence, he was promised that the police authority would write to him, but there are no further entries to confirm this happening. The entry for 2 October is the most interesting as it shows that Lees visited at least one of the murder sites for himself. This was Dutfield's Yard, where the medium makes the comment: 'Got trace of man from the spot in Berner Street'.

There is no doubting Robert Lees' sincerity but it was to be many years before a sensitive such as Gerard Croiset (who we will meet in a later chapter) would make psychic detection a seemingly viable option for the police dealing with difficult and unsolvable murders. We can now only speculate on the thought that, for one brief moment in October 1888, Robert James Lees was in fact the one person in the whole of England who may have been able to lead officers to the most notorious murderer in history . . .

NOTES

1. Eusapia Palladino (1854-1918) was a powerful physical medium from Naples who was subjected to numerous scientific investigations over many years. Despite being detected in fraud on a number of occasions, Eusapia produced undoubtedly genuine phenomena when strictly controlled and in the presence of experienced and critical researchers, particularly a committee from the London Society for Psychical Research (SPR) comprising Hereward Carrington, Everard Fielding and William W. Baggelly, who held a series of sittings in Naples in 1908. Mina Stinson (1888-1941), wife of the former Harvard Medical School instructor Le Roy Goddard Crandon, who, as noted in the Introduction, went under the pseudonym of 'Margery' for much of her career – the most controversial physical mediums of the twentieth century whose phenomena include direct voice communication, phantom lights and materialised spirit hands which exuded from her vagina. Many aspects of her mediumship, which itself caused a sixteen-year rift between factions of the American Society for Psychical Research (ASPR), and despite being championed by modern day Spiritualists, has been in all probability truthfully described as 'a most ingenious, persistent and fantastic fraud'.
2. The Mitre Square murder is one of three Ripper killings which have now entered contemporary London ghostlore. The 'Ripper Corner', the spot where Catherine Eddowes' body was found and is still discernable as such despite much alteration to the surrounding area over the years, is said to be haunted by the apparition of a huddled form glimpsed on occasion, most often on or around the anniversary of the 'double event' of 30 September. According to Jack Hallam, a 'huddled figure, like that of a woman, emitting from all over it a ghostly light', said to be the ghost of 'Polly' Nicholls, has allegedly been seen over the years near the murder site in Durward Street; while groans and screams heard in nearby Hanbury Street have been unsurprisingly attributed to the second Ripper victim, Annie Chapman.
3. There has been much debate over the years as to the exact ages of the Fox sisters at the time of the disturbances in 1848. For a comprehensive study, see 'The Fox Sisters: Riddle of the Records' by Lis J. Warwood, *Psypioneer*, Vol. 4, No. 9, September 2008. Retrieved from www.woodlandway.org on 10 September 2011.
4. *Jack the Ripper: Letters from Hell* (Sutton Publishing, Gloucestershire, 2001).
5. Carmine Mirabelli (1889-1951) was a powerful physical medium and one of the most enigmatic figures in the history of Spiritualism. His phenomena included the movement and teleportation of objects, materialised figures in full daylight and automatic writing in several languages, all unknown to the medium. One famous photograph of Mirabelli levitating during a séance in São Paulo has been shown to be faked, but there are many testimonies to the genuineness of his remarkable mediumship.

CHAPTER 4

THE WELCOMES MURDER

ERNEST DYER, 1922

Around lunchtime on 16 November 1922, the duty manager of the Old Bar Hotel at Scarborough, a popular seaside holiday town on the north Yorkshire coast, thirty-five miles north-east of York, was called through into the hotel lobby by the receptionist. Waiting for him was a man who introduced himself as Detective Inspector Abbott of the Scarborough CID and he was keen to speak with one of the guests, a Mr James Fitzsimmons, who at that moment was eating a meal in the dining room. In recent days a number of incidents had come to the attention of the local police: these included the passing of forged or 'dud' cheques and a series of newspaper advertisements that struck heavily of a confidence trick, offering business opportunities for suitable applicants in return for large downpayments in cash; all of which appeared to be connected with Mr Fitzsimmons, who was asked to come through to the front of the hotel. As Abbott waited in the lobby he had no idea that his routine visit would have such a dramatic and deadly outcome. The Yorkshire policeman was also unaware that it was just one piece of a mysterious puzzle that was to take many months and, more remarkably, a series of eerie paranormal visions that would ultimately bring about a solution.

Breaking off from his meal, Fitzsimmons seemed surprised to see the CID man but appeared cooperative and agreed to accompany Abbott to his hotel room to discuss the matter. As they reached the first floor, the policeman became instantly on his guard as Fitzsimmons reached for something in an inside pocket and, afraid he was attempting to destroy incriminating evidence, Abbott made a grab for his arms. Fitzsimmons had in fact made an effort to draw a loaded revolver; as the two men struggled together there was a shot, deafening in the confined corridor, and the hotel guest crumpled to the floor, fatally wounded.

In the immediate aftermath Abbott entered the locked hotel room and quickly came across several items which clearly showed that James Fitzsimmons, now on his way to the mortuary, had been working as a fraudster under a false identity. That name was Eric Tombe. There was a passport containing a photograph of the dead man in that name as well as several chequebooks and a leather suitcase bearing the initials 'E.T.' As Abbott examined the cheques he noticed that each bore Tombe's signature in pencil, ready to be overwritten in ink, which gave the policeman the distinct impression that Fitzsimmons had been masquerading as a real person. His few other meagre possessions showed that he had been moving from hotel to hotel, surviving on the proceeds of a well orchestrated deception.

The reality was that James Fitzsimmons was a wanted man and a warrant had been issued for his arrest; but his real name wasn't Fitzsimmons or even Eric Tombe, it was Ernest Dyer, a former employee of the Air Ministry, often known to his associates as 'Bill' Dyer. One of these was a young man by the name of Dennis Yeats Wheatley, at that time a newly married London wine merchant who had yet to embark on the future and successful literary career that was to span four decades and in a few years would transform him into the 'Prince of Thriller Writers' for several generations of the British reading public. The only son of a Mayfair wine seller, Wheatley entered the family firm when he was sixteen but turned to writing when the business stalled during the Depression. His first published novel *The Forbidden Territory* (1933) was an instant success, going through seven reprints in as many weeks, and quickly established a winning formula that would produce a total of fifty-four books, of which only eight (beginning with *The Devil Rides Out* in 1934) were the Black Magic stories for which he is now famous. Despite his imagination, talent for writing and knowledge of occultism and the supernatural, it is doubtful whether even Wheatley would have conceived a plot line such as that of the real life events into which he would eventually be drawn during the early years of the roaring twenties.

In September 1914, aged seventeen, Wheatley had received a commission into the 2nd/1st City of London Royal Field Artillery, but suffered from several periods of ill heath and caught severe pneumonia while digging gun pits at a training camp on Salisbury Plain. Following a period of convalesce at the Great Central Hotel in Marylebone, he was posted to the 6th Reserve Brigade camp at Biscot in Bedfordshire, a small village which is now a suburb of Luton. Here he met Gordon Eric Gordon Tombe, known as Eric Tombe, and they shared a billet together for eighteen months before Wheatley was finally sent to France in August 1917. Despite their friendship lasting just five brief years, Tombe would be one of the most lasting influences on the thriller writer's life: Wheatley's bookplate, self-designed and one he used throughout his life, featured Tombe as a satyr with the young author sitting enthralled at his feet, and sixty years after they first met he dedicated a three-volume set of memoirs to his memory. 'He weaned me from reading trash to books by the finest authors of all nations,' Wheatley later recalled, 'and to books about ancient civilizations and the occult'. Gordon Eric, as Wheatley called him, 'was completely immoral and immensely knowledgeable' and was twenty-four when they first met; he was also 'a crook of the first order' and that was to prove his downfall.

Eric Tombe was born in Nottinghamshire, the son of a clergyman, the Revd George Gordon Tombe. Later, the family moved to Ireland, where Tombe received his schooling, but by the time war broke out in the summer of 1914 they had returned to England and Eric, now married and with a young family of his own, was living in Stoke Newington in London and working as a motor mechanic. Tombe quickly became a private in the Public School Corps. As a lieutenant in the Royal Field Artillery he saw action in France, but was wounded when an exploding shell buried his position; he was convalescing at the Biscot Camp at the time he met Wheatley and around the time the younger man was finally posted abroad to Vlamertinghe he had taken up a desk job at the Air Ministry in Kingsway in London, monitoring the progress of factories involved in war work. In May 1918, Wheatley was gassed; his fighting days were over and, invalided out of the Army, he spent several months convalescing before finally taking up his position in the family wine business. With the war over Wheatley was also quick to renew his friendship with Eric Tombe, who, by this time, had quit his job as a civil servant and had gone into business with a former colleague from the Air Ministry; that person was 'Bill' Dyer.

Ernest Dyer, also in his twenties and originally from Brighton, had worked as a plumber fitting gas appliances before emigrating to Australia, where he followed an eclectic career path that included short-lived stints as a fruit farmer, a pearl fisherman and a horse breeder. In 1914, he enlisted as a sapper in the Australian Engineers but was wounded at Gallipoli and returned to England where, following a period of recovery, he became an officer in the Royal West Surrey Regiment and was later transferred to the Royal Engineers. Dyer saw action in France but was wounded a second time and, like Tombe, became invalided into the Civil Service, where his engineering background made him an ideal administrator, overseeing aircraft production for the RAF. Another common trait he shared with

Eric Tombe was a desire not to survive the Great War a poor man and both men were not averse to breaking the law to achieve this aim. In his *Drink and Ink*, published posthumously in 1979, Dennis Wheatley gives a pen portrait of Eric Tombe which goes some way to likening him to a kind of 'gentleman thief' along the lines of Ernest Horning's Raffles. 'He never robbed people,' Wheatley reminisced, 'but swindled insurance companies and the government out of considerable sums.' In this he was adequately aided by Ernest Dyer and soon after the Armistice of November 1918 the two conspirators put their bold and 'nefarious' plans into action.

With the cessation of fighting, Dyer's role at the Air Ministry changed from supervising aeroplane production to vetting invoices from suppliers and engineering firms, both large and small, for the cancellation of aircraft parts already in manufacture, and authorising legitimate claims for payment. Tombe was quick to realise that by setting up a number of phoney small-part businesses it would be possible to submit claims for compensation for non-existent work that Dyer could simply approve for payment with little or no chance of detection. To these ends Tombe quit his job early in 1919 and soon began putting the scam into practice: cheap office space was rented, bank accounts opened and stationery printed; the illusion was completed by installing one of Tombe's mistresses to act as a secretary, answering telephone calls and typing out letters. Soon these phantom companies were invoicing the Air Ministry for several hundred pounds worth of aborted work which Dyer promptly approved for payment; once a cheque had been banked, Eric Tombe withdrew the cash and soon after the company quietly closed down and left no forwarding address. 'It entailed extraordinary organizing ability and brought the two conspirators many thousand pounds,' Wheatley later commented, but there was a limit to how long such a scheme could operate without detection and the following year Dyer resigned from the civil service and both he and Tombe began looking around for alternative means of making money.

Ernest Dyer had been interested in horses and horse racing since his time several years before working on a stud farm in Australia. A contemporary story reported in a number of newspapers after his death stated that in 1920 he successfully gambled his entire war gratuity at odds of 33-1 on a horse called Furious which came home first in the Lincoln Handicap, and as a result received a payout of £15,000. In his *The Devil is a Gentleman* (2009), Dennis Wheatley's biographer Phil Baker concedes that there may be some truth to this but notes that a more likely explanation is that it was a cover for money laundering activities, possibly involving some of the proceeds of the recent Air Ministry scam. When a venture with Tombe selling motor cars in

Harlesden in north-west London folded, despite Eric Tombe's experience in the motor trade, the two men decided to invest in Dyer's expertise with all things connected with the race track and set themselves up as gentlemen horse trainers.

The Welcomes was a large detached house in substantial grounds with its own stable block located in Hayes Lane, Kenley, a Surrey village three and a half miles south of Croydon. Dyer bought it from Percy Woodland, a noted jockey and trainer, in 1920 for £5,000 and, moving in with his wife and children, both he and Tombe quickly built up a small operation breeding and training race horses on the nearby Downs. At this time Eric Tombe was living on the proceeds of his involvement with the Air Ministry fraud in a serviced flat on the Haymarket, but on the occasions when business called him down to the stud farm he would stay just over eleven miles away in an hotel at Dorking on the North Downs. Despite the investment, both Tombe and Dyer seemed fated to only reap the rewards of deceit as, despite starting out as a legitimate business, albeit financed with crooked money, ultimately nothing but tragedy would come out of their association with The Welcomes.

The truth was that both young men were equally capable of spending money faster than they could earn it, and in the early months of 1921 it became clear to Dyer and Tombe that The Welcomes was a financial liability that neither of them could sustain for much longer. True to form, rather than attempting to sell the estate as a going concern, Dyer's solution was more immediate and devious and one in which Eric Tombe was a willing participant. 'Neither I nor his mistress-in-chief knew anything of his nefarious activities until after his death,' Wheatley stated towards the end of his life, claiming that this was due to Tombe being able to create 'a succession of cul-de-sacs which prevented any of his associates, girl friends or men, learning anything about the others.' The reality was that Wheatley knew far more about Tombe's crooked career during the time that he knew him than he was prepared to set down fifty years later in his memoirs, particularly where the fate of The Welcomes was concerned. The property was insured for £12,000 and Dyer's answer to their cash flow problems was to arrange for the house to conveniently burn down.

Around the beginning of the second week in April 1921, Dyer sent his family off for a short break to Scotland and planned to join them a day or so later after concluding some business in Brighton. With his wife and children out of the way, he spent most of Tuesday 12 April soaking The Welcomes with petrol before catching a late afternoon train down to the south coast. With Wheatley providing a suitable alibi – the future thriller writer would later confirm that he and Eric Tombe, together with two female friends, had been dining together all evening at Tombe's Haymarket flat –Tombe made his own way (in full evening dress) to Kenley and proceeded to set the house on fire before returning to London where he joined the party shortly after midnight. When Ernest Dyer was summoned from Brighton the next day he found The Welcomes a burnt-out shell and, suitably traumatised, was soon filing a claim with his insurers.

Despite their best laid plans, the two fraudsters were to be disappointed. A sharp-eyed insurance assessor sent to Kenley to vet Dyer's claim noticed a number of petrol cans that Tombe had either inadvertently failed to clear out of the way in his haste to get back to London or assumed would be incinerated in the blaze, with the result that the company refused to pay out and Dyer had little option but to drop his claim. With The Welcomes now a blackened ruin (Dyer's wife was able to live in the one part of the building that had been untouched by the flames) Dyer and Tombe were forced in the ensuing months to fall back on what they hoped would be more successful scams to make ends meet.

Almost a year to the day after the burning of The Welcomes, on 19 April 1922, Wheatley met Tombe in London. He was in the process of buying a flat in Earls Court and was keen to get Tombe's opinion on the property. By this time Dyer was virtually bankrupt and in order to restore himself to funds was setting up a potential swindle on an unsuspecting investor. In order to see the fraud through, Tombe was obliged to act as a guarantor by transferring £2,000 of his own money into Dyer's bank account. 'I'm going down to Purley to fix it up tomorrow night,' he told him as they parted at the entrance to Earl's Court station. Wheatley was to be one of the last people who would see him alive. They had one last telephone conversation the following day: it was the same day that Gordon Eric Gordon Tombe simply vanished.

Tombe was to be missing for many months. For Wheatley and his clique of friends, which included several of Eric Tombe's mistresses and girlfriends, each assigned to their own particular 'cul-de-sac' and unaware of each other's existence, suspicion quickly fell on Ernest Dyer. Wheatley knew much about Tombe's illegal activities and although the most likely explanation for his absence was that he had been forced to lie low after one of his shady deals had got too hot to handle, even he as a privileged insider felt that Dyer was involved. Wheatley was inclined to believe that Tombe was being held against his will and made to sign over money to Dyer who, once he had got what he wanted, would vanish, leaving his former business associate free but unable to go to the police for fear of incriminating himself in their past misdeeds of glory together. This view was reinforced after Wheatley visited Tombe's bank manager who confirmed that a large sum of money had recently been transferred, at Tombe's request, to his account in Paris and that Dyer had now been given power of attorney over Tombe's affairs.

Wheatley was sure that Tombe was alive and would surface eventually, but one of his mistresses, the wife of a wealthy industrialist from Huddersfield who Tombe had met during his time working at the Air Ministry, was certain he was dead. Central to her belief was the wording of a telegram, said to have been sent to Dyer by Tombe, in which he said he had gone abroad for a few days: *'Going overseas back in Seven Days, look after things while I'm away, Eric'* – Tombe would never have used the word 'overseas'. The telegram was a fake and Dyer a murderer. The deadline of a week was soon up and still there was no sign of Eric Tombe. Wheatley continued to procrastinate but eventually gave in to pressure and as a gesture hired a private detective but the investigation lead nowhere, partly because Wheatley was economical with his information due to not wishing to incriminate both Tombe and himself in a number of his mentor's dodgy deals, including the torching of The Welcomes. When after several weeks a mutual woman friend of Tombe's who had just returned from abroad told the young wine merchant she had seen him in Madrid alive and well, Wheatley, somewhat relieved, lost interest and began concentrating on other things.

The Revd George Gordon Tombe was vicar of the small Oxfordshire parish of Little Tew, eight miles south-west of Banbury and a world away in every respect from the hedonistic London lifestyle of his son, the distress of whose continued silence eventually resulted in his giving up the living of St John the Evangelist and moving to Sydenham near Crystal Palace, where he and his wife began a concerted effort to track him down. George Tombe's involvement has been described as 'one of the romances of the crime' as, like a living embodiment of G.K. Chesterton's literary detective Father Brown, the clergyman began a systematic search to find some evidence of Eric Tombe's whereabouts.

Tombe had last seen his father at the beginning of January 1922 at the Strand Palace Hotel in London, shortly before taking a trip to Sicily. Around the middle of April he had written to the Revd Tombe mentioning a forthcoming trip to Paris and some new suits he had had made specifically for the visit. George Tombe visited the tailor in Albermarle Street and found the clothes had not been collected. He also visited the branch of Lloyd's Bank where Tombe held his account and spoke with the manager, who reassured him that they had been receiving regular correspondence from his son for some time, the last letter being dated 22 June 1922. Whereas Dennis Wheatley had felt the jagged signature on the deed granting Dyer power of attorney showed the writer had been forced against his will to sign, the Revd Tombe was more forthright and declared it and all the letters to be forgeries. Eric Tombe's account had been fleeced and was now substantially overdrawn.

Now certain that someone impersonating his son was also clearly connected with his disappearance, the elderly clergyman visited Eric Tombe's barber, who kept a list of new customers introduced by regular clients. One of these was Ernest Dyer and he had made a note of his address: The Welcomes, Kenley. George Tombe made a trip out to Surrey and found the stud farm a dilapidated ruin; there was no sign of Dyer but he met his wife, who told him her husband was dead – he had been killed in a car accident earlier in the year. This was palpably untrue, but at the time George Tombe had no idea of the violent events at Scarborough; Dyer's death had been ruled a suicide and his widow was no doubt unwilling to reveal the truth to strangers. Despite seemingly at a dead end, as he surveyed the derelict estate, the Revd Tombe felt that something about The Welcomes was forbiddingly familiar.

Like the Murder in the Red Barn almost exactly 100 years before, the evidence for paranormality in the Tombe/Dyer case revolves around the eerie prophetic dreams of Eric Tombe's mother who, over the course of several months, had numerous nightmares in which she saw her son dead. 'In my dream I heard Eric say, "Oh, let me out." I felt he was shut in somewhere and could not get free' she later told reporters. As the weeks passed this recurring dream gradually changed and became far more sinister: Mrs Tombe saw a dark damp place like some enclosure or chamber in the ground in a remote rural location, again from which the voice of Eric Tombe continued to plead for release. Haunted by these experiences, she urged her husband to go to the police again, now certain that somewhere in the wilderness of The Welcomes her son lay dead at the bottom of a well. Finally, in September 1923, like Robert Lees before him, George Tombe went to Scotland Yard.

Francis Carlin, together with Albert Hawkins, Arthur Neil and Frederick Wensley, was one of a group of Superintendents at the Metropolitan Police headquarters at Whitehall Place known as the 'Big Four'. Carlin had recently been promoted from Chief Inspector and his illustrious career at Scotland Yard later spanned over thirty years, the highlights of which he recalled in a set of memoirs titled *Reminiscences of an Ex-Detective* (1927). To the Superintendent, there was no doubting the sincerity with which the elderly cleric stated his belief in the strange dreams of his wife concerning his missing son and the lonely and derelict Surrey stud farm. Despite his earnestness, to a London policeman, the results of George Tombe's amateur investigations may have been more impressive than stories of supernatural visions and, secure in the knowledge following the events at Scarborough that through his possession of his son's cheque books and suitcase, Ernest Dyer may well have been involved in some way in Eric Tombe's disappearance, Carlin decided to act on the information.

Together with Divisional Detective-Inspector Hedges and a group of uniformed officers, Carlin visited The Welcomes. After eighteen months of abandonment, the burnt-out farmhouse and stable block were little more than rubble and weed-choked ruins and an examination of the premises revealed nothing out of place; more importantly, there was no sign of a well which Mrs Tombe was insistent contained the body of her son. However, amongst the tall grass on the edge of the paddock, Carlin noted four concrete slabs which proved to be the covers over a series of cesspits. Prising one open, the policemen found a deep circular brick-built pit; it was empty but could conceivably be mistaken for a well by someone unaware of its real purpose. Between them Carlin and Hedges lifted the covers of the remaining pits: two more were empty but the fourth was suspiciously full, almost to the top with bricks and rubble. The Superintendent sent two of the uniformed men to obtain shovels and a pickaxe and on their return they began clearing out the debris.

The cesspit was deep and as darkness fell the work continued by the light of two hurricane lamps. 'I could not help thinking to myself,' Carling later recalled, 'that the grim scene, with the flickering lights of the lanterns shining on the faces and bared arms of the workers as they swung their picks and shoveled away debris, must have looked rather like those nights some seventy years or eighty years ago when the resurrectionists, Burke and Hare, were at their nefarious work in some cemetery.' Eventually, after removing a large amount of rubble, the policemen reached ground water level and were forced to lower down a bucket. As the rank water was drawn off a sudden shout brought Carlin to the edge of the pit; by the light of a lantern they could see a man's shoe projecting up out of the rubble with a skeletal foot still attached.

Eric Tombe's body, a mass of bones only held together by his clothes, was decomposed beyond recognition and only identifiable by items still present on the body – a wristwatch, cuff links, a tie-pin and a gold crown pried from the jaw by a pathologist. The cause of death was a shotgun blast, at close range, to the back of the head and Tombe had died instantly.

At the subsequent inquest, Tombe's death was put as occurring on or around 20 April 1922, the time that he had gone down to The Welcomes to discuss financing Dyer's proposed scam on a man named Stephens. Late one night two months later, in June 1922, Ernest Dyer's wife told the Coroner's Court she had been disturbed by the sounds of stones falling outside and encountered her husband (who at the time she believed was abroad on business), in a distressed state moving about in the shadows. Dyer had ordered her back inside the house and claimed he was visiting the farm at night to avoid being seen by his creditors; the reality was that Tombe's corpse was at that moment lying in the water-filled cesspit and Dyer had returned to continue filling it in under the cover of darkness. The inquest returned a verdict of murder by Ernest Dyer, whose precarious financial difficulties had resulted in the killing of his former business partner as a short-sighted and desperate attempt to escape his mounting debts. At Scarborough, Dyer had clearly thought that Detective Inspector Abbott had come to arrest him for Eric Tombe's murder and had ultimately cheated the hangman by his own hand.

Subsequently, the Revd George Tombe tried to play down the involvement of his wife's dreams in the discovery of their son's body. The newspapers began giving conflicting statements as to who actually had the visions and ultimately the family denied that anything of the kind had actually happened. It is not difficult to see why, as any involvement with supernormal happenings of this sort would have brought him far closer to Spiritualism and even necromancy – the divination of hidden information from the dead – than would of been healthy for a Christian minister. Despite this, Francis Carlin was one of several people who acknowledged the mysterious involvement of the paranormal: it was 'one of the most remarkable things I have ever come across in my career – that a dream should have been the starting-off point in the investigations in this unparalleled mystery,' was his final comment on the case.

Despite compiling a detailed manuscript on the murder, extracts of which have only been published recently[1], Eric Tombe's death had a profound effect on the young Dennis Wheatley; the thriller writer remembered his mentor with affection for the rest of his life and adamantly refused to be drawn into talking about the murder in any way. Today there is little for the curious to see at the former site of The Welcomes. The name still survives but modern houses have been built on the stud farm grounds and much of the original farmhouse has been cleared away, although a series of cottages which once comprised the old stable block still stand.

Is it possible to give some explanation of the psychic or paranormal forces which enabled Mrs Tombe to see so accurately the grim and hidden grave of her son? During the course of his extensive examination of psychometry and paranormal crime detection, published in 1984 as *The Psychic Detectives*, Colin Wilson considered cases such as the Tombe murder and the Red Barn in terms of 'dream telepathy' between the percipient and the victim. Whereas Maria Marten may have been able to transmit an unconscious mental signal as she was being attacked by William Corder, which was subsequently picked up as a series of dreams by Ann Marten, Wilson argues that the circumstances of Eric Tombe's death – the violent and instantaneous blast from Dyer's shotgun from behind – would have been so sudden that Tombe would have been completely unable to have sent such a message. As such, a possible explanation of the paranormal revelation of Eric Tombe's body would seem to lie nearer to the spirit hypothesis of mediums such as Robert Lees and, as we will see, psychics such as Estelle Roberts. As Wilson notes, 'It is difficult to resist the inference that Eric Tombe somehow communicated with his mother after his death', although if Dennis Wheatley's suspicion that Tombe was held prisoner at The Welcomes for some time before he was killed is true, he may well have realised that Dyer intended to murder him, with the result that the 'dream telepathy' theory is still valid.

We will return to the subject of prophetic dreams in a later chapter as our next case has its paranormal element, not as a way of revealing a crime, but as a direct and chilling means of murder . . .

NOTE

1. See Phil Baker's *The Devil is a Gentleman: The Life and Times of Dennis Wheatley* (Dedalus Ltd, Sawtry, 2009). Eric Tombe was buried in a family plot in Sutton Cemetery; the memorial is to his brother, Kenneth, who died in America in 1917.

CHAPTER 5

THE ENIGMA

NETTA FORNARIO, 1929

Haunting apparitions are one of the most familiar and widely reported aspects of the paranormal world. A wealth of records exist for ghosts and ghostly phenomena occurring in and around countless buildings across the country, both humble and historic, from council houses, pubs, railway stations and cinemas, through to prisons, stately homes and ancient castles. Although their causation and reasons for appearing are at present unexplainable, these resident phantoms are for the most part benign and harmless. In his aforementioned *The Ghost Hunter's Guide* (1986), Peter Underwood considers these hauntings in terms of 'mental imprint manifestations' or 'atmospheric photograph ghosts': impressions of former inhabitants or events that have become seemingly ingrained in the building's fabric and which become active and are either able to 'play back' under suitable conditions, or are triggered into action by the presence of a psychic person. Unsettling as these experiences may be to some, they operate within their own realm oblivious to the presence of observers and are on the whole most often regarded, as writers Michael and Molly Hardwicke have described them, as 'inoffensive members of the community'.

However, the literature of psychical research is also littered with credible accounts of supernormal happenings which can best be summarised as 'extreme hauntings': paranormal experiences that seemingly involve both some form of intelligence or discarnate consciousness together with a varying degree of force or violence directed towards the percipient or observers. Although the boundaries between them are at times somewhat blurred and overlapping, they fall with some exceptions into the following three broad categories: possessions, poltergeist phenomena and psychic attacks.

Violent or 'demonic possessions' have become associated in the public mind in recent years with the disturbing and shocking imagery contained in director William Friedkin's 1973 film *The Exorcist*, whose screenplay, as well as the novel on which it was based, were both written by New York writer William Peter Blatty. Blatty's story was itself based on real life events which took place in 1949 in Cottage City, Maryland, a suburb of Washington DC, and were centred around a thirteen-year-old boy named Douglas Deen. The youth went into convulsions, screamed obscenities and spoke in Latin, a language with which he was unfamiliar, and these disturbances were also accompanied by powerful physical phenomena of a poltergeist-like nature, including scratching and banging noises together with the movement of objects and furniture. After a protracted exorcism ceremony carried out by Father William Bowdern, a Jesuit priest, the possession ended after several months in May 1949. Modern psychiatric medicine ascribes most instances of possession to personality disorders but a number of cases, such as the Cottage City incident, lend support to the argument of there being in some instances violent person-centred hauntings involving the temporary invasion of a person's organism by a discarnate 'spirit' or 'entity' from another realm or world. In Britain, a noted and high-profile exorcist was the late Revd Dr Donald Omand, who was the subject of a full length biography *To Anger the Devil* (1978) by Australian writer and ghost hunter Marc Alexander.

Supernormal happenings that today we recognise as poltergeist phenomena have a recorded history stretching back centuries to the time of Homer and Plutarch. The first book in the English language to describe poltergeist hauntings is Ludwig Lavater's *Of Ghostes and Spirites Walking by Nyght*, published in London in 1572, and there have been a number of notable cases from the British Isles since that time, beginning with the famous Drummer of Tedworth in Wiltshire, recorded by the Revd Joseph Glanville in the middle years of the seventeenth century. Glanville issued an account of his investigation in 1661 and just over 300 years separate this and the accounts of another British poltergeist incident, which is now also regarded as a landmark case. In 1977, reports of spectacular and violent disturbances of a supernatural nature in a council house in Enfield, North London, made newspaper headlines and have become one of the most famous paranormal investigations of modern times. For over a year the Hodgson family (given the pseudonym Harper in contemporary and subsequent publicity) were at the centre of bizarre and at times terrifying events which included the violent projection and movement of objects and furniture, knocks and banging sounds, the apparent levitation of family members, apparitions (including bizarrely on one occasion an apparition of one of the investigating members of the Society for Psychical Research) as well as spontaneous fires and paranormal graffiti.

Ten years before, a less well known but equally impressive period of poltergeist haunting took place in the West Riding of Yorkshire. The case of the Black Monk of Pontefract involved another working class family, the Pritchards, who, like the Hodgsons at Enfield, were subjected to several months of violent and inexplicable phenomena: deafening drumming noises, breaking furniture and crockery, the appearance of pools of water and a strange chalk-like dust, together with a tall apparition thought to be the ghost of a long-dead Cluniac monk hanged for rape in the time of Henry VIII. On one occasion twelve-year-old Diane Pritchard was dragged up the stairs by an invisible assailant, which left a series of red finger marks on her throat. The vast majority of parapsychologists have traditionally assigned poltergeist phenomena to be a form of recurring and spontaneous psychokinesis normally centred around a living person, most often an adolescent youth. However, some researchers, such as Guy Playfair, who spent several months at Enfield during the time of the disturbances, and Colin Wilson, who made a retrospective study of the Pontefract case in the early 1980s, are inclined to believe that poltergeists are actually more closely related to the popular view of possession and are the result of actual discarnate 'entities' or non-human personalities rather than the extraordinary effects of the human mind.

The subject of psychic attack has become somewhat confused in modern times, with the result that alleged contemporary cases or given examples bear only a superficial resemblance to the concept as understood and accepted by researchers and investigators in the past. Today, paranormalists are likely to group a vast array of alleged phenomena (both real and imagined), ranging from anxiety, depression and mood swings through to bad luck, curses and voodooism as evidence of some form of psychic attack, whereas in its true sense the term has more of a close kinship with person-centred poltergeist hauntings or possessions, but without an invading secondary personality and less spectacular psychokinetic (i.e. Macro-PK) effects, such as the physical movement of objects and furniture. During his experiences with the haunted skull of William Corder, Dr Kilner described to Robert Thurston Hopkins' father an incident which sounds very much like the classical interpretation of a psychic attack: of being stopped in his tracks by an enormous gust of wind while walking into the drawing-room of his house, and experiencing an unseen but tremendously powerful form which took a concerted effort, both mentally and physically, to throw off.

Psychical research has shown an awareness and interest in the phenomenon of psychic attacks since the very first days of organised investigation and discussion. At a meeting of the Ghost Club – the oldest society devoted to the study of the supernormal, having been founded in Cambridge in the early 1850s – and held in the Burlington Fine Arts Club in August 1893, Mr A.J. Hamilton Wills described several unnerving incidents that he personally experienced while staying at a country house in Somerset. Retiring to bed shortly before midnight, Hamilton Wills became aware of footsteps following him as he made his way upstairs. At the door to his bedroom he paused and heard the footsteps approach and pass by into the room. Shortly afterwards, after he had undressed and lain down in bed, he was assaulted by a powerful invisible force which tore at the bedclothes and pressed down violently on his throat and chest. The attack lasted several minutes before subsiding and Hamilton Wills likened the strength to that of three fully grown men. During his stay, there were a further two night-time incidents of a similar nature, each less powerful than the previous attack but no doubt equally as frightening and inexplicable.

One of the most famous cases of psychic attack in the early decades of the twentieth century was that involving Eleonore Zügun, a young teenage Romanian peasant girl who became known in psychical research circles in both England and Vienna during the mid-1920s as the 'Poltergeist Medium' or 'Devil Girl'. Under controlled conditions and in the presence of experienced investigators, including English-born Australian entomologist and psychical researcher Robin J. Tillyard, and Harry Price (who we will meet fully in the next chapter), raps sounded in her presence, ornaments and coins moved unaided, and small toys were apported into the test room. However, the most striking phenomena produced by Eleonore, and that for which she is most remembered today, were the painful stigmata which appeared suddenly and without warning on various parts of her body, including her face, back, neck, hands and arms. These took the form of bite marks, scratches and weals, which developed while the medium was under close and constant observation and were both photographed and filmed. A possible explanation is that these stigmata were psychosomatic in origin – Eleonore believed she was being attacked by the *Dracu*, the Romanian word for 'Devil' – in which case this would be an intriguing and protracted incident of self-induced psychic attack. With the onset of menstruation at the age of fourteen, Eleonore's phenomena ceased; she subsequently returned to Romania and went on to open her own hairdressing business in Czernowitz.

Of all psychic attacks the most extreme and controversial is that which involved an American family in Culver City, southern California, during the early 1970s. Doris Bithers, a young single mother of four children in her early thirties, living in semi-squalid conditions in a house with a local reputation for being haunted, claimed to have been physically attacked and raped by malevolent spirits for a period of several years. The case was investigated in 1974 by two parapsychologists, Dr Barry Taff and Kerry Gaynor from the University of California, Los Angeles, who reported experiencing poltergeist phenomena in the Bithers house for a period of two months. Taff later acted as technical advisor on the 1983 *Exorcist*-style film *The Entity*, which was loosely based on his own investigation.

In England during the same period, reports of unusual happenings centred on the small village of Clapham near Worthing on the South Downs also contained elements that could be described as forms of psychic or paranormal attack. Incidents of UFO sightings, missing animals, several unexplained deaths and Black Magic practices were investigated by a local man, Charles Walker, together with journalist and writer Toyne Newton, who published accounts, initially in the part-work magazine *The Unexplained*, and later as a full-length book *The Demonic Connection* (1987). Newton and Walker record several instances of visitors walking through an area of Clapham Wood being seized and temporarily overtaken by unseen and debilitating forces, while on two occasions during the 1970s, Charles Walker witnessed similar psychic attacks at nearby Chanctonbury Ring, the site of an old hill-fort on the South Downs four and a half miles north-east of Clapham village, that has become associated with the disturbances: in August 1974, a member of Walker's UFO group was suddenly levitated five feet into the air before being thrown to the ground and, five years later, another researcher was knocked off his feet by a similar unseen force.

At Clapham the inference is quite clear that both Toyne Newton and Charles Walker considered these disturbing experiences not as spontaneous events but due directly to modern day occultism and Satanic practices. As such these psychic attacks could be considered almost as by-products of intentional acts of Black Magic, involving ritual animal sacrifice, being carried out by an organised coven in the area over a period of several years; and, by surviving as localised pockets of psychic energy could, on certain occasions, cause physical and mental effects on visitors who happen to pass either into the vicinity or over a particular path or location. In this particular case there was no suggestion that psychic forces were being directed consciously by members of the occult group involved – the Friends of Hecate – but there are those who consider the ability for an adept of Black Magic or occultism to be able to create a psychic attack as a weapon or means of vengeance against an enemy to be a reality. What concerns us here is the suggestion that such a sinister and paranormal ability was in fact behind a strange and sudden death that took place on a lonely island off the west coast of Scotland in the winter of 1929.

The development of psychical research as an organised discipline in the latter quarter of the nineteenth century also coincided with an increase in the Victorian interest for ritual magic and occultism. During the 1880s, occult arts such as astrology, alchemy, ritual magic and cartomancy (the use of cards such as the Tarot to tell fortunes) were being synthesised into one unifying system of Western occultism by Samuel Liddell MacGregor Mathers, an eccentric and somewhat enigmatic Englishman in his mid thirties; this become known as the Western Esoteric Tradition. In 1888, the same year that Jack the Ripper stalked the East End of London and Cambridge philosopher Professor Henry Sidgwick presided over the newly formed Society for Psychical Research, Mathers, together with two other fellow Freemasons, founded the Hermetic Order of the Golden Dawn, a semi-secret society dedicated to ceremonial magic and the study of the 'intellectual forces behind Nature, the constitution of man and his relation to God'.

The Golden Dawn established lodges and taught its hundred or so members practical occult arts: how to set up magical circles, consecrate talismans, how to cast spells, use magical weapons and to master the out-of-body experience of astral travelling. Mathers' occultism was ceremonial rather than drug dependent or sex magic, but was none the less powerful and deadly effective: he claimed to be able to summon the demon Beelzebub, the supreme chieftain of Hell, but warned his followers that unless the magical circle was drawn with total accuracy, any mistake or slip up would result in self-destruction and the magician would be killed on the spot.

In November 1898, Mathers accepted a new student member into the Order, a twenty-three-year-old youth named Edward Alexander Crowley, who had become interested in occultism while an undergraduate at Trinity College, Cambridge. As the self-styled 'Great Beast', Aleister Crowley, as he would later call himself – and who seems to have believed he was in reality the biblical Beast whose number is said to be 666 – became one of the most notorious men in England. Known for the mantra 'Do what thou wilt shall be the whole of the law' from his prose poem *The book of the law*, a channelled text that Crowley believed he had received as a new gospel for mankind. Crowley became an enthusiastic Neophyte but tensions gradually developed; Mathers and he quarrelled and eventually Crowley was expelled from the Order. If accounts given by Crowley's biographer John Symonds in his book *The Great Beast* (1951) are to be believed, this was the beginning of a fierce astral battle between the two occultists as they launched waves of psychic attacks involving invisible vampires, bloodhounds and demons against each other for control of the Golden Dawn. Both men survived but the mystery surrounding Mathers' death – in Spain at the age of sixty-four in 1918 – makes it possible for some to speculate that the 'Great Beast' may in the end have finally succeeded in finishing off his one-time teacher; a more likely explanation is that the ageing magician in reality died of Spanish influenza.

Crowley would outlive Mathers by nearly thirty years, eventually dying in isolation and virtual obscurity in a Hastings boarding house in 1947, although the occult revival of the 1960s would ensure that his writings and his 'magick' would ultimately be encountered by a wide audience, and books, films and plays about his life and work continue to appear to this day. He was clearly a dangerous person to know and associate with: his first and second wives died insane and at least five of his mistresses went on to commit suicide. In 1911, a decade after his break with the Golden Dawn, Crowley became head of the British lodge of a German society named the Order of Templars of the Orient or Ordo Templi Orientis. Its founder Theodor Reuss, an occultist and polymath who took part in the inaugural performance of Wagner's *Parsifal*, gave Crowley the honorary title of 'Baphomet, Supreme and Holy King of Ireland, Iona, and all the Britains within the Sanctuary of the Gnosis', although for many Crowley would always be regarded as 'the wickedest man in the world', a similarly grand title bestowed upon him by the English Sunday newspapers.

The presence of the Scottish isle of Iona in Crowley's occult pseudonym is an interesting one as it was here, in the same year that the 'Great Beast' self-published his four-volume magnum opus *Magick in Theory and Practice*, that an unusual and seemingly inexplicable event took place which has strange connections with Crowley himself, with Samuel MacGregor Mathers, with the shadowy world of Victorian occultism and, seemingly, the disturbing paranormal phenomenon of psychic attack and murder.

Netta Emily Fornario (known as Norah Farnario by some authors although her real Christian name was Marie), the daughter of an Italian immigrant physician from Naples and a native Englishwoman, was thirty-two years old and from Kew in south-west London. Born in Cairo, Netta's mother had died when she was an infant after which she was raised in England by her maternal grandparents, who came from a wealthy family of tea merchants from Coventry. As a youth she spent time living in Italy, where she obtained Italian citizenship before finally returning to Britain, where she lived for a time in Bishops Stortford in Hertfordshire. In August 1928, she arrived on Iona accompanied by a travelling companion, but despite the presence of her unnamed friend, wholly personal reasons had brought her to this lonely island community, where St Columba had first arrived to begin establishing Christianity in Scotland over thirteen centuries before. The young Londoner was convinced that many years in the past she herself had lived there in a previous life, and was now searching to establish a link with her previous incarnation in the solitude and peaceful environs of this profound and remote location.

After making the ferry crossing from Mull, the two visitors took up lodgings on the east side of Iona in the house of an island woman named MacDonald, and Netta Fornario settled into the quest that had removed her both physically and spiritually from a harsh materialistic world with which she had little or nothing in common. Today, Norah's outlook would be described as being distinctly 'proto-hippie' or New Age, but back in the late 1920s she was a 'Bohemian', in both dress and outlook, whose fascination with folklore and the unseen world about us drew her apart from ordinary people and the humdrum of daily life which she eventually rejected for the solitude and enlightenment of lonely Iona, then a desolate place with neither telephones, electricity or running water. Netta Fornario was also a passionate faith-healer and Spiritualist at a time when the physical aspect of the movement was experiencing a golden age: there were many noted mediums holding blackout séances for 'spirit' communication and materialisation phenomena, and it seems that the young woman spent much time attending Spiritualist meetings in an attempt to obtain personal communication with the other side.

To these ends Netta obtained much support from a friendship and association with Mrs Moina Mathers, sister of the philosopher Henri Bergson, and wife of Samuel MacGregor Mathers, who was herself a gifted medium and clairvoyant. Moina had assisted her husband in the translation and preparation of several important occult texts and grimoires, including *The Kabbalah Unveiled*, *The Key of Solomon* and the fifteenth-century *Book of the Sacred Magic of Abra-Melin the Mage*, and with her encouragement Netta became a member of the Order of Alpha and Omega, an occult splinter group established after Samuel Mathers' death, in order to develop her own psychic abilities of faith-healing and telepathy. Mrs Mathers also had a reputation in occult and Spiritualist circles as an adept in her own right, seemingly equal to the paranormal abilities of her late husband. How good her relationship with Netta Fornario was at the time that the young woman and her friend set out on the long journey to Iona in the autumn of 1929 is not clear, although there were some who later felt that it was intimately connected with the tragic events which were ultimately to play themselves out nearly fifteen months later.

After a short time her travelling companion took the Fionnphort ferry back across the Sound of Iona to Mull and the mainland, and Netta stayed on alone. Soon she left the MacDonald house and moved in as a boarder with the Cameron family in their small cottage on the south-west side of the island. In the late 1980s, Calum Cameron, a twelve-year-old boy at the time Netta Fornario stayed in his parent's croft, remembered her to writer Richard Wilson as a restless character, much given to wandering the island moors and barren cliff tops on her own, often at night. Islanders at the time recalled she wrote poetry and although likeable talked strangely about being able to communicate with the spirits of the island's past and was known to spend much time on a large grassy mound known as the Sithean Mor or Fairy Hill near The Machair, an area of farming land on Iona's western side.

As the months wore on it became clear even to the young Calum Cameron, and more so to the rest of the family, that the young woman from London was a troubled and disturbed individual whose already eccentric behaviour was becoming alarmingly worse. Netta talked casually of succumbing to week-long trances, of seeing the faces of former 'patients' in the clouds through her bedroom window, of receiving spirit messages and seeing phantom figures. Much of her waking time was spent at night, either feverishly typing pages of now lost and unknowable script by lamplight or wandering across the island, oblivious to the darkness and the harsh Scottish weather; dishevelled and exhausted she spent much of the daylight hours asleep. Above all, the islanders felt that Netta Fornario herself seemed to believe she was being pursued by something unknown which, as it came closer, brought about an ever-growing sense of bizarre panic and personal danger.

On Sunday, 17 November 1929, Netta announced in the suitably mysterious and alarming language with which they had become familiar that instructions from the spirit world had decreed she must leave Iona immediately. The Camerons' relief at finally seeing the back of their strange lodger was somewhat tempered by the fact that, being the Sabbath, the Fionnphort ferry to Mull would not be running until the following day. Initially unable to grasp the reality of the situation, an extremely frightened and unwell Netta Fornario carried her packed bags down to the shore, where she waited in vain for some time before the realisation sank in that for another twenty-four hours she was still a prisoner on the island. Returning to the Camerons' croft, she told them that further orders from the other side had told her it was not now necessary to leave and she locked herself in her bedroom. Later that evening, when Netta appeared for supper, she gave the impression of being much recovered from the state of near panic that had gradually overtaken her in the previous weeks and, although resigned to the fact that their boarder was not leaving, the Cameron family felt that with a return to a reasonably normal state of mind it would not be so strange and unsettling to continue to have her presence in their house. When talking to Richard Wilson over sixty years later, Calum Cameron was still able to recall the sequence of disturbing events that played themselves out the following morning . . .

Netta Fornario's bedroom in the Cameron croft was an unsettling sight when Calum's sister entered after receiving no response when bringing up her breakfast: the lamps were still alight, the bed had not been slept in, and in the fire grate were the burnt remains of the numerous sheets of typescript that she had spent many months labouring in a panic to complete; and despite the fact that her suitcase and all her neatly folded clothes and belongings were still in the room, Netta Emily Fornario was nowhere to be seen.

The Cameron family immediately realised something was wrong and spent several hours looking for her. Later, when it became clear that rather than having gone off, albeit under very alarming circumstances, in one of her 'trances' or solitary walks across the windswept winter coastline, the young woman was in fact missing, Calum Cameron's parents raised the alarm. By the end of the day there was no sign of the troubled visitor from London and early the next morning several islanders went across on the ferry to Mull to alert the authorities, returning with the island policeman, who immediately organised a series of search parties to began a detailed and systematic search. During the afternoon, two farmers scouring the moorland in the vicinity of The Machair were alerted by the frantic barking of their collie dog to a spot on the side of the Fairy Hill, the one place on Iona that seemed to have attracted the New Age traveller the most, and it was here on the Sithean Mor that they made a grim discovery.

Netta Emily Fornario lay dead and it seemed that she had spent the last moments of her tortured time on Earth fighting off some dreadful and unknowable evil: her body was naked except for a black cloak decorated with the strange occult insignia of the Order of Alpha and Omega and a tarnished silver chain around her neck; the balls of her feet were bruised and cut as though she had been fleeing for her life across the rough and stony moorland, while a long-bladed steel knife had to be forcibly pried from the fingers of one hand, which held it in a powerful death grip. Tellingly, the corpse lay within a large cross-shape, which had been cut out of the moorland turf seemingly as some form of symbolic defence against an intangible assault which for Netta was shockingly real. The island doctor recorded death as being due to exposure but for those who saw it, the way her face was distorted with terror, made this verdict seem somewhat less of a representation of the truth: the young woman seemed to have been literally scared to death. Three days later, Netta was buried in the grounds of Iona Abbey, in the graveyard of St Odhrain's chapel; many of the islanders attended her funeral and the grave is marked by a simple white stone bearing the inscription 'N.E.F. Aged 33. 19th November 1929', a cryptic testament to strange events now almost beyond living memory.

What is the real truth behind the death of Netta Fornario? She was clearly a mentally disturbed and unstable woman for whom the powers of Black Magic, exacerbated by a morbid, and for her, unhealthy obsession with Spiritualism and mediumship, were a deadly reality. It is easy for those persons – the vast majority of us in fact – who do not view the world through the eyes of the clairvoyant or the psychic, to dismiss her fears as paranoid delusions, tragic nonetheless but ultimately a clinical reality easily established by modern medicine. If Netta did die from a psychic attack, then it was one she created within her own mind and that led her to venture out into the blackness of a harsh Iona winter's night dressed only in a thin cloak to unwittingly die of natural causes on the mysterious and lonely Fairy Hill, where mysterious blue lights were reported as being seen around the time the body was found.

It is easy to see how conventional science can today explain away extreme hauntings such as psychic assaults and possession. In 2008, shortly before his death from cancer, American paranormal investigator Lou Gentile spent a week with English psychological illusionist Derren Brown for the Channel 4 television programme *Derren Brown Investigates*. In line with the debunking nature of the series and Brown's sceptical approach to the subject, much if not all of the Philadelphia ghost hunter's evidence for paranormal phenomena was made to look to be the result of misinterpretation of natural events or happenings – a possessed man 'exorcised' by Gentile on a video recording was subsequently diagnosed by a consulting doctor to be an epileptic, while 'spirit' photographs and EVP recordings were put down to simulacra and static interference; Brown himself felt Gentile was sincere but sadly misguided.

But there were those, some intimately connected with the contemporary world of Netta Fornario, who were convinced that she had died as the result of a powerful and murderous psychic attack. Violet Mary Firth, more readily known by the pseudonym Dion Fortune, was an important modern occultist of the first half of the twentieth century who claimed to receive occult and spiritual teachings directly from other planes of consciousness. As a practising magician, Violet Firth joined the Golden Dawn and later became a disciple of Aleister Crowley; in the late 1920s she knew Netta well.

Violet Firth, who died in 1946 at the age of fifty-five, clearly believed paranormal murder was possible and had herself written a handbook entitled *Psychic Self-Defence* (1930) on how to combat such attacks. In the same volume she gives a personal insight into Netta's tragic demise:

> She was . . . of unusual intellectual calibre, and was especially interested in the Green Ray elemental contacts; too much interested in them for my peace of mind, and I became nervous and refused to co-operate with her. I do not object to reasonable risks, in fact one cannot expect to achieve anything worth while [*sic*] in life if one will not take risks, but it appeared to me that 'Mac,' as we called her, was going into very deep waters, even when I knew her, and that there was certain to be trouble sooner or later.
>
> She had evidently been on an astral expedition from which she never returned. She was not a good subject for such experiments, for she suffered from some defect of the pituitary body. Whether she was the victim of a psychic attack, whether she merely stopped out on the astral too long and her body, of poor vitality in any case, became chilled lying thus exposed in mid-winter, or whether she slipped into one of the elemental kingdoms that she loved, even as Swinburne swam out to sea, who shall say? The information at our disposal is insufficient for an opinion to be formed. The facts, however, cannot be questioned, and remain to give sceptics food for thought.

Accounts of Netta's death often cite Dion Fortune's apparent belief that it was a psychic murder resulting from a fall out in her relationship with the mysterious Moina Mathers, who had sent powerful forces to destroy her. Although the fact that Mrs Mathers died in 1928 at the age of sixty-three would make this impossible (unless it was an attack from beyond the grave), it would be unwise to dismiss the possibility out of hand. The Irish poet W.B. Yeats, himself a member of the Golden Dawn and also the Ghost Club, testified to the combined power of MacGregor Mathers and his wife: during visits to their house the three were said to have enjoyed a form of four-handed chess game together, with Yeats and Moina Mathers pitting themselves against MacGregor Mathers and a materialised spirit which he had specifically summoned as his playing partner.

In 2011, a stage production, *The Mysterious Death of Netta Fornario* by dramatist Chris Lee, premiered by the Mull Theatre Company, shows a continuing fascination with the case over eighty years after the events of November 1929. Lee's script was an imaginative blend of fiction and reality involving the presence of a mysterious cloaked figure reported by local newspapers as being seen at the time in the vicinity of the Fairy Hill.

Despite the enduring interest, perhaps the truth of the life and death of the enigmatic Netta Fornario will always lie between fact and fantasy somewhere out in the wilds of the enchanted isle of Iona, the place that she was ultimately never to leave . . .

CHAPTER 6

AN ENGLISH GHOST HUNTER ABROAD

HARRY PRICE AND LUDWIG DAHL, 1934

The English ghost hunter Harry Price (1881-1948) is a well known figure in the history of psychical research and any collection of writings on the paranormal seem to be lacking without either a reference to his activities or a contribution from his case files. His love of the limelight and flamboyant style of self-promotion made him controversial among his contemporaries, but he was a sincere and dedicated investigator whose great knowledge and experience in psychical matters, particularly the investigation of Spiritualist phenomena and mediumship, have become overshadowed in the years following his death by the controversy surrounding his most high-profile case, that of Borley Rectory, the 'most haunted house in England'.

An amateur magician, inventor and writer, Price, always fiercely independent, followed a career path that contained a mixture of psychic journalism and the scientific investigation of the paranormal in equal measure. He carried out controlled experiments with the leading mediums of the day, such as the famous Austrian brothers Willi and Rudi Schneider[1], but had a talent for presenting the results as part of popular digests of his adventures aimed at the general reader, something which made fellow researchers suspicious of his motives, but at the same time resulted in him becoming a household name where the investigation of ghosts and haunted houses was concerned. It is this accessible approach which continues to inspire over six decades after his death and as the 'father of modern ghost hunting', he has many admirers throughout the worldwide paranormal community of today.

The strange story of Judge Dahl is one in which Harry Price had personal interest and made reference to in a selection of his writings, notably his *Fifty*

Years of Psychical Research (1939), regarded as his most important contribution to paranormal literature. It is the closest so far in the present work to what could be described as a 'Spiritualist murder'. Price was an enthusiastic traveller and made many trips to the Continent, always trying to keep ahead with the new developments in the world of psychical research, sitting with the latest mediums, exchanging views and ideas with fellow investigators and collecting material for future books. If there was one ghost hunter who would have the opportunity to get involved in the Dahl case it would be Harry Price.

The Dahl family of Norway were one beset with tragedy. Ludwig Dahl was a magistrate in the sea-port town of Fredrikstad, just under sixty miles from the capital Oslo. In addition to being the local judge, Dahl served as mayor of Bergen and was also an amateur psychical researcher and convinced Spiritualist whose interest in psychic matters had begun around 1915 but was eventually centred around the mediumship of his married daughter, Ingeborg Köber. Ingeborg's trance mediumship had apparently developed following the deaths of both her brothers, Ludwig, who drowned while sailing in 1919, and a younger brother Ragnar, who died a few years later also in an accident. While in a trance state, the judge's daughter was allegedly able to channel both young men, and their father eventually compiled a manuscript in which he recorded details of the communications.

The Dahls embraced Spiritualism and became what was later described as a 'fanatically religious and occultist family'. The judge, however, certainly found great comfort in the movement, through which he was able to come to terms with the loss of his sons. In his manuscript he wrote: 'Our family home has not become poorer by their deaths. The passing of the two boys made our lives richer, fuller, than ever before.' Statements such as this were to have serious consequences at a later date.

In June 1927, Harry Price visited Norway and Denmark as part of a lecture tour, promoting his activities at his own London-based National Laboratory of Psychical Research. Since visiting the countries at the beginning of 1925, when he opened an International Psychic Exhibition in Copenhagen, Price had been busy carrying out experiments with several mediums including the English nurse Stella Cranshaw, Eleonore Zügun (the aforementioned Romanian 'Devil Girl'), and both the Schneider brothers, and he was keen to keep his Scandinavian colleagues up to date with his work. At the time Price was also the Foreign Research Officer for the American Society for Psychical Research, and contributed a regular series of articles to their journal.

At Fredrikstad, Price was invited to attend a private sitting with Ingeborg Köber and joined the Dahl family at their home for a pre-séance lunch. This proved to be one of the most sumptuous feasts that the English researcher had ever sat through and it was nearly four hours before the party, which comprised Judge Dahl and his wife, together with Price and Ingeborg, moved into the drawing-room where the séance was to be held. Frau Köber eschewed the usual blackout conditions often demanded by Spiritualist mediums and the sitting took place in daylight around a large table in the centre of the room.

The judge's daughter soon fell into a trance and, speaking in the voices and personalities of the two dead Dahl brothers, Ludwig and Ragnar, held several long conversations with their father and mother. Price was present throughout the sitting and was allowed to take full notes of what was said. For the judge it was an intensely emotional experience as he conversed through the entranced Ingeborg and seemingly was again in contact with his dead children. Price found the whole sitting interesting, but as the entire proceedings were in fact totally reliant on the Norwegian couple's belief that they were indeed speaking to the medium's two brothers, it was ultimately unconvincing as proof of survival after death. Interestingly, Price later described the Dahls as 'a very charming, affectionate and united family', quite at odds with the morbid picture which would be painted by others several years later.

Harry Price remained in contact with the judge and his family and four years after his visit to Fredrikstad was instrumental in getting Ludwig Dahl's manuscript detailing his paranormal investigations accepted by a London publisher. It was issued in 1931 under the title *We are Here: Psychic Experiences* to which the physicist and radio pioneer Sir Oliver Lodge (1851-1940), himself an important researcher and firm believer in survival, contributed a foreword. There the matter would have rested if it had not been for a series of truly incredible occurrences which read like something from the fiction of Agatha Christie.

Mrs Stolt-Nielsen was a friend of the Dahl family and also a trance medium. At a séance held in 1933, at which Dahl himself was present, Mrs Stolt-Nielsen entranced and, channelling her own dead daughter, spoke to the sitters and gave a grim and ultimately chilling communication. The 'spirit' had apparently been asked to pass on a message from Judge Dahl's son Ragnar, who said that his father would die from an accident which would take place in August 1934. Following the séance, Mrs Stolt-Nielsen wrote down the prophesy and kept it in a sealed envelope. The Norwegian magistrate's reaction to this startling revelation was not recorded, but through his commitment to Spiritualism he would presumably have had no fear of death and would no doubt have looked on the warning as the time that he would be reunited at last with his loved ones.

Time passed to a point where Dahl and Ingeborg were enjoying a holiday day out together on one of the beaches at Hankö, a neighbouring island and popular seaside resort a few miles from Fredrikstad. It was 8 August 1934 and the same bay where the young Ludwig Dahl had drowned while sailing his yacht fifteen years before. As his daughter relaxed sunbathing on the shore, the judge was swimming when he suddenly got into difficulties. Accounts vary as to what overcame him, possibly cramp, but it seems most likely that he suffered a stroke. By the time his daughter had reached him, the judge was unconscious and, despite desperate attempts at resuscitation, he died.

As if the Dahl family had not suffered enough, an inquest into the judge's death was the beginning of more strange and tragic events. The judge's monetary affairs were discovered to be in ruins and an audit at the Bergen town treasury revealed that large sums were missing from the public coffers, sequestered by him to prop up his own ailing finances. An insurance policy covering Ludwig Dahl's life was also found to have expired on the day following his death on the beach.

At this point Christian Apenes, the Deputy Mayor of Bergen, came forward with information about a private séance he attended with Ingeborg Köber on 4 December 1933, a transcript of which was kept by him at his office in the Town Hall. Apenes stated that Ragnar Dahl had communicated through his sister and had given a warning that their father would die within a year. The spirit said not to tell the judge or his wife anything about what was to happen and that it would provide additional evidence by giving the same information to another medium, whose spirit guide would give confirmation as well as instructions that a record was to be made of the prophesy and kept in a sealed envelope. The medium chosen was Mrs Stolt-Nielsen but, as we have seen, the communication actually took place in the judge's presence and he was aware of the warning.

Apenes subsequently produced the sealed envelope and opened it in front of witnesses, at which point a public scandal broke out and all the Norwegian newspapers were soon filled with the story. Spiritualists in Norway were quick to champion the case, citing that two separate mediums delivering the same prophesy was convincing evidence for survival after death and foreknowledge by the spirit world. Non-Spiritualists, and even some Spiritualists themselves, were not convinced and felt that the judge's death was the result of something far more sinister. Judge Bonnevie of the Norwegian Supreme Court, and a cousin of the late Ludwig Dahl, stated publicly that the magistrate had killed himself against his own free will under what he felt was a 'hypnotic influence', a 'Macbeth prophecy' which used a form of autosuggestion directed by people who wanted the judge out of the way.

Further statements by Christian Apenes at the inquest began to cast doubt in people's minds as to the truthfulness of Ingeborg's account of the death of her father. Rather than immediately going for a doctor, Ingeborg and Mrs Stolt-Nielsen, who she said she met on her way to summon help, telephoned to Mrs Dahl who was in Bergen, and it was several hours before she arrived in Hankö accompanied by Apenes. By this time two doctors had been called but there was nothing they could do except certify death by drowning. There was also a similar delay by Apenes and Mrs Dahl in informing the police of the judge's death, and rumours soon became rife that Apenes had hatched a plot to kill Ludwig Dahl by hypnotizing his daughter to murder him on the lonely beach by pushing his head under the water.

The whole matter came to a head in the Central Criminal Court in Oslo in front of Judge Trampe Broch. Ingeborg Köber brought the case to court in an attempt to clear the stigma of suicide against her father's name. Counter-charges were brought that she herself, her mother, Mrs Stolt-Nielsen and Apenes were involved in a murder plot in order to benefit from Ludwig Dahl's demise – Christian Apenes had after all become Mayor of Bergen and the family had benefitted from the large insurance policy that the judge had taken out on his life, which ended the day after the fateful day he went to the beach with Ingeborg.

The bizarre trial of the Norwegian medium lasted intermittently for three years. The Hungarian journalist and crime reporter Cornelius Tabori (1879-1944), whose son Paul would later become Harry Price's literary executor and biographer, attended the first five days of the Dahl trial and witnessed first-hand the strange situation as the foremost psychologists and psychiatrists in Norway were called as expert witnesses for the prosecution, while in their defence the Dahls and Christian Apenes quoted openly from the works of Sir Arthur Conan Doyle and Oliver Lodge in the same courtroom. 'When yesterday Ingeborg Köber spoke of the influences of the Great Beyond and of the happiness which her father achieved,' Tabori later wrote, 'the judge turned to the experts and asked them to explain these terms. But the experts just smiled; they seemed to be more interested in the life insurance policy of the late Mayor Dahl.'

In the final summing up the jury were asked to consider several possibilities. Had the judge been murdered on the last day that his insurance policy was valid to solve the dire financial situation of his own family, who had subsequently been brought to justice by forces from beyond the grave? Had Judge Dahl in fact committed suicide knowing that his embezzlement of the Bergen town funds would soon be uncovered, or was he driven to kill himself by the chilling séance room message which had in some way willed him to die. Or was Judge Ludwig Dahl's death actually a terrible accident and his son's 'message' an eerie coincidence?

Happily for Ingeborg, the jury decided on the last option and she was acquitted in December 1937. The judge's death was ruled accidental and the tragic woman found some happiness from the whole affair by marrying the chief counsel for the defence, Axel Segelcke, at the end of the trial. This was perhaps as well as the strain of the whole affair became too much to bear for Mrs Dahl and she shocked the country by taking her own life before her daughter's name was cleared.

What exactly happened in the case of Judge Ludwig Dahl will now never be known. A Norwegian criminologist at the time felt the deaths of the judge and his two sons were linked, and told Cornelius Tabori that 'under the cloak of Spiritualism an extremely cunning criminal was carrying out a series of murders'. 'The Dahl Mystery', as Tabori called it, remains one to this day.

NOTE

1. Willi Schneider (1903-71) and Rudi Schneider (1908-57), both important physical mediums, were the subject of scientific investigation by several European researchers during the 1920s and '30s. For a detailed account of their mediumship see Anita Gregory's *The Strange Case of Rudi Schneider* (The Scarecrow Press, London, 1985).

CHAPTER 7

THE DEATH OF INNOCENCE

FREDERICK NODDER AND MONA TINSLEY, 1937

The English woman Estelle Roberts was one of the twentieth century's most highly regarded and versatile of psychic mediums. Her abilities encompassed clairvoyance, healing, direct-voice communication and physical phenomena, including apports and materialisation, and she is revered by Spiritualists as one of the major figures whose quality of mediumship and steadfast lobbying at Westminster during the 1950s resulted in the movement being legalised as a religion by the British Government. Her presence in the case of Mona Tinsley and the child killer Frederick Nodder is the only redeeming factor in the entire dreadful story.

Roberts was born May Estelle Wills in Kensington, London in 1899 and claimed to have had her first psychic experience at the age of eight, witnessing a vision of a knight in shining armour floating in the air outside a third-floor bedroom window. From that time onwards she was able to hear voices and see apparitions that were imperceptible to the rest of her family, who, unsurprisingly, dismissed her claims as the result of a vivid imagination. Leaving school at fourteen, Estelle became a nursemaid to a family in Turnham Green but, despite her change in circumstances, the psychic experiences continued. Three years later she married Hugh Miles and the couple went on to have three children, but the marriage was plagued with financial hardship due to her husband's almost permanent ill health. On his deathbed in May 1919, she later described seeing the spirit forms of her husband's mother and father holding a vigil at the bedside and, at the moment of death, Miles' own etheric double leaving his body and fading away.

Following her husband's funeral, Estelle continued to work long hours to support her children. Eventually, security for her young family was achieved with a new marriage and a move to Hampton in south-west London. It was here that Estelle Roberts' psychic powers were recognised and she took the first real steps to becoming a world class medium. Having been unable to fully understand her abilities since childhood, Estelle was encouraged to visit a local Spiritualist church by a sympathetic neighbour. There, during the service, she was singled out by one of the resident clairvoyants, a Mrs Craddock, who explained that she had the potential to develop what was a natural mediumship and had great things to do in the world. The rest of her life's work began in those few moments.

Back at their Hampton home, Roberts began experimenting with table-tipping, but after a week of regular sitting became discouraged with the lack of result. On the seventh night, which again seemed to be fated to yield nothing and at the point when she made a mental decision to end her involvement with Spiritualism for good, the table suddenly became alive and rose into the air before gently descending to the floor. As she placed her hands on the table top, psychic raps sounded on the surface in a code corresponding with the letters of the alphabet and the name 'Red Cloud' was spelt out. This was the native Red Indian spirit guide who would work tirelessly through the medium for the next forty years.

For the remainder of the 1920s and through into the next decade, Estelle continued to progress her mediumship. As her clairvoyance developed she began to give regular demonstrations in Spiritualist churches across south London and the Home Counties, and quickly became a highly respected and sought after psychic. As good as her platform work became, it was in the darkness of her own home séance room that Estelle Roberts and 'Red Cloud' were able to provide comfort and convincing evidence of survival for hundreds of visitors over many years. As well as healing and psychometry, Estelle was a gifted trumpet medium, allowing sitters to receive communication from departed loved ones speaking through an aluminium megaphone-like device that floated unaided around the circle of visitors and through which discarnate spirits were able to speak again. The universality of her work was reflected in the people from all walks of life, from dustmen to knights of the realm, who came to sit with her in the séance room.

Psychic journalist Maurice Barbanell (1902-1981), founder of the long-running Spiritualist newspaper *Psychic News* and himself a gifted trance medium, was a great propagandist for the mediumship of Estelle Roberts and attended many of her séances. He claimed on one occasion to have seen the materialised face of 'Red Cloud' illuminated in the ghostly glow from two luminous plaques and to have shaken the guide's materialised hand, while in his editor's column he described many instances of convincing evidence of survival. They included an account of the widow of racing motorist Sir Henry Segrave, who was killed during an attempt to break the world water speed record on Lake Windemere on 13 June 1930, being reunited with her husband at a direct-voice séance. At another séance, and acting on instructions from a communicator, Barbanell effected a reunion between a mother, Mrs Manning, and her two dead children in what he described as 'flawless evidence for the after-life'.

On this occasion, a young twenty-two-year-old girl Bessy Manning spoke through the trumpet and gave details of her death from tuberculosis as well as the passing of her brother, Tommy Manning, in a car accident. When asked for an address, the voice gave details of a house in Canterbury Street, Blackburn, to which Barbanell wrote with details of the sitting. Mrs Manning responded and confirmed all the information given at the séance. Barbanell subsequently arranged for Mrs Manning to be brought to London and he drove her himself to a house in Teddington in Middlesex, where she again was able to speak to her deceased children, who gave information of which no person other than the mother was aware. Spiritualist newspapers of the period contain many references to communications and reunions such as these and Estelle Roberts was easily the equivalent of today's celebrity and television psychics, taking part in large organised events such as demonstrations of clairvoyance at the Royal Albert Hall in front of over 6,000 people. Roberts wrote her memoirs, which were published in 1959, and died in 1970 at the age of ninety-one.

The flowering of Estelle Robert's mediumship in the inter-war years took place during the last great phase of interest and investigation into Spiritualism, both in Britain and abroad, by paranormal organisations such as the Society for Psychical Research. Where physical mediumship was concerned it was a golden age the likes of which, both in respect of public demonstrations and the involvement of psychical researchers, will in all honesty never be seen again. High-profile controversies, such as the exploits of 'Margery' in America and the wartime 'witchcraft trial' of Helen Duncan at the Old Bailey, did much to foster an atmosphere of mutual distrust between mediums and their supporters on one side, and psychical researchers representing the scientific establishment on the other. Changes in intellectual fashion where psychical research was concerned – the Rhine revolution with its emphasis on parapsychology and statistical analysis – eventually consigned the investigation of mediums to a kind of paranormal Dark Ages. The vast majority of psychical researchers soon began to prefer statistics to the séance room while the Spiritualist movement, secure in its own beliefs, eschewed scientific investigation of any kind.

Where psychical research was concerned, the mediumship of Estelle Roberts was no different to that of say Helen Duncan, Jack Webber or Alec Harris[1].

Her refusal of an offer to be tested by the Society for Psychical Research and the need for darkness in her direct-voice séances created the usual suspicion in the minds of the ghost hunters, and the fact that Roberts was one of several mediums (including Kathleen Barkel and Maurice Barbanell) whose spirit guides gave an emphatic 'no war' prophecy in the months before the outbreak of hostilities in September 1939[1] gave the sceptics much to work with.

Events such as this notwithstanding, it is true to say that Estelle Roberts was for many years one of the most well known Spiritualist mediums in Britain, and it was this notable fact which drew her into a sequence of tragic events which took place in the English Midlands in the opening months of 1937.

Some time around the middle of May 1937, Walter Marshall, a gas-works manager from Bawtry, together with his wife and three sons was spending an afternoon boating on the River Ryton, a tributary of the larger River Idle in Nottinghamshire. Around a quarter of a mile upstream from the junction of the two rivers on the approach to Scrooby Mill, the punt ran aground on a sandbank and while attempting to free themselves they disturbed a large sack which had also been caught up in the sand. The sack gave off a dreadful smell and using one of the oars Marshall pushed it away into the silt. After freeing the punt the party carried on their way and the sack was lost to sight. Despite many recent newspaper headlines, both local and national in the previous months, its significance was not recognised by Walter Marshall and his family at the time.

Five months before, at around seven o'clock on the evening of 5 January 1937, Wilfred Tinsley, a coal carter, and his wife Lilian became concerned at the whereabouts of their ten-year-old daughter Mona, who had not returned home from school that afternoon. The Tinsleys lived in a council house in Thoresby Avenue, Newark and Mona, one of seven children, attended the Wesleyan School in Guildhall Street, which was about twenty minutes walk away. Mona had in fact been seen out of the school at the end of the day's lessons at four o'clock by her class teacher, Miss Hawley, and normally got back to Thoresby Avenue half an hour later. When she failed to appear around that time her parents were not unduly concerned as they had relations in the area and assumed that Mona had called in to see them on the way home. Two and a half hours after she should have been back, Mr Tinsley went out to check, but their family members knew nothing of the young child. At a quarter to ten Wilfred Tinsley went for the police.

The Newark Borough Constabulary quickly instigated an intensive search for the missing child. During the night empty properties in the town were checked, lorries passing along the Great North Road were stopped and examined, and officers searched the banks of the River Trent looking for some clue to Mona's disappearance. The following morning, policemen visited all the Newark schools and assemblies were called. The children were asked that if any of them had seen Mona Tinsley on the previous afternoon following the end of the school day, they should speak immediately to the police. Soon Chief Constable Barnes, who was leading the search, had his first clues.

A neighbour of the Tinsleys, eleven-year-old William Plackett who lived two doors down, said he saw Mona between four thirty and a quarter to five in the company of a man near the Newark bus station, and, later the same day, two women also came forward. One confirmed the schoolboy's sighting of Mona near the bus terminus while the second lady, a Mrs Annie Hird who, similarly to William Plackett, lived two doors away from the Tinsleys in Thoresby Avenue, said that in the quarter of an hour before the Wesleyan School was due to finish for the day she had been walking down Balderton Street (now renamed Balderton Gate) and passing the end of Guildhall Street when she had seen a man she recognised as a former lodger of the Tinsleys standing alone on the street corner looking across towards the door of the school. The policemen returned to Thoresby Avenue and Barnes spoke with Wilfred and Lilian Tinsley. The couple at first were evasive but eventually admitted that fifteen months earlier, in October 1935, a man calling himself Frederick Hudson had lodged there for a short time. He had been introduced to them by Mrs Tinsley's married sister Edie Grimes, who, like her other two sisters and her brother, lived in Sheffield, and during his time with the Tinsleys was known as Uncle Fred by their children. Hudson eventually left after three weeks having had difficulty in paying the rent. His departure had been amicable but he had at no time been given authority to take charge of Mona or her siblings.

Barnes sent officers to Sheffield while in Newark the intensive search for Mona Tinsley continued. By the late afternoon of 6 January, the police had taken a statement from Charles Reville, a local bus driver who, the previous day, had taken the regular 4.45 p.m. bus to the nearby market town of Retford, approximately twenty-two miles south-east of Newark. Reville acted as both driver and conductor and remembered seeing a young girl answering Mona's description in the company of a man who bought a half-crown return for himself but, ominously, only a tenpence single for the child. They had both got off his bus at a stop in Grove Street, Retford.

At Sheffield, policemen visited the addresses of the Tinsley's relatives and were soon knocking on the door of Thomas and Edie Grimes in Neil Road. In a similar vein to her sister, Edie Grimes and her husband were at first unhelpful and denied knowing anyone by the name of Frederick Hudson. When pressed, Mrs Grimes admitted she knew a man named Frederick Nodder but had not seen him for some time. When Barnes' men checked with colleagues at

Sheffield police station it soon became clear that Hudson and Nodder were one and the same person, who had good reason to go under an assumed name.

Frederick Colmore Nodder was a motor mechanic and sometime lorry driver from Sheffield in his early forties. Separated from his wife and two children, he was the subject of an affiliation order (known at the time as a 'bastardy warrant') for unpaid maintenance on an illegitimate child. It later transpired that soon after leaving his wife, Nodder befriended Mr and Mrs Grimes and took up lodgings with them and, in their company, had visited the Tinsleys at Newark on more than one occasion. The police returned to Neil Road and interviewed Edie Grimes again, who continued to be uncooperative and insisted that she had not seen or heard from Nodder since he left to live with her sister and brother-in-law. While one officer spoke to Mrs Grimes, another policeman questioned a neighbour and it became clear that Mrs Grimes was lying. She had good reason, as she and Nodder were having an affair, something her husband may have known about and was possibly a voyeur. Her elderly neighbour recalled seeing a lorry with the word 'Retford' painted on the side parked in Neil Road close to the Grimes' house the previous month, over the Christmas period. When confronted with this statement, Thomas Grimes admitted that Nodder had called on them around that time but insisted that he had no idea of his present whereabouts. This may have been true but his wife certainly did know where Nodder was living.

During the afternoon of 6 January, Chief Constable Barnes established through enquiries at public houses and motor garages in Retford that a man by the name of Nodder was living on Smeath Road near the village of Hayton, some three and a half miles from Retford. The house, called 'Peacehaven', was recently built and still stands today, although the surrounding area was not so built up. When Barnes together with a detective-sergeant, two other officers and their driver arrived at around seven in the evening, they found it lonely and isolated; it was also in darkness with no immediate sign of the occupier.

The policemen, having checked with the next-door neighbour and finding that Nodder had been seen there during the day, decided to wait and took up positions near the house and in the roadway. The night was dark with a gale-force wind. After nearly four hours Nodder appeared and, after Barnes had established his identity, went with him into the house using the back door, the front being fixed shut with screws. When questioned, Nodder denied any knowledge of Mona Tinsley or her whereabouts, although he admitted he knew her and claimed to have spent the day in Newark looking for work. The bastardy warrant enabled Barnes to hold Nodder while the police searched for evidence that might connect him with the child's disappearance, and he was taken to the cells in Newark police station.

The following day the police returned to 'Peacehaven'. The house was searched thoroughly, floorboards were lifted and, aware that what had begun as an enquiry for a missing person could develop into a murder hunt, officers dug up the garden and opened the attic. Amongst a pile of newspapers and magazines a piece of paper was found covered with a child's handwriting and, similarly, a child's fingerprint was discovered on a plate on the kitchen draining board. The immediate neighbours were also interviewed and the daily maid – a woman living two doors down from 'Peacehaven' – stated that the previous morning, while taking rubbish to the dustbin, she had seen a young girl wearing what she thought was a blue dress standing in the back doorway of Nodder's house; Nodder himself was digging in the garden at the time.

While the police were turning over 'Peacehaven', Frederick Nodder was taking part in an identification parade at Newark police station. The Tinsley's neighbours, William Plackett and Annie Hird, together with the bus driver Charles Reville confirmed that Nodder was the man they had seen on 5 January, but, when questioned again, the motor mechanic denied having taken the Retford bus that afternoon.

Realising that the search for Mona was stalling for lack of new evidence, Barnes organised an appeal for information to be broadcast on national radio and statements were issued to the Press with a request for maximum publicity. Notices were sent to police stations and posters with the child's photograph and description were circulated. Three people quickly came forward – a passenger on Charles Reville's bus together with two labourers, both acquaintances of Nodder – who stated they had seen a man and Nodder himself respectively in the company of a small girl resembling the missing child the previous Tuesday afternoon. Nodder's drinking buddies noticed that he appeared to have come from the Retford bus stop and was walking with the girl along the road to Hayton village.

The following evening, just after ten o'clock, Nodder made a request to see a detective sergeant. William Francis, who was on duty, went to the cells and Nodder stated that if Edie Grimes was brought to the police station he would make a statement that would lead to Mona Tinsley being found alive and well. Francis telephoned to Sheffield and a car was sent to Neil Road. At a quarter to one in the morning, Nodder was brought into Chief Constable Barnes' office, where Mrs Grimes was waiting. Indicating the policemen, Nodder said to his mistress, 'They know about us,' and asked if Mona was with her in Sheffield, to which Edie Grimes said no.

Nodder then made a statement in which he admitted seeing Mona in the street in Newark on Tuesday afternoon. She had asked after her Auntie Edie in Sheffield and asked if he would take her to see her baby cousin Peter, who she had not yet met. As he expected to see Mrs Grimes the following day (they were meeting regularly once a week at the time), Nodder said he reluctantly agreed and took Mona back to 'Peacehaven', where she stayed the night. However, his meeting with Edie did not take place, so he took her in the evening on the 6.45 p.m. bus to Worksop with instructions on how to get to Neil Road in Sheffield, together with a letter explaining his actions to Mr and Mrs Grimes. After seeing her off on the 8.15 p.m. bus to Sheffield, he drank at two pubs in Retford before returning home, where he was met in the road by Barnes and his men. His excuse for not taking the child to Sheffield himself was fear of trouble due to the warrant for non-payment of his illegitimate child maintenance. If anything had happened to Mona Tinsley, then it must have been during the time that he was travelling back to Retford or drinking ale in the Sherwood Foresters Arms.

Worksop, then as now, is nineteen miles by road from Sheffield, and the Grimes' house in Neil Road was a twopenny tram ride from the Pond Street bus terminus. Anyone taking the trip would have had to walk to the tram stop and also have a long walk at the other end down the length of Neil Road to number nine. It was a black winter's night, Mona Tinsley was ten years old and had not visited her aunt's house for several years. 'Uncle Fred', it seemed, was happy for her to do this entire trip alone, despite the fact that ten days previously he had driven to Sheffield in his lorry seemingly without fear of arrest. Chief Constable Barnes was unconvinced and by the end of the following day, with no progress in the hunt for Mona, Nodder was charged with abduction and removed to a cell in Lincoln Prison.

Soon the entire country was caught up in the desperate search for the little girl from the Midlands. Newspapers reported the tireless efforts of search parties and volunteers: the searching of left luggage lockers and unopened parcels, the beating of woods and remote places around Retford by a search party of nearly 900 people, the dragging and draining of a five-mile stretch of the Chesterfield Canal, which ran suspiciously within fifty yards of 'Peacehaven' and Nodder's garden, the opening up of cesspools and gravel pits, the countless statements taken by police forces across Britain from people who felt they had seen or knew where she was.

It was in this atmosphere of intrigue and fearful expectation that Estelle Roberts entered into the story of Mona Tinsley and Frederick Nodder. Douglas Sladen, a friend of the medium who had been following the story, spoke to Roberts and asked if she would be willing to help in some way in the search. She agreed on the understanding that there would be no publicity of her involvement. Sladen contacted the police and the request was put to Barnes in Newark. Roberts' standing in the Spiritualist movement was such that the policeman was disinclined to view Sladen as a crank and he put the request to Wilfred and Lilian Tinsley, who agreed and sent a pink silk dress which belonged to Mona to the medium in Hampton. Estelle Roberts was 150 miles away from the centre of the search for the missing child, but as soon as she held the dress in her hand she knew Mona Tinsley was dead. At the same moment, the medium's dog, which had been sleeping in front of the fire, howled mournfully and began charging around the room.

We will encounter this kind of experience, the reading or psychometrizing of an object by a sensitive for information, again in later chapters. All these cases are unique, but what makes this one stand out is that as well as psychometry, Roberts later claimed to have actually made contact with the dead child's spirit and obtained first-hand information about the murder from the victim herself. After handling the dress, Roberts went into a trance and, making contact with 'Red Cloud', asked him to bring the spirit of Mona Tinsley to speak with her. The child told her how she had been taken to a small house and strangled, her body had been put into a sack and taken 'on wheels to the water and thrown in'. She gave a description of the house and its location and Douglas Sladen wrote it down. When this was passed to the Newark police they realised the uncanny similarity to the lonely 'Peacehaven' – a small house with a water-filled ditch on one side (the way a child might describe a canal) and a field behind which lead on to a graveyard; there was an inn nearby and more fields and a river to which the medium felt compelled to move towards.

Barnes took the description seriously enough to request the medium to travel to Newark, and sent a car to pick her up from the railway station. At 'Peacehaven', Estelle Roberts walked around the garden and the house, a striking figure in her long black cloak. The house was exactly as she had seen it, seemingly through the eyes of little Mona Tinsley. She said that the child had spent some time inside the house copying writing from a book; she had slept in the first floor back bedroom and been killed there, and, specifically, the murderer had taken the body out through the back door. This corroborated details only the police were aware of – the writing discovered in the living room and the front door fixed shut with screws.

Outside, Estelle took the police down through Nodder's garden and across the adjoining countryside – the graveyard and the layout of the fields were all as she had seen it remotely back at her home in Hampton. She told Chief Constable Barnes that the body of Mona Tinsley would be found in a river which lay beyond the fields and was not visible from where they were standing. The nearby River Idle had already been dragged but the continuing heavy rain had turned the stream into a raging torrent and had made the work incredibly difficult and dangerous.

Despite a police embargo at the time on the medium's visit, corroboration of Estelle Roberts' vision did come from local sources. A Newark Spiritualist medium told Wilfred Tinsley that Mona would eventually be found in the River Idle as, in trance, she had tasted mud in her mouth, while another psychic told the police that the child's body would be recovered from water 'thirty miles in a north-westerly direction from Newark'.

On 9 March 1937, two months after Mona Tinsley's disappearance, Frederick Nodder appeared in front of the Warwick Winter Assizes at the Victoria Courts in Birmingham. The trial lasted a day and the jury took sixteen minutes to find Nodder guilty of abduction. The presiding judge, Mr Justice Swift, told Nodder: 'It may be that time will reveal the dreadful secret which you carry in your breast. I cannot tell, but I am determined that, as far as I have part or lot in that dreadful tragedy . . . I will keep you in custody.' Nodder was given seven years and returned to Lincoln Prison.

It was to be three months before both the judge's and Estelle Roberts' prophesies were to come true. By the beginning of June 1937, the weeks of inclement weather which had plagued the hunt for Mona Tinsley had finally subsided. On the afternoon of Sunday 6 June, Walter Marshall and his family were again enjoying a boat trip on the River Idle in the company of some friends. About a quarter of a mile below Bawtry, Mr Marshall noticed an object in the water about five yards in from the river bank on the Nottinghamshire side and steered his punt towards it. As they came alongside, Marshall was horrified to see the trunk of a small body, the legs floating in the water, the whole corpse held in position by the head, which had become buried in the silt. Mona Tinsley had been found at last.

Marshall sent his son to the nearest police station at Austerfield and officers removed the body to an outhouse at the Ship Inn at Newington, where Wilfred Tinsley was able to make a formal identification. The body was then taken to Retford Mortuary where Dr James Webster, the Director of the West Midland Regional Laboratory, carried out a post-mortem. Due to the extended time the corpse had been in the river there was extensive adipocere formation, which had prevented destructive decomposition or disintegration and Webster was able to state that death had been due to strangulation by a ligature (there was a dark circular mark around the neck) and that Mona had been dead before she was put in the water. A funeral service was held on Thursday 10 June at the Methodist Church where Mona used to attend Sunday school, and she was buried the same day at Newark Cemetery; several hundred people lined the streets and stood in silence as the coffin was laid to rest. Eighteen days later Frederick Nodder was charged with murder.

Nodder's second trial opened at the Nottingham Assizes at the Shire Hall on 22 November 1937 in front of Mr Justice Macnaghten (the judge at Nodder's first trial had died a month before) and lasted two days. Among the many witnesses for the prosecution was Sir Bernard Spilsbury, the troubled genius of British forensic medicine, who confirmed that the child had been killed from behind, strangled by a bootlace or similar item. Nodder clung to his original defence that an unknown person had killed Mona Tinsley after he had seen her off on the Sheffield bus at Worksop, but the retiring jury only took an hour to find him guilty. Sentencing Nodder to death, the judge made a notable reference to Mr Justice Swift's summing up at the previous trial by saying: 'Justice has slowly but surely overtaken you . . . '. An appeal was quickly dismissed and Nodder, who entered criminal history at the time as a man who, for all practical purposes, was tried twice for the same murder, ate his last Christmas dinner in the condemned cell at Lincoln Prison. He was hanged by Tom Pierrepoint and Stanley Cross at 8 a.m. on 30 December 1937.

What drove Nodder to kill Mona Tinsley will now never be known, although it seems most likely that the motive was sexual. It was impossible to ascertain any evidence for this due to the advanced state of decomposition of the body but, tellingly, a packet of sweets and a tin of Vaseline were found under the pillow of the bed in the front bedroom at 'Peacehaven'. Writing about the case in the early 1980s[3], Colin Wilson was of the opinion that Nodder had developed a sexual obsession with Mona during the time he lodged with the Tinsleys at Newark. Nodder was a known drinker (he had been dismissed from several jobs due to drunkenness) and may have abducted the child on an impulse after drinking heavily during the day. The attraction of Edie Grimes to Nodder was clearly sexual despite his filthy personal hygiene and dirty way of living. He had been thrown out of the lodgings he moved into after leaving Neil Road and before moving to Hayton for lack of cleanliness, and when the police searched 'Peacehaven' they found it in a squalid state. He had a strange hold over the woman and to a certain extent her husband; amongst other things successfully persuading Thomas Grimes to buy a second-hand car in which he drove the couple around.

Over the next twenty years the involvement of mediums and psychics in criminal cases, particularly those of murder, was to achieve greater public prominence and several will be discussed in detail later in this book. Before we encounter the first of these paranormal detectives, we move forward in time some twenty years after Estelle Roberts walked around lonely 'Peacehaven' to a time in post-war Britain during the 1950s, where the dreams of two ordinary London women were to become mixed with stories of strange crimes and with wife murder . . .

NOTES

1. Helen Victoria Duncan (1898-1956), Scottish materialisation medium and prominent Spiritualist martyr famously imprisoned for nine months during the Second World War for 'pretending to recall spirits of deceased persons'. Her death has been attributed to the effect of a police raid on one of her séances in Nottingham although there is no direct medical evidence for this. John (Jack) Boaden Webber (1907-40), Welsh miner and physical medium who was the subject of an investigation and biography by Spiritualist healer Harry Edwards. Webber's mediumistic career was cut short by his premature death at the age of thirty-three. Alexander Frederick (Alec) Harris (1897-1974), Welsh foreman painter and highly regarded materialisation medium. Harris gave many séances in his native Cardiff and later in Johannesburg, and, like Helen Duncan, his death has been attributed to the effects of an attempted exposure by South African journalists in the mid-1960s.
2. On 7 January 1939, two months before Hitler's invasion of Czechoslovakia, *Psychic News* published details of a communication from 'Red Cloud' which, with specific reference to the growing international disaster, included the famous phrase: 'We have returned from the spirit world to succeed and not to fail.'
3. *The Psychic Detectives* (Pan Books, London, 1984), pp. 205-7.

CHAPTER 8

THE WHISPERING WOMAN

DORIS HARRISON, 1957

The 'Black Museum' at Scotland Yard seems to epitomise in its title more than anything else the human fascination with true crime and classic murder cases of the past. More correctly known as the Metropolitan Police Crime Museum, this notorious collection of criminal memorabilia was established in the early 1870s as a centre of instruction for detectives and policemen using the Prisoners Property Act of 1869, which gave the police power to retain items of evidence and personal property belonging to convicted felons for the purposes of training and education. For many years the Black Museum – a suitably macabre name credited to a disparaging remark by a disgruntled journalist from *The Observer* newspaper who, in April 1877, was refused access to view the exhibits – was housed at the New Scotland Yard building in Whitehall Place. In the late 1960s, the collection was relocated to new premises and today occupies two rooms on the first floor of the Metropolitan Police Headquarters at Victoria Street, SW1. Its exhibits, un-viewable by the general public, every one a tribute to the dark and sinister side of the human psyche, contain connections to some of the most notorious names in the annals of British criminal history: the bathtub used by 'Brides in the Bath' killer George Joseph Smith to drown three women; a human vertebrae held together by tree roots recovered from the garden of 10 Rillington Place, where officially seven people were murdered by necrophile John Christie; and the gas stove from a Muswell Hill bedsit on which homosexual mass murderer Dennis Nilsen boiled human flesh.

In September 1957, there was much speculation in the British tabloid press that an incomplete handwritten manuscript was to be deposited in the Museum's archive by detectives from the 'X' Division at Harrow Road police station.

If Frank Harrison's short story 'The Mad Killer of Vermin Alley'[1] did make it into this unique collection of death masks, blunt instruments and hangmen's ropes, it would have been the only artefact in the Black Museum which crosses over into the strange twilight world of crime and the paranormal through which we are currently journeying. Its author, his crime and the eerie circumstances surrounding its discovery are now almost completely forgotten.

Francis Charles Alfred Harrison (known as Frank) was born on 7 November 1920 in Hampstead. A spoilt child, he left school at the age of fourteen and worked as an office boy before being employed as a stores assistant at the Arrons Electricity Meter factory in Salusbury Road, Kilburn. In 1941, Harrison enlisted in the RAF and served until 1946, rising to the rank of Corporal. Most of the war years were spent uneventfully guarding aerodromes although at one point he received twelve weeks' detention for fighting with civilians and, in March 1944, was unconscious for a period of twelve hours after falling down an escalator in an Underground station and, as a result, was hospitalized for a month. After de-mob, Harrison returned to Arrons and took up an office job as a progress chaser.

In March 1948, Frank Harrison married Doris Purkiss, the sister of a friend from the RAF, but the marriage became an unhappy one that was marred by frequent quarrelling and rows, often over money but also due to Doris's decision not to have children, which Harrison resented. The couple moved into a small terraced house at 11 Dagmar Gardens, Kensel Rise, which was divided into two flats; the Harrisons lived upstairs and sub-let the ground floor. Doris Harrison found a job as a meter tester at Arrons and worked there until November 1956. Early on she became friendly with a factory colleague, Myrtle Hughes, and she and her husband subsequently moved into the ground floor flat at Dagmar Gardens, where they stayed for seven years before eventually moving to West Sussex. Another worker at the Arron factory who knew the Harrisons well was Miss Mavis Welch, who lived nearby in Gordon Road, Kilburn. The two women often went shopping and to West End shows together and after Doris Harrison resigned from Arrons in November 1956, Mavis visited her at Dagmar Gardens regularly every Thursday. All three became close but none of them could have envisaged the future events that lay ahead.

In 1955, the Harrisons' stormy marriage took a turn for the worse. Doris threatened suicide and move temporarily to her parents' house in Southampton, where she was treated for depression by the family doctor. The couple eventually agreed to a reconciliation and Frank Harrison arranged to join his wife and in-laws for a holiday. However, shortly after arriving in Southampton, Harrison appeared to have a breakdown of his own and went missing for six days, eventually returning with amnesia and totally unable to

The lonely Clachen of Inverey, photographed in the early years of the twentieth century, over 150 years after the death of Sergeant Davies. (Author's collection)

Sir Walter Scott (1771-1832), who published an account of the ghost of Arthur Davies in the 1830s. The great Scottish novelist felt the story of the haunting was an invention. (The Walter Scott Digital Archive)

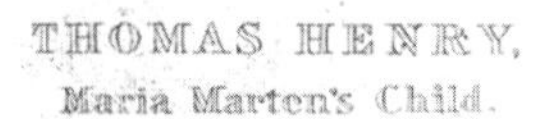

The execution of William Corder outside Bury Gaol on 11 August 1828.

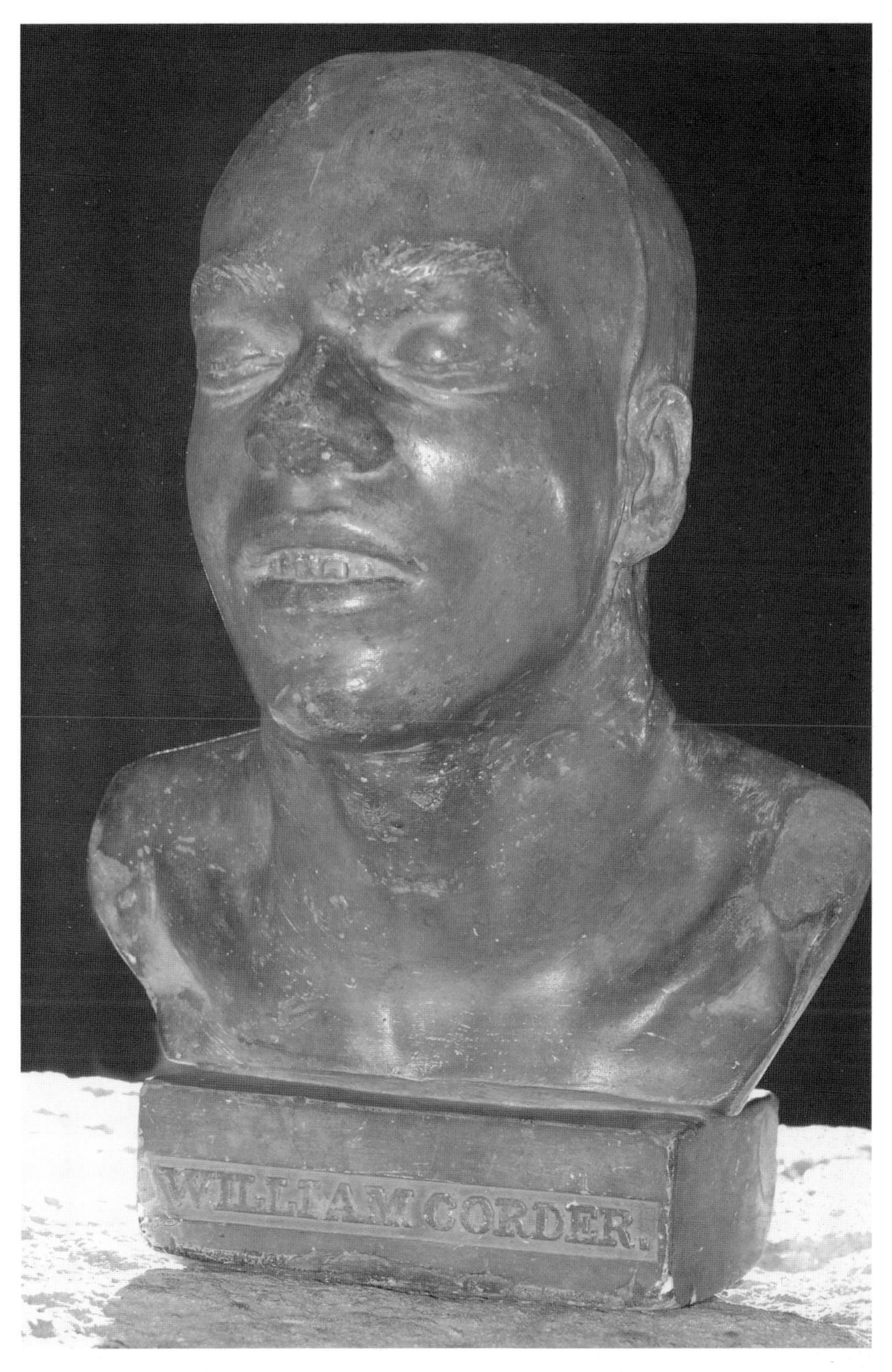

A death mask of William Corder, perpetrator of the infamous Murder in the Red Barn – other surviving relics include a section of his pickled scalp and a published account of the murder bound in Corder's own skin. (St Edmundsbury Borough Council)

English ghost-hunter Robert Thurston Hopkins (1884-1958) examining one of the haunted Warbleton Priory skulls. Thurston Hopkins' father at one time owned the death's head of William Corder. (Peter Underwood Collection)

Robert James Lees, photographed in the studio of Philips and Lees at Ilfracombe sometime between 1911 and 1925. (Stephen Butt)

Ernest 'Bill' Dyer, whose crime of murder was revealed by the eerie dreams of his victim's mother. (Author's collection)

Eric Tombe (right) photographed with the young Dennis Wheatley in the years immediately following the First World War. Wheatley described Tombe as 'a crook of the first order' but revered his memory all his life. (Charles Beck)

The entrance to The Welcomes, photographed in 2011. (Paul Adams)

The graveyard of St Odhrain's chapel on Iona, the last resting place of the troubled Netta Fornario. (Donald Whannel)

Harry Price (1881-1948), English ghost-hunter extraordinaire, demonstrating a séance room controlling device in the late 1920s. (Author's collection)

Judge Ludwig Dahl and his daughter Ingeborg, the main players in the Norwegian Spiritualist murder trial. (Author's collection)

Above: Estelle Roberts (1899-1970), in her distinctive black cloak, gives a platform demonstration in front of a packed hall. Through her spirit guide 'Red Cloud', she seemingly made contact with the spirit of the murdered Mona Tinsley. (*Sunday Pictorial*)

Right: Child-killer Frederick Nodder, hanged for the murder of Mona Tinsley in December 1937. (Author's collection)

MONDAY, JUNE 7, 1937

Daily Mirror

No. 10455 Registered at the G.P.O. as a Newspaper. ONE PENNY

MONA TINSLEY'S BODY FOUND IN RIVER AFTER FIVE MONTHS

The body of Mona Tinsley wa s recovered from the River Idle, at Bawtry, South Yorkshire, yesterday, by a special constable rowing down the river in a bo at for a picnic with his three sons and a friend.

IT was taken to the Ship Inn, Newington, and late last night was identified by Mona's father, who had been rushed from his Newark (Notts) home in a police car.

He broke down as he saw the body, identifying it as his daughter by the sodden clothes.

Mona Tinsley.

Mr. W. Marshall, Bawtry gas manager and special constable, was in a rowing boat when he saw the body floating in the water.

He pulled it into the boat, brought it to the bank and warned the police.

The River Idle earlier had been searched yard by yard without result.

Notts and West Riding police last night communicated with the Home Office, and in all probability a post-mortem examination will be made to-day.

Mona Tinsley, ten-year-old schoolgirl, disappeared from her home last January. An intensive police and civilian search all over Nottingham failed to trace her.

Two months later Frederick Nodder, forty-nine-year-old motor-driver, was sentenced at Birmingham Assizes to seven years' penal servitude for decoying the girl

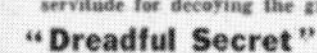

"Dreadful Secret"

Sentencing him, Mr. Justice Swift declared: "It may be that time will reveal the dreadful secret which you carry in your breast.

"I cannot tell But I am determined, as far as I have part or lot in this dreadful tragedy, that I will keep you in custody.

"What you did with the little girl, what became of her, only you know.

"It may be that something will happen which will show other people that you ought to be released.

Mr. Norman Birkett, K.C., outlining the case for the prosecution, said that when Mona left school for her home at 4 p.m. on January 5, Nodder was seen close to the school building.

Next morning Nodder borrowed a spade and fork from a neighbour. A child is seen at his back door, wearing a pale blue dress, as was Mona. Then Nodder is seen digging

"From that moment," Mr. Birkett dramatically told the Court, "no human eye has ever seen Mona Lilian Tinsley."

3-HOUR FIGHT TO FREE MAN TRAPPED IN LIFT SHAFT

FOR nearly three hours firemen and ambulance men worked to release twenty - year - old garage attendant B. Walters, of Boston-road, London, N.W., trapped between a lift and the floor last night at Longman's Garage, Rossmore-street, London, N.W.

Brickwork round the lift-shaft was cut away and a doctor crawled through the hole to give chloroform to the tortured man while the work went on.

Rescuers were called by eleven-year-old Edward West, who was passing the garage and was horrified to see the man trapped in a rapidly ascending motor lift.

"I was just walking past when I saw Mr. Walters," he told the *Daily Mirror*. "I know him well. He lives just near my home.

"He was waving people clear of the gates and suddenly the lift shot up. He fell down, and I saw his arm caught in the railings. He screamed and screamed. There were some girls there, but they were so frightened that they ran away."

Walters was taken to hospital with arms and legs badly crushed and lacerated.

Picture on back page.

13,000 MILES TO SEE UNCLE—LOST ADDRESS

MISS Ella Norman, of New South Wales, travelling 13,000 miles to visit her uncle in Edinburgh, has arrived at Australia House, London, to find she has lost his address.

She kept it in an address book which she must have dropped when she was touring the Belgian battlefields.

Now she has written to Edinburgh police asking assistance in tracing her uncle, Mr. T. Norman, who is about seventy years old.

JEAN HARLOW RECOVERING

Miss Jean Harlow, who has been ill in Hollywood for some time, is now recovering, according to her doctors. But she will not be fit to resume film work for several weeks.

Doctors describe her illness, says British United Press, as an internal inflammation

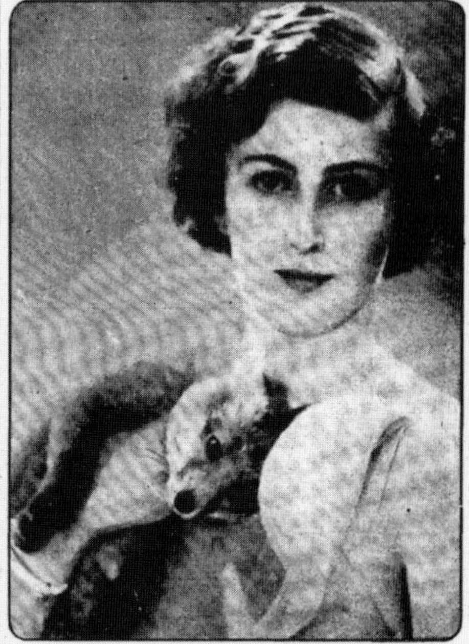

Miss Diana Battye, twenty-one-year-old Society girl, who is missing.

RICH GIRL VANISHES AFTER KIDNAP THREATS

BY A SPECIAL CORRESPONDENT

WITH only £5 in her handbag and no luggage at all Miss Diana Battye, well-known twenty-one-year-old society beauty left the home of Viscountess Long in Oxford-square, W., last Tuesday and has not been seen or heard of since.

Behind her she left her jewellery worth £500.

She is the daughter of Captain Percy Battye, formerly of the Welsh Guards, and Mrs. Leonard Hackett, of West Winds, Woodley, Berks.

Her parents are frantic because for months Miss Battye has been receiving a series of anonymous letters threatening to abduct her.

Their anxiety is increased by an assault which was made on her by a man on Coronation night.

She was walking along Cambridge-street, W., when a man suddenly sprang at her. She resisted him and he cut her forehead with a razor, inflicting two wounds.

was felt it was the act of a drunken reveller.

The police were not told of this because it Now the event has taken on a more serious significance.

Last night Mrs. Hackett told me: "My daughter received seven of these letters in all. The first came in March and the last in April.

"They were all the same—typewritten on a half-sheet of notepaper and unsigned."

Miss Battye is engaged to Mr. Michael Asquith, son of Lady Cynthia Asquith.

Mr. Asquith is at Oxford and he has also heard nothing from his fiancee since she vanished.

Scotland Yard has been asked to search for Miss Battye.

Before she left, Miss Battye made two 'phone calls. One was to her old nurse at Billingsbear Lodge, Binfield, near Ascot, which was her home.

The other call has not been traced.

Miss Battye, blue-eyed and fair-haired, is one of the best-liked girls in society. She is a popular figure at the smartest parties, restaurants and night clubs. Her friends call her "Didi."

The front page of the *Daily Mirror* for 7 June 1937, reporting the discovery of Mona Tinsely's body in the River Idle. (Chris Hobbs)

Doris Harrison, the victim in the 'Body in the Cupboard' case, and (inset) her husband Francis Harrison. (Author's collection)

Number 11 Dagmar Gardens, Kensel Rise, where a whispering ghost revealed a brutal murder. (Paul Adams)

Dutch super-psychic Gerard Croiset (1909-1980), known as the 'Wizard of Utrecht'. The clairvoyant received many calls both day and night from the parents of missing children. (Henri Croiset)

'at McAdam, who went missing in 'ebruary 1967. Her body has never een recovered. (Author's collection)

Anne Noblett – her bizarre 'Deep Freeze Murder' remains unsolved. (Paul Heslop)

A modern view of the derelict pig farm at Marshalls Heath Lane, Wheathampstead, said to have been haunted by the ghost of Anne Noblett during the 1970s. (Paul Adams)

The full court story—See Pages 2, 3, 4, 5 and Jean Rook on the Centre Pages

The Ripper

Peter Sutcliffe goes by prison van to the Old Bailey yesterday where he admitted killing 13 women

Picture by John Rogers

TV Guide Pages 24, 25 • Weather Page 4 • William Hickey Page 13 • Pop Page 26 • Starline Page 31 • Letters Page 32 • Finance Pages 36, 37 • Sport starts Page 38

Left: Face of Evil – the front page of the *Daily Express* for 30 April 1981, showing Yorkshire Ripper Peter Sutcliffe returning from the Old Bailey after being charged with thirteen murders. (Author's collection)

Below: Article from the *Daily Mirror* for 21 November 1980, showing the Yorkshire Ripper predictions of psychic Nella Jones. (Author's collection)

'He will strike again within a few days'

STARTLING PREDICTION OF A RIPPER CLAIRVOYANT

By BRIAN CROWTHER

THE Yorkshire Ripper will strike again within the next few days.

This frightening warning came yesterday from clairvoyant Nella Jones—who forecast with astonishing accuracy the death this week of the Ripper's thirteenth victim, Jacqui Hill.

"It's tragic, but I feel he will strike again almost immediately," Nella said. "I see him coming back to claim another victim within the week."

She said the next victim would be a youngish woman, but refused to give further details. "I do not want to frighten the life out of some poor young girl with a similar description," she said.

Six weeks ago, Nella told the Yorkshire Post newspaper that the Ripper would strike twice within a few days.

Brutal

She forecast that the first murder would be in Leeds on November 17 or 27 . . .

Jacqui, a 20-year-old student, was brutally murdered in Leeds on Monday, November 17.

Nella also forecast: "The murder will take place on a damp, misty night when it is raining. The body will be found amid the undergrowth and near leaves."

Jacqui was attacked on a rainy night and her body was found lying in undergrowth on wasteland.

The Yorkshire Post revealed her astonishing predictions yesterday.

It said it had kept the forecast secret because of fear that it might incite a killing by the Ripper or an imitator.

Ron Thompson, of the Yorkshire Post's London office, said that Nella had also warned about the twelfth murder fourteen months ago.

Mistake

Nella, a 48-year-old mother of four, had another prediction to make yesterday:

The Ripper is going to make a mistake that could lead to his capture.

She said at her home in Freta Road, Bexleyheath, Kent, that she receives mental "images" about the Ripper and his victims.

A drawing of how she sees the Ripper has been sent to police.

The Daily Mirror office in Manchester yesterday received a phone call from a man claiming to be the Ripper saying he would kill again in Leeds next week.

JACQUI: Victim No. 13

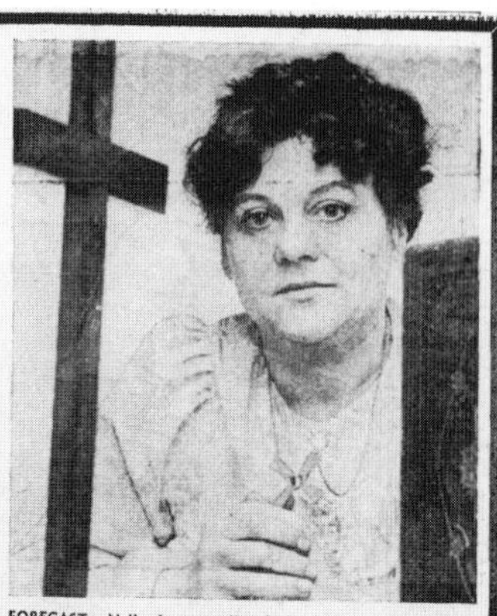

FORECAST: Nella Jones predicted the Ripper's latest murder.

Did killer travel on Jacqui's bus?

By MIRROR REPORTERS

THE Yorkshire Ripper may have met his 13th victim on a bus.

This possibility was being investigated by police last night. Detectives know that 20-year-old student Jacqui Hill caught a green Metro bus from Cookridge Street, Leeds, for her two-mile ride home to Headingley.

At least 15 passengers were on the bus. Five got off at the same stop as Jacqui.

Talk

Minutes later she was murdered by the mass killer.

Detective Superintendent Alf Finlay said yesterday: "We are anxious to talk to all the passengers who travelled on the bus, especially the five who got off at the same stop."

Jacqui's flatmate, student Andree Proctor revealed last night that she walked past the murder scene seconds after the killer struck.

Andree, 19, said: "If I had been a fraction further up the road, it would have been me he pounced on."

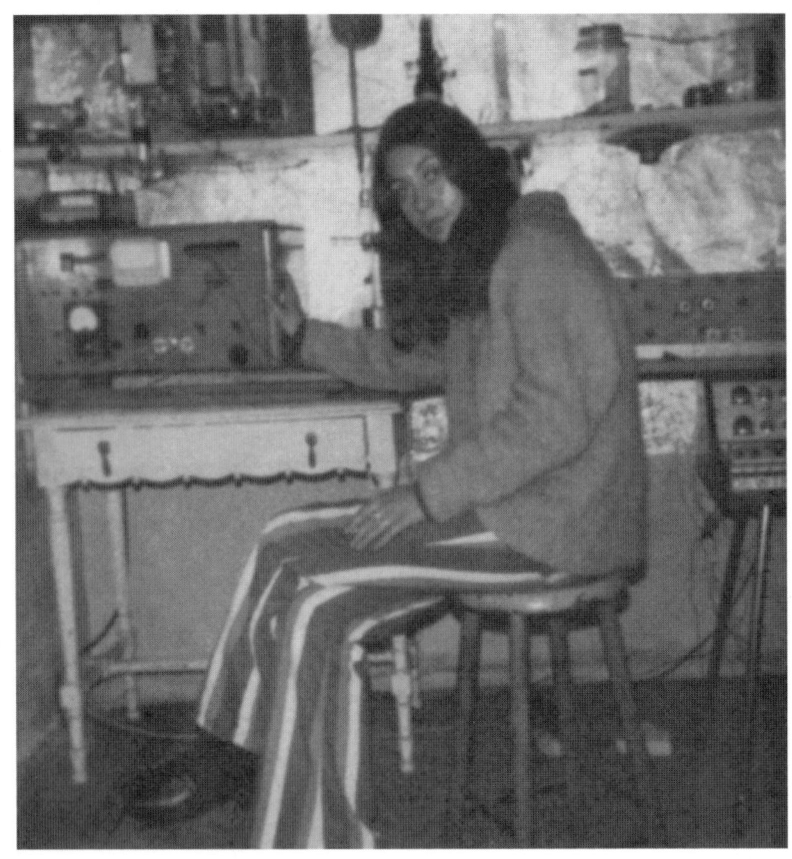

Clairvoyant Suzanne Padfield, photographed in the Paralab in the early 1970s. Through remote viewing she was able to reveal information about the Moscow ice rink murder. (Author's collection)

Number 16 Wardle Brook Avenue, Hattersley, photographed shortly before its demolition in 1987. (Richard Lee-Van den Daele)

[Cr]awley Harvey Crippen and his mistress Ethel Le Neve in the dock at Bow Street Police Court. [(A]uthor's collection)

[Ja]cqueline Poole, who seemingly [co]mmunicated information to medium [C]hristine Holohan in the days following her [de]ath in 1983. (Author's collection)

Kousar Bashir, the tragic twenty-year-old victim in the Oldham exorcism case. (Author's collection)

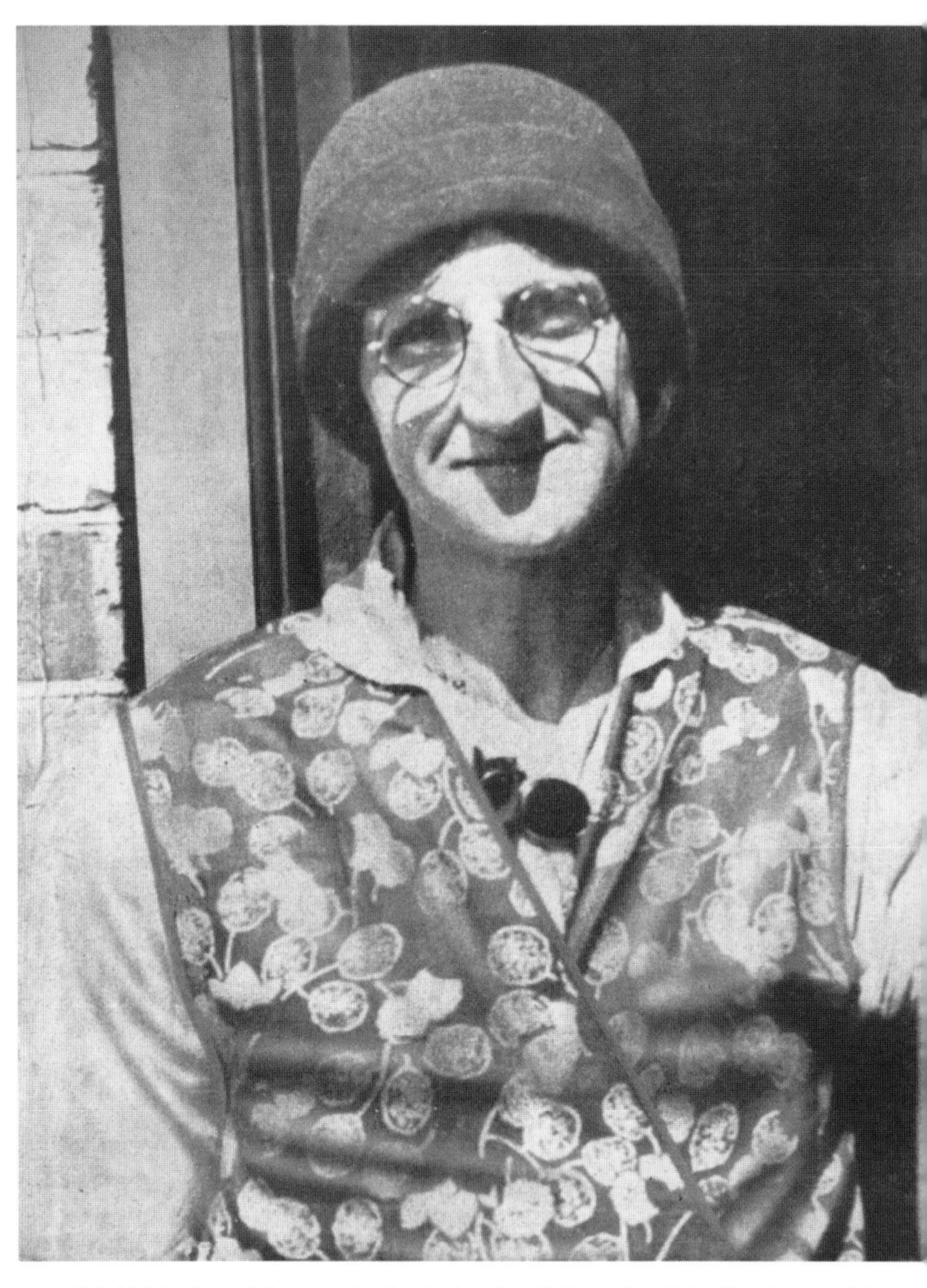

Ethel Major, hanged for poisoning her husband on 19 December 1934. Her ghost is said to haunt Hull Prison to this day. (Steve Fielding)

explain where he had been or what he had been doing. Back home in north-west London, Harrison's own doctor was inclined to believe that he had lapsed into a dissociative state or hysterical fugue as a reaction to the stress of his wife's illness; the reality was that Harrison had earlier began an affair with a work colleague, Margaret Daly, and the two had spent the time touring Devon as man and wife.

Harrison, a budding poet and short story writer, was able to use his clerical position at Arrons to spend lunch hours in Margaret Daly's company, as office rules dictated that factory workers like Doris and Myrtle Hughes were required to take their breaks in the works' canteen on the other side of the building. Whether Harrison wrote poetry for Margaret is unclear, but at some point he spent time writing a murder mystery thriller which he felt enough of to show to Myrtle Hughes when they first moved to Kensel Rise, asking for her opinion as he intended to try and get the manuscript published. The surviving text of 'The Mad Killer of Vermin Alley', a clumsy cross between *The Murders in the Rue Morgue* and Mickey Spillane's *The Death Dealers*, as held on microfilm at the National Archives, runs to twelve pages of double-spaced typescript and describes the crimes of a hook-handed killer who stalks the seedy alleyway of the title. The following extract gives a fair example of Harrison's literary style, as the tragic hero, Paul Garnet, defends himself and his wife against a night-time attack by the deranged murderer:

> . . . Creeping into a recess at the head of the stairway, Paul stood waiting with his gun gripped firmly in his hand. As the figure grew [*sic*] level with him, he rapped out, 'Stick em up, whoever you are!'
>
> The intruder's only reply was to raise an arm and Paul saw a cruel hook start to descend! He tried to leap out of the way but the hook caught his shoulder and threw him heavily onto the stairs. Before he could stop himself he was rolling down them with the sound of horrible laughter above! It was the killer!
>
> As Paul crashed into the hall, he heard his wife screaming upstairs! Picking himself up, he rushed madly upstairs, praying and hoping that he would get there in time to save her!
>
> On entering the bedroom, he heard the smash of broken glass. He raced to the window and saw the attacker tearing down the street. Paul emptied his gun at the creature but it got clean away.
>
> He walked over to the door and switched on the light. Looking towards the bed he swore vengeance!
>
> His wife was lying on the tangled bedclothes ripped wide open! Her nightdress was torn from her body and her blood ran freely on to the carpet!

Paul's lips set in a thin line and he silently reloaded his gun! He went downstairs and out into the street, straight to where Steve Carter lived! Knocking on the door, he stood there waiting. He didn't have to wait long for Steve was awake already. He opened the door and saw Paul standing there with the revolver in his hand.

'What's wrong Paul?' he asked.

'Molly's dead!'

'Dead!' Steve's eyes opened wide. 'You don't mean that the monster – '.

'Yes, Steve,' replied Paul hollowly. 'The fiend killed her in cold blood! It isn't a monster; it's a man, a madman!'

'Are you sure?' asked Carter.

'Quite sure!' answered Paul. 'I can't explain the hooks where his hands should be, though. But we're wasting time standing here, anyway. Let us call the people and track the swine down!'

'You're right Paul,' said Steve. 'We must destroy the devil before anyone else dies.'

Soon a vigilante mob roused by the two men have cornered the killer in a local haunted house and the hero is happy to join his wife in the afterlife as he and the claw-handed 'demon' fall to their deaths down a stairwell. Unfortunately for the author, Myrtle Hughes was nonplussed by the story, which was consigned to obscurity in Harrison's desk drawer at Arrons and where it was subsequently recovered by the police. On at least one occasion during a lunch hour, Myrtle Hughes unexpectedly came across Harrison and Margaret Daly in a compromising situation that made it quite clear there was some intimacy between them, something she may or may not have confided to Doris Harrison.

In February 1957, Myrtle Hughes gave notice at the Arrons factory and she and her husband Jack left Dagmar Gardens and relocated to Chelwood Gate, near Haywards Heath. The three women – Harrison, Hughes and Mavis Welch – kept in touch by letter. Now with complete vacant possession of the downstairs flat, the Harrisons decided to sell the house with the intention of moving into a more modern property and made arrangement with a local estate agent to put the house on the market.

Mavis Welch continued to visit Doris Harrison at Dagmar Gardens and spent the evening of 21 March in her company. The following Thursday she went to Kensal Rise as arranged but, unusually on this occasion, the house was in darkness and there appeared to be no one at home. Early in April she wrote to Doris but the only response was on 6 April, when Frank Harrison came round to Gordon Road to tell her that he had seen the letter but his wife was not there; they had had a row, and she had walked out and had gone to stay with her parents in Southampton. The following week the Harrisons' estate agent, Clive Woods, visited Dagmar Gardens to take down sales particulars of the house but was unable to get into the upstairs bedrooms, both of which were locked. Over the next few weeks through April and into May, Woods made several visits to show prospective buyers over the house and on each occasion noticed a particularly bad smell in the downstairs flat, which seemed strongest in the vicinity of the stairway. When this was mentioned to Frank Harrison, he put it down to problems with the drains and said they were in the process of getting them cleared. In an effort to alleviate the problem, Harrison set out air fresheners around the ground-floor flat.

In the early part of the week before Easter, Mavis Welch saw Harrison leaving the Arrons factory in Salusbury Road and asked after his wife. Harrison told her he hadn't heard from Doris and said he was going to spend the holiday with an old friend from the RAF. This 'old friend' was actually Margaret Daly and the couple spent the Easter weekend together at Matlock Baths.

The following month, Harrison received a worried letter from his father-in-law, William Purkiss; neither he nor his wife had heard from their daughter for some time and an Easter egg present they had sent to her at Dagmar Gardens had been returned after three weeks by the Post Office undelivered. On 18 May, Harrison went down to Southampton and admitted that he and Doris had had a terrific row, that she had walked out on him and he had not seen her for some time, although he felt she had been back to the house on one or two occasions while he had been out at work. In the hope of encouraging Doris to get in touch with them, Harrison agreed to the Purkiss's writing a letter, which he promised to leave on the hall mat so that his wife would recognise the handwriting and postmark. Soon afterwards he wrote: 'You don't know how worried I have been . . . Please try to look for the silver lining in our dark clouds, as I am really trying to do, although it is not easy', and also placated them by agreeing to contact the Salvation Army, who helped locate missing persons.

Two days after going to Southampton, Harrison again saw Mavis Welch in Salusbury Road; on this occasion he told her that he had been to Southampton but Doris had walked out after rowing with her parents and he had no idea where she was, although he would contact her as soon as he had any news. After a fortnight, during which time she neither saw or heard anything from Frank Harrison, and now understandably concerned, Miss Welch wrote to the Purkiss family on 3 June 1957 asking if they had any news of their daughter.

Around the same time, the beginning of June, in Haywards Heath, sixty miles away from their former home in Kensel Rise, Myrtle Hughes began to be troubled by a series of distressing nightmares. On each occasion she woke up crying. In the dreams she saw a vision of a red fireplace, which she recognised as being the one in the front room of their old flat at Dagmar Gardens. Chillingly, beyond the fireplace, in a bricked-up alcove, was her friend Doris Harrison, who was calling out to her in a soft, whispering voice: '*Come and find me . . . come and find me.*' The nightmares continued regularly for two weeks and in every one, Myrtle Hughes was haunted by the echo of the sad and pleading, whispering voice. Jack Hughes was dismissive but his wife became convinced, as the dream returned night after night, that something dreadful had happened and this seemed to be confirmed when, in the second week of June, she received a letter from Mavis Welch asking if Doris Harrison was staying with her in Sussex. Myrtle Hughes wrote back immediately (on 14 June) but by this time she had already made up her mind to take the train to London and see Mavis herself.

Arriving at Mavis Welch's house in Kilburn, the two women discussed their missing friend and were stunned when it soon became clear that they had both shared the same eerie dream. Already distressed by Doris Harrison's disappearance, Mavis Welch had herself in the previous week experienced a nightmare in which she heard a voice calling out to her from some dark unknown place: '*Come and find me, Mavis . . . come and find me. You know I'd do it for you . . .* ' It seemed too much of a coincidence and, although not inclined to any great beliefs in ghosts or the supernatural, they went the same day, 19 June, to Harrow Road police station. How much credence the duty officer gave to the two women's strange story is debateable; however, when their statement was passed through to detectives of the 'X' Division at the same station, the mention of the name Doris Harrison twice within the space of less than a week was enough for officers to want to speak with the missing woman's husband, and Detective Inspector Henry Cox went that afternoon to Arrons factory in Salusbury Road.

Three days before, on 16 June, the police in Southampton had passed on a letter they had received from William Purkiss, who had written expressing his concerns for the safety of his daughter as well as the seeming lack of urgency on the part of his son-in-law in making enquiries as to her whereabouts. The same day, WPC Joy Plane called at Dagmar Gardens and Frank Harrison accompanied her back to the Harrow Road station, where he gave an interview about his missing wife, with a promise that should he obtain any information he would contact her parents immediately. Now at Salusbury Road, Detective Inspector Cox saw Harrison for the first time and, after some perfunctory questions about Doris's disappearance, told him he intended to go with him to Kensel Rise where he would search the house, after which

Harrison was to make a full statement about the reasons for his wife leaving. 'I'll do whatever you think is right,' was Harrison's response.

Just before five o'clock in the afternoon, Harrison let Cox into 11 Dagmar Gardens and watched as the policeman looked around the first-floor flat before taking him downstairs. As they walked along the hallway, Cox commented on the peculiar smell, which was immediately apparent. Again Harrison blamed the drainage system but the Detective Inspector was not convinced and told him bluntly, 'We are going to trace the source of that smell even if I have to take the floorboards up.' Harrison made no reply. Cox realised that the smell was strongest by the door leading to the cupboard under the stairs. Inside, wrapped in a blanket and hidden by bed linen and a stack of timber boarding, he found the rotting body of Doris Harrison. 'What is it? How did it get in there?' Harrison asked with some amazement. 'We shall have to go to Harrow Road police station now, I have a lot of enquiries to make before I can answer that,' Cox replied. The house was locked up and Harrison was taken into custody.

Dr Robert Teare, a Harley Street physician, along with Professor Francis Camps of the London Hospital Medical College and Keith Simpson from Guy's Hospital, made up a trio of celebrated post-war forensic pathologists known to the medical and police professions of the day as 'The Three Musketeers'. In 1951, Teare had presented the forensic evidence at the enquiry into the Harrow and Wealdstone train crash and would later carry out an autopsy on the body of celebrated musician and guitarist Jimi Hendrix. The three men had all been involved in the 1953 exhumation of Beryl Evans, the former tenant of 10 Rillington Place, in the aftermath of the revelations brought about by the Christie trial. At 6.30 p.m., Teare accompanied Detective Inspector Cox and Superintendant Davis to Dagmar Gardens, where he supervised the removal of the body of Doris Harrison to Kilburn Mortuary and, later the same evening, carried out a post-mortem. The body was in an advanced state of decomposition but Teare was able to state the cause of death as being due to multiple fractures of the skull carried out in 'a frenzy of violence'; the murder weapon was most likely an axe which had been found in an upstairs cupboard in the house and which bore signs of having been recently cleaned. Subsequently, a bloodstained mattress was discovered in the first floor back bedroom in the Harrisons' flat and the police found clear evidence of one of the bedroom walls having been recently wallpapered to cover up splashes of blood. 'It is all like a dream – it seems utterly fantastic,' Frank Harrison told Detective Inspector Cox. On 20 June 1957 he was charged with murder and the following day was remanded in custody in the hospital wing at Brixton Prison.

At Willesden Magistrates Court on 11 July 1957, Harrison was committed for trial at the September sessions of the Central Criminal Court. 'We had been rowing for weeks,' Harrison had told Detective Inspector Cox, continuing:

> We had a terrific row one morning, which morning is beyond me, I seemed to black out, it's very difficult to describe, it just seemed to get the better of me . . . I got hold of something, it was metallic, and I remember hitting her on the head although I didn't see her face. I was in a frenzy and after I hit her my mind must have gone completely blank . . .

He stated he had come round at ten o'clock later the same morning on a bus on his way to his parents' house at Neasden, but had no recollection of events before that time and was unable to explain how the body of his wife had come to be found in the cupboard under the stairs. While on remand, Harrison was interviewed by Dr Denis Leigh of the Maudsley Hospital. 'He is . . . a man of hysterical personality, who reacts to stress by the manifestation of amnesiac manifestations,' Leigh commented, while the prison psychiatrist at Brixton, Dr J.C.M. Matheson, who had an extensive experience of violent criminals and murderers including Christie, also felt that Harrison's loss of memory was genuine. They also both agreed that he was sane and fit to stand trial.

The case of Regina vs. Harrison opened at the Old Bailey on 10 September 1957. Prosecuting for the Crown was Mr Christmas Humphries assisted by Mr Griffith-Jones, while Mr William Henning acted for the defence. Much emphasis was placed on Harrison's hysterical personality and his allegedly morbid and unwell state of mind, as demonstrated by the surviving pages of 'The Mad Killer of Vermin Alley', which had been recovered by Detective Inspector Cox from his desk drawer at Arrons and extracts from which were read out in court by William Henning, quickly prompting sensational newspaper headlines such as the *Daily Mirror's* 'Husband Wrote a Story of Horror'. Despite his early episode of hysterical fugue being shown to be a lie, the defence insisted that Harrison was mentally ill and the proper verdict was one of manslaughter. The jury disagreed and Harrison was found guilty and sentenced to life imprisonment. A few months earlier in March, the Homicide Act 1957 had come into force, which reduced the death penalty to acts of premeditated murder as well as a new charge of capital murder, i.e. murder during the course of or furtherance of theft.

The case of Francis Harrison, like those of Maria Marten and Eric Tombe, puts forward in a compelling way the idea of some form of supernormal contact from beyond the grave. Sceptics would of course argue vigorously against this. Writing in 1980 in his essay 'Parapsychology: Science or Pseudoscience?'[2],

Anthony Flew, Emeritus Professor of Philosophy at Reading University, made the comment 'that the content of visions, dreams, and misperceptions is always in part a function of the wishes, beliefs, and expectations of the subject', a level-headed approach against jumping to seemingly obvious supernatural conclusions: Anne Marten knew of William Corder's unsavoury reputation, which may have lead her to suspect that a murder had taken place in the Red Barn; the suicide of Ernest Dyer, a known associate of Eric Tombe, and revelations of his crooked career, could have caused the Revd Tombe to conclude that his missing son was buried somewhere at the site of their failed business venture together at the deserted Welcomes farm; and Myrtle Hughes and Mavis Welch, both worried about their missing friend, may have imagined they had had the same dream of her whispering ghost. But to dismiss things simply out of hand as being just impossible is clearly unscientific, and Professor Flew acknowledged this when, in the same paper, he made the personal observation 'that, although there was no repeatable experiment to demonstrate the reality of any of the putative psi phenomena, and although the entire field was buried under ever-mounting piles of rubbish produced by charlatans and suckers, nevertheless one could not with a good academic conscience dismiss the case as closed.' Colin Wilson, originally a sceptic, and after much study of the subject, came to the conclusion that there was as much evidence for the paranormal as there is for atoms and electrons, although it must be said that evidence for the paranormal does not always automatically equate to proof of survival after death.

However, if the paranormal contents of cases like the murder of Doris Harrison are in fact spontaneous flashes of post-mortem communication, or the fleeting whispers of passing ghosts, what evidence exists (outside of the world of mediums and Spiritualism) for crimes that have actually been solved by direct professional investigation and contact with the spirit world? As the occult revolution of the 1960s began to gather momentum, this question took several steps closer forward to being answered – the time of the psychic detective had arrived.

NOTES

1. The actual title of Frank Harrison's story is unknown as its opening pages were never recovered and the typescript, prepared from it for use as an exhibit at his trial and now held on microfilm at the National Archives, is incomplete. For the purposes of the commentary in this book I have taken the liberty of giving it a title as befits the writing style of its author. The whereabouts of the manuscript original, if it still survives, is today unknown as, despite notices published in the press at the time, the record of acquisitions for the Black Museum for the year 1957 show no record of it being added to the collection.
2. Reprinted in *The Skeptic's Handbook of Parapsychology*, Edited by Paul Kurtz (Prometheus Books, New York, 1985).

CHAPTER 9

THE POWER OF THE PSYCHIC DETECTIVE

GERARD CROISET, 1960s

If Uri Gellar was the psychic superstar of the 1970s, then it would be true to say that the Dutchman, Gerard Croiset, was easily his equal during the Swinging Sixties. The 'wizard of Utrecht' became a familiar figure in the public eye as newspapers, magazines and television programmes regularly documented his astonishing powers of clairvoyance and telepathy. It was not without foundation that he was also known as 'the man who mystifies Europe' and 'the man with the X-ray mind'; and much of this popular reputation was due in no small way to his own particular application of his psychic talents to the field of murder and crime detection. Almost singlehandedly, Croiset established the figure of the psychic detective in Europe and lived the role to the full. As we will see, he was and remains, a pioneering figure in the history of twentieth-century paranormal research.

As with other mediums and sensitives such as Estelle Roberts, Gerard Croiset's psychic abilities became apparent at a young age, but for him these childhood years were unhappy ones and culminated in a nervous breakdown when he was in his early twenties. Born Gerard Boekbinder on 10 March 1909 in the northern Dutch city of Laren, he was given up to foster parents at the age of eight by disinterested parents – his father, a philandering actor, was rarely at home while his mother was unable to cope with bringing up Croiset and his younger brother practically singlehanded. Around 1920, Croiset and his mother, who had divorced his father and remarried, effected a reconciliation but the young boy was uneasy around his new stepfather and ran away several times. At home, Croiset found solace in prayer, despite the fact that, although being Jewish, his mother was by choice an atheist and, being disinclined to allow any kind of religious instruction in the home, looked on her son's acts of faith with contempt, thereby driving a wedge through what little relationship they had managed to rebuild.

During the early 1930s, after a series of 'dead end' jobs, Croiset married and started a career as a self-employed grocer in Enschede, close to the border with Germany, with money borrowed from his wife's parents. The couple eventually raised a family of four children, three boys and a girl; Croiset was imprisoned twice by the occupying Nazis during the Second World War but was released and, during these periods of freedom, worked for the Dutch resistance. Throughout these difficult years, from the time he was a small child at school through to the end of the war years, psychic experiences and contacts with the twilight world of the unseen were also a part of Gerard Croiset's difficult life.

An often repeated account of the beginning of Croiset's psychic awareness concerns an incident during the 1930s, when the Dutchman visited the shop of a local watch repairer. As Croiset casually picked up a ruler that lay on a workbench, a series of images connected with the horologist's youth and early years, subsequently confirmed by the watchmaker as being wholly accurate, came into his head, in the same way that Estelle Roberts had been able to hold Mona Tinsley's pink dress and know instantly that the child was dead. In fact, Croiset would recall an even earlier incident when, at the age of six, he told a schoolmaster who had been away from the classroom for a day, that he had been visiting a blonde lady who wore a red flower; this was the teacher's fiancé to whom the day before he had successfully proposed marriage with a gift of a red rose. Croiset was able to make many predictions using his increasing clairvoyant abilities in the years that followed, but it was to be in the period immediately following the end of the war in Europe that he would begin to lay down the foundations that would enable him to build a career as one of the most well known of post-war psychics.

Wilhelm Heinrich Carl Tenhaeff, born in 1894, became one of Holland's foremost psychical researchers. In 1933, he successfully submitted a thesis on 'Clairvoyance and Empathy' to obtain a doctorate from the University of Utrecht and twenty years later, in 1953, held the first ever Chair of Parapsychology at Utrecht, the first academic to obtain such a position, beating Hans Bender at Freiburg by a year. Professor Tenhaeff's department, although funded by the Danish Society for Paranormal Research, was a major step forward for the fledgling discipline of parapsychology, and Tenhaeff's pioneering status ultimately made his later fall from grace that much more difficult and painful to accept, both by Tenhaeff himself and particularly for the academic world of psychical research. Although he carried out Rhine-style card experiments, Tenhaeff's real interest lay in examining clairvoyance and he coined the term 'paragnost' (from the Greek *para* 'beyond' and *gnosis* 'knowledge') for people able to demonstrate and be tested for these abilities. In 1946, Tenhaeff gave a lecture on parapsychological subjects at Enschede; in the audience that day was Gerard Croiset.

Croiset's meeting with Professor Tenhaeff was a watershed moment for both men; it marked the beginning of a close working association that would make both the psychic and the scientist famous. Croiset offered himself as a subject for investigation by Tenhaeff's Department of Parapsychology and, after a time, he became the one 'paragnost' with whom the researcher had the most success. It is his involvement with cases of missing persons, and with crime and murder, that Gerard Croiset is most remembered today, and this association began soon after his contact with Tenhaeff.

In the winter of 1946, a twenty-one-year-old girl was attacked and beaten with a hammer while cycling home along a country road near the town of Wierden, around twenty miles from where Croiset was living. Fortunately the girl survived and in his haste to escape, the assailant dropped the hammer, which was recovered by police. It was put on display in a Wierden shop window in the hope that someone might identify it, but after several weeks the police investigation drew a blank and, when the police contacted the Parapsychology Department at the University of Utrecht with a request to involve a clairvoyant, Wilhelm Tenhaeff suggested the hammer should be shown to Gerard Croiset. When Croiset held the hammer he described a tall, dark person of around thirty years of age who was connected with the attack on the girl; but the tool did not in fact belong to him and was the property of an older man, in his mid fifties, in whose cottage it normally hung with other tools. Croiset's impressions were noted but provided the police with no new leads. However, six months later, in June 1947, the Dutch police arrested a twenty-eight-year-old youth for another crime and, under interrogation, he confessed to carrying out the hammer attack at Wierden; he admitted to taking the weapon from the house of a neighbour and descriptions of the assailant, the owner of the hammer and his cottage all fitted those previously taken down by Croiset.

Two years later, in July 1949, Croiset was asked to give his impressions on a rape case that had taken place in the northern province of Drenthe. A retarded girl had been enticed away from a folk festival near the town of Assen by two brothers, who had taken her to a nearby hay barn and assaulted her. The men had intended to follow through the attack by tying the girl inside a sack and throwing it into a river, but at the last minute they baulked at committing murder and dumped the sack in a ditch. The two brothers were later reigned in by police as probable suspects but the case stalled for lack of evidence, prompting the public prosecutor at Assen to put a call through to Professor Tenhaeff at Utrecht. In a room at the Assen courthouse, Croiset examined several items associated with the two brothers and immediately began reeling off impressions: from a tobacco box and a cigarette holder he described the two middle-aged brothers in some detail, while after holding the sack in which the young girl had been found, Croiset was able to correctly describe the particulars of the attack (which previously had been withheld from him) as well as the fact that it had been used previously as a cow blanket. The same day, Croiset and Tenhaeff drove to the crime scene. When they were several kilometres away from the hay barn, Croiset began giving a description of the building, which the psychical researcher found was wholly accurate once they had arrived and were able to look round. The two brothers had been involved in other crimes and Croiset attended a separate hearing for one of the men. After the hearing, Croiset told Tenhaeff that he felt certain the accused man would die by hanging, a prediction which came true several weeks later when the Dutchman committed suicide.

As the 1950s progressed, Croiset became nationally acclaimed throughout Holland for his abilities to help with the tracking down of missing persons. The case that firmly established this reputation took place in 1954. On 18 April, Easter Sunday, a four-year-old boy named Jacob Klerk was found to be missing, believed kidnapped, from his home in the town of Haarlem. Police stations throughout Holland were informed of the disappearance and a countrywide search for the child was soon underway. The Haarlam Police Commissioner, William Gorter, was interested in the fledgling subject of psychic detection and, off his own back, made a decision to telephone Croiset personally. The clairvoyant told the policeman over the line that he had an overwhelming impression that the missing Klerk boy was dead; he had drowned in the River Spaarne near a bridge and the body would be recovered within the week. Croiset described the setting: there was a caravan and some lorry trailers with bails of compressed peat, while beyond the river was a shipyard with a crane. The river was dragged but nothing was recovered and as the days began to pass the truth of Croiset's vision began to fade. However, on 4 May 1954, the Dutchman was vindicated as, tragically, Jacob Klerk's body was found floating in the Spaarne; the surroundings were as Croiset had described and it seemed likely the corpse had become fouled on a submerged root or other obstruction which had kept it submerged for nearly two weeks.

Gerard Croiset's reputation as one of the world's leading clairvoyant detectives or 'paragnosts' was firmly established in his native country by the work of Wilhelm Tenhaeff, but the person who played the most part in establishing the Dutchman's international reputation was American magazine journalist, Jack Harrison Pollack. In February 1961, Pollack wrote an article entitled 'Crime Busting With ESP' on the use of psychics in police work for *This Week* magazine, which was syndicated to over forty big-circulation American Sunday newspapers including the New York *Herald Tribune*. The publication of the article, which included accounts of some of Croiset's work with the Dutch police, coincided with the disappearance of a four-year-old girl, Edith Kiecorius, nicknamed 'Google', who was last seen playing outside her uncle's Manhattan home at 170 Eighth Avenue on the afternoon of 22 February. An official of the KLM airline, who had read Pollack's article, offered to fly both Croiset and Professor Tenhaeff out to New York but the psychic settled on working from his own home using a street map of the city plus articles belonging to Edith which were flown out by courier to Utrecht where, by this time, Croiset had been living for five years. The American police were following several lines of enquiry, one of which was that Edith Kiecorius had been seen with a woman at Chicago airport, but Croiset was adamant that she was still in New York; like the case of Jacob Klerk, the Dutchman also warned that the child was dead and had been taken away by a small man with sharp features in his mid fifties, who had taken her to a room on the second floor of a grey stone building in a neighbourhood that Croiset was able to describe in some detail.

Four days after she was reported missing, two New York policemen kicked down the door of a second floor room in a boarding house at 307 West Twentieth Street and found the body of Edith Kiecorius; she had been raped and bludgeoned to death. Three days later, a New Jersey farm worker, Fred J. Thompson, who detectives had found had rented the room the previous week, was picked up by police; he admitted the crime and was committed to the Mattewean Hospital for the Criminally Insane. Pollack subsequently checked details of the case and visited the area where the abduction had taken place. He found that Croiset had been highly accurate on a number of points including the description of the murderer, the boarding house where the body had been discovered and details of the surrounding area, while other points which were incorrect seemed to be more in the nature of near misses rather than total inaccuracies. Pollack later included the Kiecorius case among nearly a hundred other accounts of Croiset's work reported by Tenhaeff and preserved by him in the archives of the Parapsychology Department at Utrecht in his book *Croiset the Clairvoyant*, which was published by W.H. Allen in 1965. For many in the English-speaking world, this was their first introduction to the psychic adventures of 'The Miracle Man of Holland'.

During the 1950s and '60s, as well as Gerard Croiset, other noted 'paragnosts' were gradually being brought to the attention of the public at large. In Sweden, a contemporary of Croiset was Olof Jonsson, an engineer by profession, who became known as a highly accurate clairvoyant and sensitive. Jonsson's finest hour was to come in February 1971, when *Life Magazine* published an article about ESP experiments that had taken place through space between the psychic engineer (who at that time was living and working in Chicago) and the American astronaut Edgar Mitchell, then in orbit around the Earth in the Apollo 14 spacecraft. Much earlier, in 1952, Jonsson had assisted a Swedish journalist, Leif Sunde, who was writing an article about a series of violent murders that had taken place in and around the southern village of Tjörnarp. Thirteen people, all unconnected, had been attacked in their homes – stabbed or shot – and then robbed, after which the houses had been set on fire in an attempt to destroy any incriminating evidence. By the beginning of March 1952, when Jonsson accompanied Sunde to Tjörnarp, the police investigation had stalled, but when the psychic engineer was handed the charred remains of a rifle that had been recovered from one of the crime scenes, he instantly knew that the killer was one of the actual policemen assigned to work on the case and who had been acting as a guide to the visiting journalists. The following day, Officer Hedin, the man named by Jonsson, was found drowned in a local river; a suicide note contained a full confession to the crimes.

Another Dutchman who became something of a psychic celebrity, particularly in America, during the 1960s was Peter Hurkos (real name Pieter Van der Hurk), a former house painter and Dutch resistance fighter, who developed a vaudeville stage routine in the years following the Second World War psychometrizing photographs while blindfolded. Hurkos' act impressed Dr Henry (known as Andrija) Pulharich, an American medical inventor and radical psychical researcher, who, in 1948, invited the Dutchman to the States to take part in laboratory experiments. While in America, Hurkos became involved in several high-profile murder cases including that of Melvin David Rees, a twenty-eight-year-old professional jazz musician known as the 'Sex Beast', who was executed in 1961 for killing nine people in Maryland and Virginia, including a family of four; and the case of the Boston Strangler, a notorious series of sex crimes carried out between June 1962 and January 1964 for which Albert DeSalvo (who was stabbed to death in prison in 1973) was regarded as the perpetrator. Hurkos in fact considered a Boston shoe salesman, subsequently detained permanently in a mental institution and known by the pseudonym Thomas P. O'Brien, to be the real killer. Hurkos, who died in 1988, often performed on television and described himself in his own autobiography as 'the greatest psychic in the world'.

As the 1970s began to gather momentum, super-psychics like Hurkos, Croiset and Jonsson found themselves effortlessly eclipsed by the headline-grabbing activities of one man, an ex-Israeli soldier, fashion model and nightclub entertainer who became an instant media sensation as newspapers, radio and television, first in Germany and later Britain and America, quickly succumbed to the phenomenon of the 'Geller Effect'. The alleged paranormal abilities of Uri Geller (born in Tel Aviv in 1946), whose powers famously include metal-bending, mind-reading and the ability to stop and start clocks and watches at will, are so well known that it is hardly surprising that middle-aged 'paragnosts' like Croiset and Hurkos, despite their impressive back catalogues of psychic crime busting, were unable to compete with such a young, dynamic and instantly controversial psychic star. With no exaggeration was the late John Beloff able to state, in his *Parapsychology: A Concise History* (1993), that 'as with no other psychic of modern times is it harder to separate fact from fiction or to decide whether to treat him [Geller] as an ingenious entertainer or as a genuine purveyor of the paranormal'; particularly as under hypnosis, the spoon-bending Geller revealed (to Andrija Pulharich, who brought him to America in 1972) that his supernormal abilities came from a cosmic super-computer called 'Spectra' built by aliens from the planet Hoova.

If media coverage of psychic superstars like Uri Geller, together with sensational cases of haunting such as the 'Amityville Horror' (America's very own Borley Rectory – see Chapter 14) and the Enfield Poltergeist, readily demonstrate an explosion of popular exploitation of the paranormal throughout the 1970s, for the world of parapsychology it was in reality a decade of crisis as academics struggling to make ghost hunting a respectable science faced some of their greatest challenges to date. In June 1974, Dr Joseph Banks Rhine, founder of the Institute for Parapsychology in Durham, North Carolina, one of the most respected and influential figures in twentieth-century paranormal investigation and often regarded as the 'Father of Parapsychology', discovered that one of his most trusted colleagues was faking the results of laboratory ESP experiments. Dr Walter Levy, whom Rhine had made Director of the Institute, and who was considered one of the rising stars of experimental psychical research, was caught falsifying data by two other staff members. Levy, who blamed his actions on the stress he had put himself under to produce successful results while carrying out his work, resigned; he claimed he had resulted to fraud 'for the good of parapsychology' but the damage was done. Four years later another bombshell exploded, this time on the other side of the Atlantic, when Betty Markwick, a member of the Society for Psychical Research, published conclusive evidence of similar data manipulation, this time by noted British mathematician and parapsychologist Samuel George Soal, during landmark ESP experiments he had carried out during the 1940s with South African photographer Basil Shackleton as the subject. Psychical researchers have since argued whether Soal's actions (he died in 1975) were intentional, but it was enough to blot the posthumous copybook of not only Soal himself, but the respectability of organised paranormal investigation as a whole which, by the mid-1970s, had suddenly found itself under close and critical investigation. In 1976, Paul Kurtz, an American author and professor of philosophy at New York's State University, had founded the Committee for the Scientific Investigation of the Claims of the Paranormal (CSICOP), in effect an anti-paranormal thought police, whose concerted mission was (and still is) to expose as 'flim flam' and 'pseudo-science' what its sceptical members considered to be the threat posed by the public interest and acceptance of mediumship, astrology, ghosts and hauntings, on rational thought in both the United States and elsewhere. Scandals such as the Levy and Soal exposures were grist to the CSICOP mill, and there was to be more coming its way.

Piet Hein Hoebens, the chief editorial writer for Holland's largest circulation newspaper *De Telegraaf*, was appointed as Chairman of the Netherlands branch of CSICOP, and in the late 1970s began looking closely at the University of Utrecht's Parapsychology Department, and in particular the published work of the department's head, Wilhem Tenhaeff, and his claims for the amazing psychic feats of his favourite 'paragnost', Gerard Croiset. After much consultation with police officials across Holland, the journalist discovered that practically all of Tenhaeff's statements regarding Croiset's successful solving of crimes and murder by psychic detection could not be substantiated. In 1983, by which time both Tenhaeff and Croiset were dead, Hoebens was able to state with supreme confidence that the Dutch psychical researcher 'was not the cautious, dispassionate and honest scholar his many admirers believed him to be' but was in fact 'an extremely sloppy investigator who not infrequently indulged in outright manipulation of the data'; while his pet clairvoyant 'was a master in the stock-in-trade techniques of the "prophet": collect information by normal means and feed it back as "telepathic impressions".' CSICOP had claimed two more impressive scalps: Tenhaeff died in isolation in 1981, 'a disgrace to the field', while the psychic sleuthing of the 'miracle man of Holland' was seemingly nothing more than plain old 'double Dutch'.

Sadly, there is often little that can be done to rehabilitate the reputations of those persons who resort to fraud, be they mediums or researchers, as they are condemned by their own actions. A convenient 'get out clause' for psychics and clairvoyants is that of 'mixed mediumship', whereby a genuine sensitive, faced with failing powers or the pressure to perform successfully at every séance, will resort to trickery on occasions. Some psychical researchers have faced similar problems, a prime example being Harry Price over his reporting, in the latter part of his career, of the Borley Rectory haunting. Piet Hein Hoebens, however, was of the opinion (in following the ultra-sceptical party line of Paul Kurtz's organisation) that all mediums and psychics are fakes and nothing they say can be trusted, a viewpoint which is totally unrealistic, as anyone who has looked in any detail at the evidence will come to realise. Wilhelm Tenhaeff may have been economical with the truth and some of his methods suspect, particularly as with other researchers such as Harry Price and Hans Holzer, he had a good relationship with the press and knew the value of popular publicity to his work, but to dismiss the case for genuineness in such a psychic as Gerard Croiset solely because of the reporting of one researcher is an unfair and illogical approach to establishing the truth. At Borley, the case for paranormality at 'the most haunted house in England' does not stand and fall with the work of Harry Price and, likewise, the posthumous reputation of 'the wizard of Utrecht' is not solely reliant on Wilhelm Tenhaeff. In both cases there exist testimonials independent of the principle investigators. This book is primarily concerned with British cases of murder and their association with paranormal, and in this respect we are fortunate in that what could be considered to be one of Gerard Croiset's finest demonstrations of his power as a psychic detective is inextricably linked with one of Scotland's noted unsolved cases of modern times.

The publicity generated by Pollack's *Croiset the Clairvoyant* brought about an inevitable involvement with the Dutch 'paragnost' and British crime. In early 1970, Croiset was asked to assist in the case of the Hosein brothers, two bungling but ultimately murderous immigrants from Trinidad who carried out the very first instance of kidnap and ransom in Britain when they unsuccessfully tried to effect the abduction of the wife of millionaire newspaper mogul Rupert Murdoch. On the evening of 13 December 1969, Arthur Hosein and his younger brother Nizam took by force Muriel McKay, the wife of Murdoch's deputy Alick McKay, from their house in Arthur Road, Wimbledon, in the mistaken belief that she was Mrs Murdoch. The kidnappers made contact demanding £1m for Mrs McKay's safe return but days went by with no progress and, after press and television appeals had failed to elicit further response, the McKay family sent details to Croiset in Utrecht. The Dutchman psychometrized maps of the home counties and felt Mrs McKay was being held on a farm somewhere on the border between Hertfordshire and Essex. The British police acted on the information but eventually drew a blank. Forty days after Muriel McKay went missing, the Hosein brothers were arrested at Rooks Farm at Stocking Pelham in Hertfordshire. The police recovered evidence linking the two men to the abduction but Mrs McKay was never found and Arthur and Nizam Hosein were charged with murder and subsequently sentenced to life imprisonment. Croiset had been correct with the farmhouse setting but his powers had failed to pin down the exact location. The Hoseins never confessed to the crime, although it was believed at the time that Muriel McKay had been shot and her body disposed of by being fed to pigs on the farm.

One person who followed Croiset's involvement in the McKay kidnapping with interest was Frank Ryan, a journalist on the staff of the Scottish *Daily Record* newspaper based in Glasgow. In February 1970, only a few weeks after Croiset had made headlines searching for the newspaperman's wife, Ryan realised he would be in Holland for a short period and decided to try and visit the clairvoyant in Utrecht personally. Before he left he had the forethought to take with him some material that he was keen for Croiset to look at. This related to a disappearance that had taken place in Dumfries exactly three years before that Ryan had covered for the *Record* and with which the police had been unable to make any progress.

Patricia McAdam was a seventeen-year-old factory worker with an outgoing personality from Dumfries. On Saturday, 18 February 1967, she and a friend, Hazel Campbell, who lived in Annan on the Solway Firth, decided to spend the day clothes shopping in Glasgow. The two girls went by bus to Gretna after which they hitched a lift to Glasgow, where they bought new handbags, shoes and other items. Pat and Hazel spent Saturday evening at a dance hall, The Flamingo, after which they went on with some people they met at the hall to a house party, where they ended up staying the night. In the morning, the girls decided to hitchhike back to Dumfries and, after a short time in the London Road, a heavy articulated lorry stopped and picked them up. The lorry driver took the A74 road towards Lockerbie and twenty miles from Glasgow stopped at Lesmahagow, where he bought Pat and Hazel a meal at a transport café. Afterwards, Pat allowed the driver to kiss and cuddle her in the cab while her friend dozed in the back. Eventually the three got underway again; Pat McAdam sat in the front talking to the driver while Hazel continued to rest in the rear of the cab. Keeping to the A74 the lorry passed Gretna and then at Kirkpatrick Fleming took the road south-west towards Annan. At two o'clock in the afternoon the driver pulled up in Annan High Street and Hazel Campbell got out and waved her friend off. The lorry pulled away and continued on in the direction of Dumfries. Two days later, with no word or contact from their daughter, Pat McAdam's worried parents went to the police.

Detectives at Dumfries quickly put out a national appeal to find the goods lorry and its driver. Several people came forward who remembered seeing an articulated lorry matching the description given by Hazel Campbell passing with some difficulty along narrow country lanes north of the A75 Dumfries road near the village of Dalton that weekend. At one point it was seen north of Dalton parked off the road near a place called Williamwath Bridge. The police began an intensive search of the Dalton area but, as the days passed, found nothing. Finally, three weeks after Pat McAdam was reported missing, a driver whose lorry resembled the search vehicle admitted to giving Pat and Hazel Campbell a lift on the Sunday afternoon in question.

Thomas Ross Young was a Glaswegian in his early thirties and, as officers in Dumfries quickly found out, was also a man with a violent past who had been known to the police from an early age. In 1944, at the age of nine, Young had been arrested for theft and four years later was sent to a borstal for indecent assault. By 1962 he had married but that year served a sentence for burglary and in 1963 was imprisoned for three months for failing to pay maintenance on his children. A strongly built volatile man with a violent temper, Young's real danger lay in his compulsive and vicious sex drive, which had become apparent at the age of thirteen and had resulted in his commitment to an approved school. By the mid-1960s, he was a lorry driver, a job which allowed him to pick up women passengers like Patricia McAdam with relative ease. Young told police that Pat had agreed to have sex with him and he had parked the lorry in a convenient spot in a country lane. Afterwards, he said he had dropped the teenager off near her home in Dumfries and then carried on his way. With no evidence to suggest that Pat McAdam was dead, Detective Inspector Cullinan of the Regional Crime Squad in Glasgow, who now had become involved in the search, had to let Young go. Ominously, later the same year, Young (who would later boast to police of having had sex with over 200 women in the cab of his lorry) was sent to prison for eighteen months for raping a girl in Shropshire and by the time Frank Ryan made his way to see Gerard Croiset in Utrecht, he had begun an eight-year sentence for picking up and raping a fifteen-year-old girl.

Throughout March and April 1967 the hunt for the missing girl intensified. Police held press conferences and combed the countryside and farmland around Dalton. Ditches and rivers were dragged and digging was carried out in wooded areas and fields, but nothing came to light. Both Pat's parents and the police were disinclined to believe she had left home on purpose. The *Daily Record* printed hundreds of leaflets and posters with Pat McAdam's photograph and description and distributed them throughout the country, but as the weeks went by with no breakthrough, it seemed almost inevitable that the young factory girl would never been seen alive again. Like Frederick Nodder forty years before, the one man who seemingly knew the real truth of what happened on the afternoon of 19 February 1967 had taken it with him to a jail cell, in this case one in Peterhead Prison. All this would have been running through Frank Ryan's mind as, on 16 February 1970, almost three years to the day that Pat went missing, the journalist walked into the small consulting room at Croiset's house at 21, William II Street in Utrecht and came face to face with Holland's most famous psychic detective.

Through an interpreter, Croiset agreed to try and help and looked at one of the *Daily Record's* 'Have You Seen This Girl?' posters that Ryan had brought with him. As the Dutchman looked at Pat McAdam's photograph, Ryan confirmed she had gone missing three years before but through the interpreter, Croiset asked only if her home life had been happy and the location of where she was last seen; he was quite adamant that he didn't want to know anything else. The journalist took out a map of Scotland and pointed out the general area between Annan and Dumfries where Pat lived and also where Thomas Young had dropped off Hazel Campbell before driving away. Croiset immediately began describing and sketching on paper the impressions which were coming into his mind and which related to the young Scottish girl's disappearance: there was a café where Pat had had a meal, then an area where a river ran between the slopes of hills that were wooded with fir trees; in particular the river banks were eroded and the roots of the trees that grew near the water were exposed in a distinctive way; then there was a flat bridge over the same river at the foot of one of the hills – the bridge had a balustrade made from lengths of grey tubular steel, part of which was bent down, and the road over it led to a building like a cottage which had advertising hoardings on it and was surrounded by a white-painted wooden fence. Croiset stated that to get more he would need to handle something that had belonged to Pat McAdam personally. He also asked that nothing be made public until the journalist had checked the area and seen if his impressions were accurate. Ryan thanked the Dutchman for his time and, taking the drawings, he started on the trip back to Scotland.

Back in Dumfries, Frank Ryan together with Jack Johnstone, a local photographer, went on an excursion out to Dalton. Thomas Ross Young's lorry had been seen parked off the road at Williamwath Bridge and Ryan thought this was the location that Croiset had viewed remotely, but when they arrived they immediately saw that the setting was wrong although the bridge was similar to the way the Dutchman had described it. Unlike Ryan, Jack Johnstone knew the area well and said that around three miles away at Middleshaw was another bridge crossing over a river known as the Water of Milk. Getting back into the car, the two men drove on. A short time later, Frank Ryan got out of the car and realised they had entered into the scene of Gerard Croiset's vision. Everything was as the clairvoyant had described hundreds of miles away in his consulting room in Utrecht: the wooded hillside, the eroded river bank, the bridge with the tubular railings, the cottage with the advertisements, while a chain-link fence attached to the bridge sagged in just the way that Croiset had sketched. Ryan was stunned and realised that he had to contact Pat's parents in order to obtain the personal item that the clairvoyant had requested.

Ryan went to Lochside Road in Dumfries and introduced himself to Matthew and Mary McAdam. After he had shown them the results of Croiset's psychometry, the couple allowed him to take away Pat's Bible and Frank Ryan returned with it to Utrecht, together with Jack Johnstone's photographs and a larger-scale map of the area he had visited. Croiset was pleased that Ryan had confirmed what he had 'seen' but when he picked up the Bible his expression changed. Like Jacob Klerk and Edith Kiecorius before, Croiset had the overwhelming impression that the young Scottish woman was dead. He then turned to the map and described his impressions: at a place called Broom Cottage (unvisited by Ryan and Johnstone) there was a wrecked car; it was being used for something but Croiset couldn't tell what, but he described a wheelbarrow leaning against the side; Pat had been killed and her body hidden on the river bank among the exposed tree roots; there they would find items of clothing that belonged to her.

With high expectations Ryan returned home and, together with his wife and another *Record* journalist, drove out to Middleshaw. Broom Cottage was three quarters of a mile downstream from the bridge over the Water of Milk that Croiset had described during his first visit, and as the party got out of their car they realised that again the Dutchman had been unbelievably accurate. In the garden of the cottage was an old car, a green Ford Poplar that the farmer was using as a hen house and leaning against the back was a rusty wheelbarrow. Ryan knew Detective Inspector Cullinan, who had headed the enquiry to locate Pat three years before, and, realising it was possible a breakthrough on the case was imminent, contacted the policeman. That evening Cullinan sent two officers with Ryan back to Broom Cottage and the three men searched the river bank looking for the clothing that Croiset had said would be there. Finally, after a long search, Ryan recovered a woman's long-sleeved black dress, a stocking, and the remains of a handbag caught up in the mud and undergrowth, which were taken back to Dumfries.

Ryan's reporting of the discoveries for the *Daily Record* made front page news across Scotland and it seemed only a matter of time before Pat McAdam's body would be recovered. It was not to be. Further searching of the river bank revealed nothing and the clothing could not be matched to the missing girl: the dress was unlike anything Pat had been wearing when she disappeared and Hazel Campbell was adamant that her friend had only bought a handbag in Glasgow, not the dress that Ryan and the police had found.

Disappointed but convinced of the reality of the Dutchman's psychic powers, Frank Ryan returned to Utrecht and, four days after the discovery of the discarded clothing, asked Croiset to put on record his impressions of the events that led up to Pat McAdam's death. Croiset said she had walked with a man along the river bank near to Broom Cottage and a place where trees had been recently cut down and it was there that she had been beaten to death with a large metal spanner and her body thrown into the river, where it had become entangled in the tree roots exposed by the action of the water. The killer was in his early thirties, five feet four inches tall, with one ear noticeably larger than the other. Ryan made careful notes and contacted his editor in Glasgow, who agreed to the newspaper paying to fly Croiset to Scotland to see the area in person. The Dutchman, who had never visited Scotland before, spent a day around Middleshaw accompanied by Ryan and a local policeman. He confirmed his previous impressions of the disappearance and claimed that after a time, Pat's body had become dislodged and had been washed out to sea. It was known that the Water of Milk was subject to periodic flash flooding during episodes of heavy rain and anything picked up by such fast-moving water would soon be swept away out into the Solway Firth. Despite the great efforts made by Frank Ryan and Gerard Croiset, the McAdam case remained unsolved.

In 1975, Colin Wilson and producer Colin Godman interviewed Croiset for an episode of the BBC's paranormal-themed television programme *A Leap in the Dark*. During the course of filming, Croiset told Wilson that the case was a personal triumph for him as through his involvement the police had recovered the missing teenager's body. The broadcaster knew this was not the case and the two men argued until Wilson, sensing that nothing would convince the Dutchman otherwise, decided to let the matter drop. Later it became clear that Croiset had been misled by a friend, who had told him that the Scottish police had found a woman's body in the same area – they had, but it was that of a married woman in her forties who had change in her pocket which had been minted after Pat McAdam had disappeared. Gerard Croiset died in 1980 at the age of seventy-one. Many people, including the clairvoyant himself, have considered his collaboration with Frank Ryan, despite the fact that ultimately Pat McAdam's body was never traced, to be his finest hour as a psychic detective.

Who did kill Pat McAdam and why? The prime suspect, Thomas Ross Young, was released from prison in 1975 after serving two-thirds of his sentence for assaulting a teenager. In June 1977, police investigating the rape of a sixteen-year-old girl at an address in Ashley Street, Glasgow, were given his name by the victim, who claimed he had held her by force inside the house for ten hours and subjected her to a repeated and violent assault. Ross was traced to the house of his estranged wife, where he was arrested. Police found a secret hideout under the floorboards where the lorry driver had been concealing himself, which contained a number of items including a make-up compact. This was found to belong to thirty-seven-year-old bakery worker, Frances Barker, who had gone missing from her home in Maryhill Road, Glasgow earlier the same month. Her decomposing body, naked from the waist down and with her hands tied behind her back, was subsequently discovered in undergrowth near a service road leading to Inchneuk Farm at Glenboig on 27 June. Forensic analysis of hairs collected from the cab of Young's lorry revealed they were the same as those from Frances Barker's body and on 25 October 1977 at the High Court in Glasgow, a jury took an hour to find him guilty of murder and Young, the 'Monster of the highway', was sentenced to life imprisonment. At the time of her disappearance, Hazel Campbell had told police that Pat had refused to sleep with someone at the party they went to on the Saturday night in Glasgow as she was on her period and most commentators have concluded that she would have dissuaded her killer from having sex for the same reason. It probably cost her her life.

On 23 September 2007, over forty years after the disappearance of Pat McAdam, Young was officially charged with her murder by Sheriff Kenneth Ross via a video link with the Dumfries Sheriff Court. The petition alleged that Ross had carried out the killing, by means unknown, at or near Charlesfield Farm on the B7020 road between Annan and Dalton on 19 February 1967. However, despite the indictment, closure in the McAdam case was not made possible as it was subsequently found that Ross, then aged seventy-two, was too ill to stand trial due to a suspected heart condition, and the hearing was dropped. Two months later, in November 2007, the case of Thomas Young took a new twist when it was announced that the Scottish Criminal Cases Review Commission had referred his conviction for the murder of Frances Barker to the High Court of Justiciary as being unsafe. In the Commission's view, a study by two forensic pathologists at Glasgow University together with a report submitted by FBI profilers at the Behavioural Analysis Unit at Quantico, Virginia, on the killings of six young Scottish women during the 1970s made it highly likely that either one or more men had carried out all six murders. The reports had been prepared as part of the prosecution case against another Scotsman, serial sex killer Angus Sinclair, who was accused of killing two Edinburgh women, Helen

Scott and Christine Eadie, in 1977 in what became known as the World's End pub murders. Scott and Eadie, along with Frances Barker, were three of the six 'cold cases' which were reviewed at the time by the FBI, all of which, according to profiler Mark Safarik, were carried out by the same killer or killers. Sinclair's trial collapsed in August 2007 due to lack of evidence but it paved the way for a review of Young's conviction, who was in prison during the times that the other five women were killed, although the Commission acknowledged that there remained a strong body of evidence that continued to implicate Young in the murder of Frances Barker. To date the High Court has not pursued the Review Commission's case and Thomas Ross Young remains behind bars in Peterhead Prison, now one of Scotland's longest-serving prisoners.

The story of Pat McAdam continues to arouse periodic interest. In January 2011, the discovery of a woman's skeletal remains in a disused quarry near Longtown in Cumbria brought the case again briefly into the spotlight, but forensic examination soon discounted any connection with the forty-four-year-old mystery. Writing about Croiset's role in the investigation in the early 1980s, Colin Godman concluded that if Pat McAdam's body *had* been discovered in 1970, the case would have become 'the classic work of psychic detection'. Even Croiset's most ardent critic, Piet Hein Hoebens (who died in 1984), admitted that it was one of the clairvoyant's greatest triumphs. However, Hoebens preferred to believe that the wealthy Croiset had in fact paid his secretary to travel to Scotland to collect the information on his behalf, a somewhat desperate attempt at debunking given the wealth of independent evidence that supports the genuineness of the case. 'A few hundred pounds is a bargain for a classic ESP hit' was his rather short-sighted comment, a response that goes a long way to proving that on occasion, a belief in paranormality is far more credible than the 'rational' explanations of the sceptics.

For parapsychologists intent on obtaining the smoking gun evidence that would give psychic detection the satisfaction of a convincing 'case closed' scenario, the Croiset-McAdam story was a frustrating one. Colin Godman's 'classic work' seemed to be forever tantalisingly out of reach, but as we shall see, it was coming. It would just be a matter of time . . .

CHAPTER 10

GHOST OF THE FROZEN GIRL

ANNE NOBLETT, 1974

We have already seen how the alleged ghost of a murder victim was the catalyst that brought about the revelation of Modern Spiritualism in the middle years of the nineteenth century. What is often cited as the first ever instance of the investigation of a haunted house, a hundred years before the birth of Christ, may also have involved the apparition of a murdered man. This is the well-known account, attributed to Pliny the Younger, who described the discovery of the skeleton of a man, bound hand and foot in rusted chains, from under the floor of a courtyard in a villa in Athens. The appearance over several years of the fettered figure of a grey-haired old man, so Pliny recorded in a series of letters to a friend, had so frightened several occupants that the house had a sinister reputation in the immediate neighbourhood and the owner had considerable difficulty in finding tenants who would stay for any length of time. A philosopher, attracted by the local tales and the disarmingly low rent, moved in and observed the appearance of the ghost, which disappeared at a particular spot in a corner of the courtyard. When this was excavated, by workmen in the presence of the philosopher and a magistrate, a shallow grave was found which must have lain undisturbed for many years. After the skeleton was given a proper burial, the sinister apparition of the mysterious man in chains was never seen again.

Unlike the ghost of Hamlet's father, who revealed to his son how he was murdered in his sleep (with poison poured into his ear) by his brother Claudius, Pliny's spectral Athenian, if he was the victim of an ancient murder, did not reveal the identity of his killer or give any indication of how he came to be bound and buried in such a way. The world of literature abounds with vengeful spectres who materialise to denounce killers and reveal secrets from beyond the grave. Much nearer to our own time than Shakespeare's tale of the tragic Danish king, writers Geoffrey Palmer and Noel Lloyd, in their book *Ghost Stories Round the World* (1965), a collection of accounts based on allegedly true happenings, tell the story of one such purposeful shade, that of the doomed Henry Edwards, 'The Ghost of Anngrove Hall'. Edwards, an under-coachman in the service of Charles Stanford, is dismissed and later murdered by the Master of Angrove for revealing his love for the Squire's daughter, Catherine. Henry's ghost later appears to his sister Polly and denounces his former master as a killer. Polly, in the tradition of the tale of the Red Barn with which it is contemporary, dreams of her brother's body buried in a grave under a haystack on the Anngrove estate. Labourers from a neighbouring country house dig at the site and unearth a heavily decomposed body dressed in a coachman's uniform, but by this time Charles Stanford himself has disappeared, presumably at the ghostly hands of his former servant, and Anngrove Hall, located near Stokesley, a small market town in North Yorkshire, has become a derelict ruin.

Palmer and Lloyd's book contains a number of stories previously collected by Charles Lindley Wood (1839-1934), 2nd Viscount Halifax, and published in 1936, with a foreword and annotations on the contents, by his son as *Lord Halifax's Ghost Book.* The book, which contains a broad cross-section of reported cases of supernormal phenomena including crisis ghosts, phantasms of the living, phantom guardians and haunting apparitions, is one of the first major collections of allegedly true ghost stories and should be read by any serious investigator interested in the history of the paranormal. Lord Halifax was an avid collector of supernatural encounters and gives the provenance for the vast majority of the accounts he preserved, these often being the experiences of personal acquaintances. Sadly, the authority is missing for one such tale, 'The Passenger with the Bag', which interestingly features the ghost of a murdered man whose appearance results in the eventual apprehension of the killer: an unnamed gentleman is travelling on a train out of Euston and falls into conversation with a fellow passenger, who reveals himself to be the director of the particular railway company on whose line they are travelling. The director, a Mr Dwerringhouse, discloses he is carrying a substantial amount of money to a local bank which will be used to finance the construction of a new branch line. When Lord Halifax's correspondent mentions he is attending a dinner party at a particular house in the district, the traveller declares the owner to be his niece and asks to be remembered to her, mentioning a previous visit during which he stayed in the Blue Room and complained of the over-large fire which had been lit in the grate.

When the train pulls up at a station and the director gets off carrying his bag, the passenger realises he has dropped his cigar case and, following him out onto the platform, observes Mr Dwerringhouse talking under a lamp-post with a man with sandy-coloured hair whose face he clearly sees. However, the two men have unaccountably disappeared when the narrator reaches the spot and a nearby porter declares that no persons matching their description were standing on that part of the platform at the time. Arriving at his destination, the traveller dresses for dinner and during the meal passes on the message to his hostess, who is clearly distressed at hearing the news. After the ladies have retired, leaving the men to their brandy and cigars, her husband takes the narrator to one side and reveals that his wife's uncle is missing and under investigation by the police, having apparently absconded with £70,000 of the railway company's money. Their conversation is overheard by two fellow guests, also directors of the same company, who request the narrator give a statement about his encounter to the Railway Board. At the meeting a few days later, the narrator recognises the man with the sandy hair, who turns out to be the company's Chief Cashier. When questioned he eventually admits to robbing and murdering Mr Dwerringhouse in a quarry on the way to the company's bank, although the killing itself was not planned: in the struggle to gain possession of the bag, the railway director fell and died instantly after striking his head on a rock.

The story sounds almost too good to be true and at this distance of time there is much to be suspicious about the uncorroborated account as presented by Lord Halifax in his *Ghost Book*, particularly as all important dates, locations, as well as the names of all but one of the participants are missing. However, Charles Lindley Wood was a careful collector of allegedly true paranormal experiences and in this respect 'The Passenger with the Bag' is an exception; the vast majority of the stories included in the collection (which includes a detailed account of the famous poltergeist haunting at Hinton Ampner in Hampshire) contain details of dates and witnesses. Rather than dismissing the account out of hand, it serves as a good example of the importance in obtaining accurate information concerning reports of supernormal experiences in order to make the reported facts that much more credible. As we have seen with the case of Gerard Croiset, the sceptical opposition to the paranormal has reached almost professional status in recent years, one that can only be challenged by a meticulous and similarly professional presentation of convincing evidence.

Not all ghosts that are said to be the victims of violent crimes and murder, however, are as obliging as the apparitions of Henry Edwards and Mr Dwerringhouse in revealing the identity of their killers. An interesting modern case that involves both a murder, the appearance of an apparition thought to be that of the victim, and also where specific details of witnesses and events, both natural and supernatural, are readily known, remains a mystery to this day.

The Hertfordshire village of Wheathampstead lies on the B653 road between Welwyn Garden City and Luton in neighbouring Bedfordshire. In the autumn and early winter of 1974, a series of strange and inexplicable events at a business premises on the northern outskirts of the village had become so regular and notable that by the beginning of the following year they made front page headlines in the local press[1]. Staff at a plant hire company operating from outbuildings at a former pig farm in Marshalls Heath Lane, a quarter of a mile north of the main Lower Luton Road, became convinced that the workplace was haunted, so much so that two employees refused to work shifts there after dark. The phenomena, which lasted for a number of months before gradually petering out, comprised incidents of a poltergeist nature and psychic touches, as well as the opening and closing of doors and the appearance of a mysterious female figure.

Several employees working at the old farm site all reported unusual happenings. Bob Shambrook, a twenty-four-year-old workman from Ware, was alone one night when a stable door adjacent to the company building began opening and shutting by itself. Disturbed by the noise, Shambrook fastened the latch securely on three occasions, but each time the door seemingly came open unaided and repeatedly banged against the wall. There was no wind and Shambrook was certain no one could have played a trick on him without being seen. Another employee, Alfred Spink, a mechanic in his mid-forties from nearby Harpenden, also reported strange experiences. Alone in one of the outbuildings one evening, he was feeding a local cat when he had the unmistakable impression of something brushing against the side of his head. Immediately turning round he saw he was quite alone, but the experience was convincing and unsettling. Another worker at the farm also reported the same cat hissing and arching its back at an apparently empty space on several occasions. Similar happenings continued at Marshalls Heath Lane for several weeks, almost as though they were building up to what became the most notable phenomenon associated with the haunting.

One evening a workman noticed a young girl standing by a single-storey storage shed near to one of the old farm outbuildings. Assuming it was a local child playing about, he shouted out and walked towards her, but by the time he reached the spot the figure had disappeared. Like his colleagues, he was convinced that no one could have hidden in the vicinity of the outbuildings without being seen or, likewise, have passed by him unnoticed. The shed itself was locked as was the barn immediately adjacent, the only other building in the immediate vicinity. The workman was not close enough to describe the face of the figure in any detail but Alf Spink, convinced by his own experiences that something genuinely paranormal was taking place, was also, as a local man, certain that he knew the identity of the apparition and also the reasons for her haunting the old farm. Its origins seemed to lie, so he subsequently told Roger Mackenzie, a reporter for the *Herts Advertiser*, in sinister events that took place in the same area exactly seventeen years earlier . . .

On the evening of Monday, 30 December 1957, Anne Noblett, the seventeen-year-old daughter of local farmer and company director Thomas Noblett, arrived back in Wheathampstead after attending a dance class in neighbouring Harpenden. The Nobletts were a reasonably affluent family: earlier in the year Anne had returned from a Swiss finishing school near Montreux and was now intent on pursuing a career as a children's nurse. Carrying a paper bag filled with mushrooms, she got off a bus outside the Cherry Tree pub on the Lower Luton Road and set out to walk home to her parent's somewhat isolated farmhouse, Heath Cottage, a quarter of a mile from the main road. Somewhere along Marshalls Heath Lane, a narrow road unlit and overhung with trees, she met her killer.

Anne was expected home just before seven o'clock. When over two hours had passed and she had not arrived, Thomas Noblett began calling her friends on the telephone and, with no news as to her whereabouts, eventually called St Albans police station. The following day, the police began a major search operation in the Marshalls Heath area. Groups of officers with dogs and reinforced with members of the public began combing the surrounding woods and fields, and a temporary headquarters was set up next to the roadway outside Heath Cottage. By the end of the day, and with no clues as to the whereabouts of the missing teenager, the search was turned over to Hertfordshire CID and Detective Inspector Leonard Elwell took charge of the operation. Over the next few days, Elwell organised a massive search involving 300 soldiers and over a thousand civilians; newsreels were shown at local cinemas, house-to-house searches were carried out and the police took down over 2,000 statements. One volunteer who gave his time to look for Anne Noblett was twenty-seven-year-old Alfred Spink, but despite the intensive operation that involved Scotland Yard and requests for information in newspapers across the country, several weeks passed with no sign of a breakthrough.

On the afternoon of 31 January 1958, exactly a month after the teenager disappeared, a young RAF serviceman in his early twenties together with his younger brother, were dog walking at Rose Grove Wood on the outskirts of Whitwell, a small village four miles due east of Luton, when in a clearing amongst the trees they came across what at first appeared to be a sleeping person. On closer inspection they saw it was a young girl who was clearly dead and immediately hurried back to the village to raise the alarm. Soon police were converging on the quiet rural spot but the circumstances of the discovery of Anne Noblett were to make it one of the most mysterious and baffling of post-war British murders.

The teenager's body was found lying on its back, fully clothed, with hands folded across the chest and still wearing her glasses; her purse lay alongside her and still contained the same amount of money – thirty shillings – with which she had left the house on the day she went missing. What became immediately apparent to the police as they organised the moving of the body was the remarkable state of preservation: Anne Noblett had been missing for a month but her corpse showed no sign of the extensive decomposition which would have been expected in a body that had lain out in the open for that amount of time. Putrefaction, caused by the migration of bacteria from the intestines through the body tissue via the blood-vessels, normally begins within a period of two days after the effects of *rigor mortis* have worn off and after around three weeks a dead body is normally bloated and unrecognisable. Given the fact that Anne had been missing for a month and her body was in no way as grossly disfigured as would have been expected made it appear at first as though she had been held against her will and kept alive for some time after she went missing from Marshalls Heath Lane at the end of the previous December. It is doubtful whether Detective Inspector Elwell and his officers would have suspected the real reasons behind the remarkable preservation of the young girl's body, which soon became apparent once it had been taken to the mortuary.

We have already briefly encountered Professor Francis Camps, one of the twentieth century's most distinguished forensic pathologists. Camps carried out over 88,000 post-mortems during the course of his professional career, but the one that he performed on Anne Noblett must rank as one of the most intriguing. The cause of death was manual strangulation and from the undigested stomach contents it was clear that the girl had been murdered on the day she went missing. Camps suggested that the puzzling lack of decomposition was due to the fact that the body showed all the signs of having been kept at an extremely low temperature, such as would be consistent with being stored in a refrigerator. The 'Deep Freeze Murder' seemed almost unprecedented but the reasons behind the killing were plain enough: Camps noted interference of a sexual nature and from the arrangement of buttons on Anne's underclothes the police were certain she had been stripped and later redressed in her own clothes prior to being laid out in Rose Grove Wood. Immediately, Detective Inspector Elwell ordered a check on establishments with deep freezers within a thirty-mile radius of Whitwell large enough to take a human body, including poulterers and butchers storing meat. It was to be in vain as, despite the new leads the autopsy provided, the police failed to make any progress and the killer of seventeen-year-old Anne Noblett was never caught. Today, over fifty years since her death, it is only possible to state that her killing was a planned sex murder, possibly by someone she knew, who had a good knowledge of the local area.

Did the ghost of Anne Noblett return, seventeen years after her mysterious and tragic death, to haunt the farm only a stone's throw from the house where she lived a happy and normal life? People working in Marshalls Heath Lane at the time were convinced that she did and others since then have expressed the same opinion. The first person to document the case was Tony Broughall, a Luton-born office worker in his mid-forties who, during the 1970s, was making a name for himself as a serious local ghost hunter and intrepid investigator of the paranormal. Together with his wife Georgina, a natural clairvoyant, Broughall, who during his working life had an eclectic mix of careers which included a jazz drummer, a cinema projectionist, civil servant and funeral director, began visiting allegedly haunted locations throughout Bedfordshire and Hertfordshire, compiling accounts of ghosts and strange occurrences. Christened 'The Ghost Man' by the *Luton News*, who featured him in a number of articles, he gave lectures on his numerous investigations, which included Chicksands Priory, Farnham Castle and Borley church, and was a member of the two most prestigious paranormal organisations of the day, the Society for Psychical Research and the Ghost Club. Between 1974 and 1978, Broughall compiled the first systematic survey of provincial hauntings, both historic and contemporary, for both counties, a full-length report which remained in typescript until it was finally published in an edited and updated edition in 2010[2]. Soon after the disturbances at Marshalls Heath Lane appeared in the Hertfordshire press, Broughall visited the farm but found the workers he met at the plant hire firm as well as local residents, no doubt upset by some aspects of the publicity, unwilling to discuss recent events concerning both the haunting and the murder of Anne Noblett, and his requests to interview witnesses and carry out an on-site investigation was turned down. As a result the case never received a contemporary examination by a competent investigator and for some it remains an interesting seasonal ghost story not to be taken too seriously. In retrospect, Tony Broughall's inability to investigate the

Marshalls Heath haunting is frustrating in that the case resembles, to a lesser degree, a well regarded case of haunting, the so-called Cardiff Poltergeist, which took place in 1979 at similar industrial premises (a lawnmower repair workshop) and which also involved both physical phenomena and the appearance of an apparition[3].

Tony Broughall himself was no stranger to unusual happenings. In 1963, he had experienced a series of bizarre and seemingly inexplicable incidents while walking home along a deserted road in Houghton Regis, which in a personal way opened his mind to the reality of paranormal activity. In his memoirs he describes a scene not dissimilar from events portrayed by director Jacques Tourneur in the classic 1957 film *Night of the Demon* – of seeing an insubstantial black figure and being pushed to the ground by an unseen force, as well as hearing an eerie whistling noise which followed and eventually overtook him as he walked alone on two separate occasions along lonely Sundon Road in the early hours of the morning. When recalling the incident several years later, Broughall stated that he had subsequently been unable to discover anything which might explain these strange incidents, although a local woman in Houghton Regis had apparently taken a dislike to him and a short time before had threatened to put him under a curse. The fact that around the same time the ghost hunter had chanced to speak to a young man who had himself encountered similar strange happenings along the same road, including being thrown off his motor scooter into a ditch in a similar way that Tony Broughall was struck down by an invisible blow, makes it unlikely that the phenomena was the successful result of a personal black magic vendetta; that it was and remains an intriguing and bizarre event cannot be denied.

Today, the former farm premises in Marshalls Heath Lane, now derelict and abandoned, remains private property but, despite the passage of time, the Anne Noblett haunting continues to arouse periodic interest from members of the local paranormal community. In the early 2000s, a séance involving a planchette and ouija board was held by a group of Hertfordshire spiritualists in one of the old outbuildings close to where Alfred Spinks' work colleague saw the apparition of the young girl in 1974. During the sitting, an alleged communicator identified itself as the murdered teenager and passed on information concerning the murder including what amounted to details of the killer, who was identified as a man, at that time still alive, and living at nearby Whipsnade in Bedfordshire. The credibility of information obtained in this way, involving as it does the asking of leading questions by people who subconsciously may know a substantial amount of information about a particular case or haunting beforehand, is debateable and controversial, although there is no doubting the sincerity of the people involved, who often wish to help or 'rescue' what they consider to be earthbound spirits that are confused or trapped on the earth plain to move on to higher realms. Where the case of Anne Noblett is concerned, the facts are that both the 'Deep Freeze Murder' and the Marshalls Heath haunting remain a mystery, both to the criminologist and the psychical researcher.

NOTES

1. 'Murdered Girl: Ghost Haunts Farm', *Herts Advertiser*, 10 January 1975.
2. *Two Haunted Counties: A Ghost Hunter's Companion to Bedfordshire & Hertfordshire* (The Limbury Press, Luton, 2010).
3. For a concise account of the Cardiff case, see *Ghost Hunters: A Guide to Investigating the Paranormal* by Yvette Fielding & Ciarán O'Keeffe (Hodder & Stoughton, London, 2006), pp. 77-93.

CHAPTER 11

THE PSYCHIC SEARCH FOR THE YORKSHIRE RIPPER

1979-1980

The serial sex murders of Peter Sutcliffe, the so-called 'Yorkshire Ripper', brought the frightening and brutal reality of his Victorian namesake's 'Autumn of Terror' into the lives of ordinary people living in the late twentieth century like no other catalogue of modern British killings. Beginning in October 1975 and ramping up with chilling intensity through the second half of the decade and on into the early part of the 1980s, what became a total of thirteen savage murders of young and middle-aged women – the youngest a teenager of sixteen – was to keep towns in the north of England in a grip of fear, ending only at the beginning of January 1981 when Sheffield police arrested a thirty-five-year-old Bradford lorry driver who, it later transpired, was only minutes away from claiming his fourteenth victim. Sutcliffe had cruised the red-light districts of towns including Leeds, Manchester, Huddersfield and Bradford for five years, defying all attempts by the Yorkshire police to run him to ground, subjecting his lone victims to frenzied assaults, mostly with a hammer, often following the initial crippling attack with a series of horrific mutilations using either a knife or screwdriver. The majority of victims (eight in total) were prostitutes, but the Ripper also attacked women who clearly were not street-workers – a civil servant, a doctor, a university student – meaning that all women in fact were targets. As well as the sickening violence, the killer's disturbing anonymity and the increasingly worrying way he continued to evade capture, there was another parallel with the infamous Whitechapel killings of nearly a century before in that, like Robert Lees before them, contemporary mediums and psychics also attempted to use their supernormal powers to assist the police in what still remains the largest criminal manhunt in recorded British history.

Early in July 1975, thirty-seven-year-old Anna Rogulskyj was struck down from behind by a man wielding a hammer as she walked through an alleyway in the town of Keighley, five miles north-west of Bradford. As she lay stunned on the ground, her attacker slashed her across the stomach and then ran off. Despite the brutality of the assault, Anna survived but required brain surgery. The following month, on 15 August, forty-five-year-old office cleaner Olive Smelt was attacked in a similar way near her home at Boothtown in Halifax. A man in his thirties with whom she had struck up a conversation suddenly turned on her, hitting her twice with a hammer on the top of the head and cutting at her back with a knife before running away. Luckily, like Anna Rogulskyj, Mrs Smelt recovered. Another survivor of the early days of the Yorkshire Ripper's reign of terror was Tracey Browne, a fourteen-year-old schoolgirl from the village of Silsden, on the fringe of the Pennines north of Keighley. Only a few days after the attack on Olive Smelt she was left with a fractured skull after being repeatedly beaten about the head by a man who fell into step beside her as she walked home late one evening to her parents' house after visiting friends in Silsden. Her attacker was apparently frightened off by an approaching car and the teenager, covered in blood, was rushed to Chapel Allerton Hospital in nearby Leeds, where surgeons removed bone splinters from her brain.

Early on the morning of 30 October 1975, a milkman and his brother passing along Scott Hall Road in the Chapeltown area of Leeds noticed what they took at first to be a bundle of rags lying in the grass on the Prince Philip playing fields. Going closer, they saw it was the body of a woman lying on her back, her clothes saturated with blood. Police identified her as twenty-eight-year-old Wilma McCann, a Scotswoman separated from her husband and originally from Inverness, who supported herself and her four children through prostitution. She had been struck down by two violent blows to the head with either a hammer or an adjustable spanner and then stabbed fifteen times in the neck and body. At the time, West Yorkshire police had no idea it was the beginning of a campaign of unremitting and shocking violence that had claimed its first victim and would last for over half a decade.

In the opening month of 1976 the Ripper struck again. Unbeknown to her husband, a Leeds-based roofing contractor, and the rest of her family, Emily Jackson, a forty-two-year-old housewife and mother of three children, supplemented her husband's wages by soliciting from Sydney Jackson's Commer van while he was out at work. When on the evening of 20 January she failed to pick up Mr Jackson as arranged from a job, he was forced to take a taxi home. The following morning a passer-by found Emily Jackson's body lying in a narrow alleyway off Manor Street in the Sheepscar district of Leeds;

her head had been battered almost beyond recognition, and the killer had inflicted over fifty stab wounds to the body with a sharpened screwdriver. Soon after the murder of Emily Jackson, an eighteen-year-old shop assistant was struck down from behind while walking along the edge of a field at Queensbury in Bradford. She was left for dead with serious head injuries but survived. Four months later, on the evening of 19 May, Marcella Claxton, who had come to Britain from the Caribbean island of St Kitts in the mid-1960s, was accosted while walking home in an intoxicated state from a West Indian drinking club in Leeds city centre. She was driven to Roundhay Park, where she was struck by a flurry of powerful blows from a hammer. The twenty-year-old only escaped certain death by pretending to be unconscious and her assailant, believing her to be dead, got back into his car and drove away. She managed to crawl to a public telephone box and dial 999. Later, in Leeds General Infirmary, doctors were able to successfully treat her dreadful head injuries but Marcella, three months pregnant, miscarried her baby. For most of the long hot summer of 1976 the Ripper laid low, although an assault later in August at Lister Hills in Bradford that left a twenty-nine-year-old housewife with head trauma and stab wounds to her body had all the hallmarks of another attack. It would be over twelve months following the death of Emily Jackson before the Ripper killed again but, as if making up for missed opportunities, the following year an explosion of murderous violence took place in both Leeds and Manchester which stunned the country and left the north of England under a palpable cloud of fear.

The twelve months of 1977 saw six separate attacks, four of them fatal, and the killer, christened the 'Yorkshire Ripper' by the British tabloid press, entered the public consciousness for the first time. On the morning of 6 February, an early morning jogger passing through Roundhay Park, where nine months before Marcella Claxton had been violently assaulted, came across the body of Irene Richardson lying on the grass near to the sports pavilion; the twenty-eight-year-old prostitute had been killed with a hammer and her body slashed with a knife. On 24 April, Bradford police were called to a small flat at Oak Avenue in Manningham, where the boyfriend of Patricia 'Tina' Atkinson had found the thirty-two-year-old battered and stabbed to death. As with the killing of Mary Kelly by his Victorian namesake in the autumn of 1888, this was to be the only murder that the Ripper carried out indoors. Jayne MacDonald was a sixteen-year-old Leeds schoolgirl with film star looks who lived only a few doors from Wilma McCann. It would seem highly likely that, on 26 June 1977, while walking home from an evening out dancing at Leeds' city centre Hofbrauhaus, she was mistaken for a prostitute and ambushed while passing by an adventure playground in Reginald Street. The following morning her body was found by two young children. The killer had knocked her down with brutal efficiency using hammer blows to the head and had then dragged her to the spot where she was discovered, stabbed over twenty times in the front and back with a thin-bladed weapon. Her death sent shockwaves across the county as the general public, seemingly ambivalent to the violent and mounting deaths of street-workers, now realised that every woman out at night in the north of England was a potential target for a psychopathic killer. This became chillingly clear a month after the murder of Jayne MacDonald when residents of a gypsy caravan site near Bowling Back Lane in Leeds heard cries for help coming from a patch of wasteground. Police called to the scene found forty-two-year-old Maureen Long, a mother of several children separated from her husband, lying with severe head injuries and several stab wounds. The Ripper had left her for dead but she survived. The penultimate attack, and what would be the final killing of 1977, took place three months later at the beginning of October, when the Yorkshire Ripper crossed the Pennines to Manchester. There he picked up twenty-year-old Scottish-born prostitute Jean Jordan and took her to an allotment in Chorlton near to the city's Southern Cemetery. Nine days later her heavily decomposed body, heaving with maggots and savagely mutilated, was discovered by Bruce Jones, a local dairyman who was collecting bricks to build a shed base on an adjacent allotment. Jones, then aged twenty-three, would later find national fame as an actor in the long-running television soap opera *Coronation Street*, but his experience that day was one that would haunt him for many years. It later transpired that Jordan's body had lain hidden under a nearby hedge for over a week, after which time the killer had returned looking for a new, and therefore traceable, £5 note which he had given to the woman before attacking her. Frustrated in his search, the Ripper had attacked the body again, cutting open the abdomen and partially severing the head with a hacksaw blade. Ten days before Christmas, on 14 December, the Ripper returned to Leeds, where he picked up twenty-five-year-old Chapeltown prostitute Marilyn Moore and took her to a quiet factory site in Buslingthorpe Lane. As with all the previous victims, Marilyn was beaten mercilessly with a hammer from behind but, seemingly disturbed by the noise of a barking dog, the Ripper curtailed the assault and, getting back into his car, drove away. The mother of two managed to stagger out to the main road, where passers-by came to her aid and, like Maureen Long, she survived after emergency neurosurgery.

The opening month of 1978 saw the Ripper claim two more lives amid a massive police hunt that, despite vast resources and a dedicated team of detectives (known as the 'Ripper Squad' and lead by Assistant Chief Constable George Oldfield), seemed powerless to prevent further killings.

On the night of 21 January, Yvonne Pearson, a twenty-one-year-old prostitute, disappeared from the streets of Bradford after leaving her two young children with a babysitter in order to carry out an evening's business. Her decomposed body was found nearly two months later on Easter Sunday, 26 March, partly concealed by an overturned settee on wasteground off Arthington Street in the city's Whetley Hill district; at Bradford public mortuary the pathologist found her skull had been smashed into over twenty separate pieces. At this point four of the Ripper's total of seven victims had been murdered in Leeds, but the intense police presence in the city was to drive the killer to nearby Huddersfield where, ten days after Yvonne Pearson was reported missing, eighteen-year-old street-worker Helen Rytka was stabbed to death at a timber yard in Great Northern Street. On 17 May, over three months after the killing in Huddersfield, the Ripper returned to Manchester. Early the following morning, Jim McGuigan, a landscape gardener working on a contract at the city's Royal Infirmary, saw what he assumed to be a large doll or dummy lying on the grass next to a wire fence in the hospital grounds. The area was known as a favourite spot for prostitutes to take their clients. Forty-year-old Vera Millward, a Spanish-born street-worker, had taken the Yorkshire Ripper there the previous evening. She was killed by three hammer blows to the head and then stabbed repeatedly as she lay dying on the ground. Weeks passed with no further attacks and by the end of the year, as the region held its breath, it seemed that possibly the atrocities had come to an end. However, as the lull continued into the spring of 1979, police were well aware that it was simply that – by his very nature the man they sought would never stop killing and for the people of the north of England it was to prove to be the eye of the storm.

The Ripper ended his near year-long hiatus in Halifax. Josephine Whitaker was a nineteen-year-old bank clerk who, around midnight on 4 April 1979, walked home alone after spending the evening watching television at her grandparents' house. As she crossed a football pitch in Saville Park, she was attacked and struck down by a single powerful hammer blow that fractured her skull and left her defenceless. The killer then stabbed her repeatedly in the torso and vagina with a sharpened screwdriver. Six months later, at the beginning of September, the Ripper claimed his eleventh victim back in Bradford. In the early hours of 2 September, university student Barbara Leach left the Manville Arms pub – not far from the university campus – after an after-hours lock-in with some fellow students. Barbara was renting a small bedsit in Grove Terrace and decided to walk back there alone. When it became clear, around teatime later the same day, that she was missing, a police search began in earnest. The following morning her body was found leaning against a dustbin in an alleyway at the rear of 13 Ash Grove, partly covered with a discarded carpet weighed down with bricks. Like Josephine Whitaker she had been felled by a single hammer blow from behind and then stabbed; pathologist David Gee found eight wounds to the torso, which had been carried out using the same screwdriver weapon that had been used in Halifax earlier in the year. Unbeknown to the police and the public, the Yorkshire Ripper was to enjoy a further fifteen months of freedom, during which his murderous crusade would kill two more young women and leave another two severely injured.

Nearly a year passed before the Ripper struck again – then, the late summer and autumn days of 1980 became filled with a savage frenzy of killing. Marguerite Walls was a forty-seven-year-old unmarried civil servant who worked as an officer for the schools inspectorate at the Department of Education at Pudsey on the western outskirts of Leeds. On 20 August, after working late and eating a takeaway meal at her desk, she left her office around a quarter to eleven and set out to walk the mile and a half to her home on a new estate in the city's nearby Farsley district. The following morning, a couple arriving to carry out gardening work at 'Claremont', a detached house in its own grounds in New Street, Farsley, noticed a pair of women's shoes and a torn skirt, as well as a shopping bag and a chequebook, lying discarded on the grass. Concerned they alerted the police, who discovered Marguerite Wall's naked body close to a garage building and covered with grass cuttings. A post-mortem showed she had put up a terrific fight after being initially struck down and dragged into the garden of 'Claremont', where her killer had knelt on her chest, breaking three ribs, before strangling her with a ligature and stripping off her clothes. Although the initial assault had begun with a blow to the head, at the time the lack of stab wounds gave detectives the impression that the murderer was a local man and it was not until the Ripper's arrest five months later that Marguerite Walls was officially classed as the Yorkshire Ripper's twelfth and penultimate victim.

The next two victims, attacked within a few weeks of one another in Leeds and Huddersfield, both survived. Around eleven o'clock, thirty-four-year-old Dr Uphadya Bandara, a postgraduate student at Leeds University on a scholarship from the World Health Organization, was walking home alone after spending the evening visiting a friend in Headingley. As she turned into Chapel Lane, a bearded man came up behind her and strangled her into unconsciousness with a length of rope. The attacker then seemingly changed his mind and ran away, although it is likely he was unsettled by the presence of a passing police patrol car, whose officers found Dr Bandara lying prone and bleeding from a head wound in the cobbled road. On 5 November, Bonfire Night, James Furey, a Huddersfield millworker in his mid-twenties watching fireworks from a window of his house in Willwood Avenue, saw what he took to be two youths scuffling further down the street. It was in fact his teenage girlfriend, sixteen-year-old Teresa Sykes, fighting for her life against a mystery assailant who had struck her from behind as she was returning from buying cigarettes at a local off-licence. Furey shouted out, causing the Ripper to break off his attack. He ran off with Furey in pursuit but managed to hide under a hedge and get away. Teresa Sykes spent five weeks in hospital and required brain surgery. It was the closest the Yorkshire Ripper ever came to being caught red-handed. Twelve days later, a shop manager making an early morning visit to a bank in Leeds' Arndale Centre saw a woman lying on a patch of wasteground behind a wire fence off Alma Road in Headingly. Around ten o'clock the previous evening, a blood-spotted handbag had been found by a student returning to the nearby university hall of residence and police called some two hours later briefly searched the area where the bag had been picked up, before being called away to attend a burglar alarm alert. Jacqueline Hill, twenty years of age from Middlesborough attending Leeds University as an undergraduate studying English, lay dead in the darkness on the other side of the street. Beaten with a hammer and stabbed in the body and once through the right eye, she was to be the thirteenth fatal and ultimately final victim of the Yorkshire Ripper[1].

Just before eleven o'clock on the evening of Friday, 2 January 1981, Sergeant Robert Ring and Constable Robert Hyde, a probationary, became suspicious of a car parked in the driveway of an office building on Melbourne Avenue in the Broomhill district of Sheffield. The area was well known to the police as a place where street-workers took their clients and, as they pulled the patrol car up in front of the Rover saloon, the two men saw that the occupants were a bearded man in his early thirties and a young black woman. The driver, who gave his name as John Williams from Rotherham, claimed the passenger was his girlfriend but PC Hyde was unconvinced, especially when Williams was unable to tell him his companion's name. Sergeant Ring radioed the car's numberplate through to divisional headquarters and soon a check with the computer database showed that the registration actually belonged to a Skoda owned by an Asian man. The policemen found the Rover's plates were false and, arresting the couple on suspicion of stealing a vehicle, they were taken in the patrol car to Hammerton Road police station. Twenty-four-year-old Olivia Reivers had at that point just escaped with her life by a matter of minutes.

In the interview room at Hammerton Road, Robert Hyde quickly felt that there was something not right about the arrested man, who now admitted his real name was Peter Sutcliffe and gave an address at Heaton in Bradford. When the prisoner had been searched at the police station, Hyde had found a three-foot length of knotted rope in his pocket. Sutcliffe said it was for repairing cars but the policeman noticed there was a more than passing resemblance between the arrested man and a photo-fit of the person who had attacked Marilyn Moore in Leeds just before Christmas in 1977. The following morning Sutcliffe was taken by car to Dewsbury police station and, as he ate breakfast in the cells, detectives from the Ripper Squad were contacted. The interview with Sutcliffe occupied most of the day and it soon became apparent that he had been questioned several times over the past five years in connection with the Ripper murders; his car had also been recorded dozens of times in the red-light areas of Leeds, Bradford and Manchester. Sutcliffe lied fluently but by ten o'clock in the evening he was still at Dewsbury and was returned to the cells, while detectives from the Ripper Squad made arrangements to check a number of his alibis.

Around the same time, Sergeant Robert Ring came on duty for the nightshift at Hammerton Road in Sheffield. Learning that the man he had picked up the previous evening for car theft was still in custody and had been interviewed all day by the Ripper Squad in Leeds, Ring decided to take a trip back to Melbourne Road. The sergeant recalled that while he and Constable Hyde had been waiting for their vehicle check to come through, the driver had gone off on his own for a brief time to relieve himself behind a wall a short distance from where the two cars had been parked. It was to prove a crucial decision and a pivotal moment in the long search for the Yorkshire Ripper. Ring took a patrol car and drove up to Broomhill. Searching around by torchlight in the area where Peter Sutcliffe had slipped away, he found a ball-pein hammer and a knife lying on a pile of leaves over a grating in a gap between the stone wall and an oil storage tank. Some time later a check was made in the lavatory that Sutcliffe had used just prior to his initial interview at the Hammerton Road station, and another knife was found submerged inside the toilet cistern. When told of the discoveries, Sutcliffe immediately confessed and over the next fifteen hours dictated a thirty-four page statement admitting to a string of violent attacks and murders: a half-decade campaign of evil had finally come to an end. Protected by a police cordon from a huge crowd baying for his blood, Sutcliffe appeared at Dewsbury Magistrates Court on 5 January 1981 charged with thirteen murders and was remanded in custody in Armley Gaol. Four months later, on 5 May, his trial began in Court No. 1 at the Old Bailey in London. Sutcliffe pleaded not guilty on the grounds of diminished responsibility, claiming he had been on a mission from God to rid the world of prostitutes by a campaign of organised murder. The jury were unconvinced and on 22 May 1981, Peter William Sutcliffe was jailed for life with a recommendation that he serve a minimum of thirty years.

Much has been written since that time concerning the Yorkshire Ripper and what drove him to carry out his crimes. Sutcliffe, a 'manipulative psychopathic liar', clearly derived powerful sexual satisfaction during the act of killing, unobtainable during normal intercourse – a sweater worn under his trousers with the V-neck exposing his genitals allowed him to kneel and masturbate over his victims as they lay dead or dying, and he furthered a morbid fascination with red-light areas and the world of the street-worker. Sutcliffe was also able to live a double life: his wife Sonia, five years his junior and the daughter of Czech and Ukrainian immigrants, was completely unaware that she was living with a killer. They first met in 1967 and later married in August 1974, but although the relationship was at times stormy and marred with arguments and the problems associated with Sonia's schizophrenia, Sutcliffe never laid a finger on his wife during all the time they were together. This parallels the life and crimes of Peter Kürten, the sadistic 'Monster of Dusseldorf', who carried out a similar series of sex crimes directed at women and young children during the 1920s, and whose wife at no time suspected her husband's vile and hidden perversions. Unlike the Yorkshire Ripper, Kürten went to the guillotine on 2 July 1931. Sutcliffe had in fact been interviewed a staggering nine times in connection with the Ripper murders, but he was one of thousands and had evaded detection on each occasion, his file buried under the vast information overload that afflicted the West Yorkshire police's investigation in the days before extensive computerisation and DNA technology would revolutionise crime detection. During the early months of 1979, the investigation took a dramatic turn when the Ripper Squad received a number of letters and a cassette tape recording that purported to come direct from the killer, a man with a distinctive Geordie accent that was narrowed down by phonetic experts to the Castleton district of Sunderland. As the West Yorkshire police concentrated a proportion of their enquiry in the hunt for 'Wearside Jack', anyone not from the region was dismissed as a suspect and Peter Sutcliffe, who was born in Bingley, later admitted that he felt safe during this period[2]. In the dark days of the late 1970s, with police unable to make the breakthrough that would trap the vicious perpetrator of a seemingly endless series of killings, the psychic angle offered by clairvoyants and mediums may have appeared to some to be able to succeed where the forces of the Ripper Squad were failing.

The psychic search for the Yorkshire Ripper was one that was driven by both local and national newspapers. During the second half of the 1970s, one medium who became firmly established in the public eye as one of the country's major psychics was Essex housewife Doris Stokes. Born in Grantham, Lincolnshire in 1920, Stokes claimed to have had paranormal and mediumistic experiences from childhood. During the Second World War she enlisted in the WRAF and in 1943 married John Stokes, a sergeant in the paratroops who became a prisoner of war following the raid on Arnhem in 1944. Their son, John Michael, died in infancy and the Stokes later adopted a young orphan, Terry, who they subsequently brought up as their own. The Stokes household was a poor one, due in no small part to the head injuries that John Stokes had received during his time in Holland and which affected his ability to work throughout his life. Inspired by the Scottish materialisation medium Helen Duncan, who supplemented her husband's income as a postman by giving séances throughout the country, and one of whose sittings she attended around the time that they adopted Terry, Doris decided to train as a medium and support the family in the same way. Developing her natural ability as a clairaudient at a local spiritualist church, she eventually passed a 'test séance' at Nottingham and in 1949 was registered as a practising medium by the Spiritualists' National Union. Stokes later became a State Enrolled Nurse but continued to give séances privately and, in 1975, at the age of fifty-five, became one of the resident mediums at the Spiritualist Association of Great Britain's headquarters at Belgrave Square in London.

Doris Stokes' major fame outside of the Spiritualist movement was precipitated by a visit to Australia in 1978, when she took part in *The Don Lane Show* on television. This generated a huge public interest in her platform work and, like Estelle Roberts before her, Stokes began to give large scale demonstrations of her mediumship before capacity audiences at prestigious venues such as the London Palladium and Barbican Hall in England and Australia's Sydney Opera House. Assisted by her invisible spirit guide, a Tibetan lama named 'Ramanov', Stokes seemed to be able to provide and pass on convincing evidence for survival after death to people from all walks of life around the world: she issued a number of autobiographical volumes – beginning with the 1980 book *Voices In My Ear: The Autobiography of a Medium* – that chronicled much of her psychic work, and on her death, following an operation for a brain tumour in London on 8 May 1987, Stokes had easily been the public face of mediumship in Britain throughout the 1980s up until that point.

On 1 July 1979, just over three months after the murder of Josephine Whitaker in Halifax, the *Sunday People* newspaper ran a dramatic front page story entitled 'Face of the Ripper' featuring Doris Stokes' attempts to identify the unknown killer following the broadcast of the 'Wearside Jack' tape recording on television. The article was accompanied by a prominent sketch of the murderer drawn by the tabloid's resident artist Bob Williams, who had been guided by the medium's psychic description as he drew his portrait, and the clairaudient's profile was passed on by the newspaper to West Yorkshire police. Through a link with the spirit world, Stokes revealed the Ripper was aged between thirty-one and thirty-two, five feet eight inches tall, was slightly built and lived on Tyneside or Wearside in a street named Berwick or Bewick. His name was either Johnny or Ronnie and his surname began with the letter M, while Edwards' portrait showed a clean-shaven man with collar-length straight hair parted on the right with 'a small bald patch which he tries to cover up'. Stokes also felt that the killer had at some point received mental treatment at the Cherry Knowle psychiatric hospital at Ryhope, just outside Sunderland. At one point it seemed that the police might have got their man in the shape of Ronnie Metcalf, a long-distance lorry driver from Berwick Avenue in Sunderland's Downhill neighbourhood, but Metcalf was quickly eliminated and, with hindsight, it is plain to see that the voices in Doris' ear were hopelessly wide of the mark: as well as the complete inaccuracy of the name, Peter Sutcliffe was thirty-four at the time of Doris Stokes' sitting for the *People*, wore a distinctive full beard and lived at 6 Garden Lane, Heaton in Bradford, and, not surprisingly, detectives acting on her information got nowhere.

Like many television and celebrity psychics, Doris Stokes remains a controversial figure nearly twenty-five years after her death, with sceptics putting much if not all of her mediumistic abilities down to 'cold reading' and luck. Ian Wilson, a historian and writer on paranormal subjects from Bristol, attended one of Stokes' sell-out platform demonstrations at the London Palladium in November 1986, not long before the medium's death, while researching for a book on the evidence for life beyond the grave, and together with two television journalists, Beth Miller and Siobhan Hockton, came away unimpressed. In his *The After Death Experience* (1987), Wilson notes that the reality of the medium's performance that night (split into two parts separated by an interval) was not all that it seemed: members of the audience who in the first half received lengthy messages, ostensibly from beyond, were known to the medium and had been invited to attend the performance, while enquiries with the Palladium management revealed that Stokes booked the front three rows, where some of these people were sitting, 'for her own purposes'. 'No longer was there need to believe that Doris's information in any way came from the dead,' Wilson concludes. 'All the hard and really impressive material Doris produced during the show had been known or available to her beforehand . . . It was no accident that Doris's second-half free-for-all messages for non-pre-arranged individuals were much less convincing. For these she had to rely on intelligent guesswork and "fishing".' For those working at the CSICOP level of scepticism these kind of revelations are grist to the mill, but to explain away the entire mediumship of Doris Stokes (and platform mediums in general) in this way is giving the subject only superficial consideration. The workings of mediumship, whether it be clairvoyance, clairaudience or even materialisation, are a subtle and seemingly unknowable, but ultimately real, process and the experiences of Ian Wilson and his colleagues go to show that when this process is elevated to the level of 'psychic entertainment' the pressures for a medium or sensitive to deliver the goods at every sitting are enormous, particularly as in this case at such a prestigious and sold-out venue as the London Palladium. We have already discussed 'mixed mediumship' in this context, and, as there exists many supportive testimonials to the genuine psychic abilities of Doris Stokes that the people involved were adamant could not have been picked up or effected by trickery or 'cold reading', it is best to leave the medium, and the subject, there for the moment.

Another psychic who turned detective in an attempt to bring the Yorkshire Ripper to justice was none other than the 'wizard of Utrecht', Gerard Croiset. Working with *The Sun* newspaper, the Dutchman gave a profile of the killer which was passed on to West Yorkshire police and also appeared in the paper on 28 November 1979. Croiset said the Ripper lived in the centre of Sunderland in a block of flats over a garage. He wore his hair long and cut straight across the neck, had a squashed nose and, due to a damaged right knee, walked with a limp. Like Doris Stokes, Croiset felt that the murderer had received some form of psychiatric treatment in the past, possibly in a children's home; he was also fooled by the 'Wearside Jack' hoaxer and his pronouncement was one of several high-profile late-career failures that were to give Piet Hein Hoebens the ammunition he needed to shoot down the clairvoyant's posthumous reputation not long afterwards. Where the Yorkshire Ripper was concerned, Croiset was no more successful than medium Patrick Barnard, who had stated four days before in the Southend *Evening Echo* that the killer was a crewman on a submarine, clairvoyant Flora MacKenzie who was certain the Ripper lived in Barnsley, Wim Virbeck, an engineer from Holland who claimed he was a washing-machine repair man from Aberdeen, Dutch psychic Dono Meijling who felt he was related to the temporary head of the West Yorkshire CID, Detective Chief Superintendent Jim Hobson, and occultist Alex Sanders, the self-styled 'King of the Witches' from Notting Hill Gate who, through magical divination, described him as a single man living alone near railway arches in South Shields.

Amidst all the conflicting statements and false leads were two psychics, however, whose contemporary pronouncements on the Ripper case cannot, with what we now know in hindsight about the murderer Peter Sutcliffe and his crimes, be dismissed so easily. Robert Cracknell, a private detective and former finance company investigator at that time in his mid-forties, has been described as 'the leading psychic detective of the 1980s'. Much of this notoriety is based on his involvement, during the autumn of 1980, with the hunt for the Yorkshire Ripper. An illegitimate and unwanted child, Cracknell's father died before he was born and he was brought up in London by foster parents. Evacuated to Nottingham to escape the Blitz, Cracknell spent the war years lonely and unhappy, being beaten and ill-treated for bedwetting. Later, at fifteen, he joined the RAF but was discharged in 1956 aged twenty-one on medical grounds and suffered a nervous breakdown. After spending time living in London as a down and out, Cracknell managed to pull his life around and began working as a case assessor for an insurance company and later went on to found his own detective agency. Throughout this time, Cracknell had nurtured and developed a natural clairvoyant ability that had made itself apparent even before he enlisted in the air force.

During the 1970s, Robert Cracknell's psychic abilities came to the attention of Kevin McClure, then the President of the Oxford University Society for Psychical Research, who arranged a series of controlled experiments, the so-called 'chair tests', in front of an audience of university students. Cracknell was able to predict, with a high degree of success over and above what would be considered as achievable by chance, the details of occupants of certain seats in the audience of future university meetings, a form of ESP experiment that Tenhaeff had undertaken on a number of occasions with Gerard Croiset. Later, he provided evidential information when a homosexual friend of McClure's was murdered by a partner, data which was later confirmed by police working on the case. McClure introduced Cracknell to Colin Wilson and the two men became involved for a short time in the still unsolved disappearance of thirteen-year-old Aylesbeare schoolgirl Genette Tate, who vanished while on a paper round on 19 August 1978. Ultimately, despite some early impressions which had impressed the Devon police, Cracknell was unable to say who had abducted Genette and his prediction that her body would be found within ten days of her disappearance proved to be wrong. The following year Robert Cracknell became drawn into the case of the Yorkshire Ripper.

Cracknell was convinced that the Ripper was from Bradford. Soon after the murder of Barbara Leach, the *Daily Mirror* pre-empted the *Sunday People's* investigation with Doris Stokes by asking Cracknell if he was able to pick up anything in connection with the Bradford student's death. Despite living in London, the investigator stated the killer was a local man and although having not visited the city before, correctly described several landmarks that he felt were on the route that the Ripper would have passed on his way back to his own home. Subsequently the *Yorkshire Post* invited Cracknell to come to Bradford, where he was driven around the area in an attempt to identify the location of the murderer's house. Cracknell felt that the killer had some past connection with a terrace of latterly demolished houses in Rayner Terrace in Pudsey, Leeds and at some point had lived there, but this has proved not to be the case. However, when driving around Bradford, Cracknell, following his own psychic intuition, took the reporters to within 100 yards or so of Peter Sutcliffe's house in Garden Lane, but was unable to pinpoint the actual address. He did, however, provide the newspaper with a description of the house.

In his book *The Psychic Detectives* (1984), Colin Wilson describes the final stages of Robert Cracknell's involvement with the Ripper case. On 11 November 1980, both he and Bob Cracknell were invited to lunch by Christopher Watkins, the sales director of the Hamlyn publishing house, who had accepted the psychic's autobiography *Clues to the Unknown* – Wilson had assisted in placing the manuscript and had agreed to contribute a foreword. During the course of the luncheon, Cracknell made a prediction that the Yorkshire Ripper would commit his last murder in a fortnight's time, after which he would soon be caught. The murder of Jacqueline Hill took place six days later but the rest of his statement, including the description of the killer's house in Bradford, proved to be correct. Robert Cracknell was present in Colin Wilson's house in Cornwall when a television newsflash announced the arrest of the Ripper on 5 January 1981.

The second psychic who it later transpired delivered accurate information about the Yorkshire murderer, and in fact was the most successful of them all, was clairvoyant medium Nella Jones. Born in a shack on Belvedere Marshes in Kent on 4 May 1932, she tells in her autobiography *Ghost of a Chance* (1982) of her impoverished upbringing as one of six children to casual farm labourers. Her mother was a Romany gypsy of fairground stock while her father, a violent man, had worked in the past as a miner. The family was poor and lived at various times in a gypsy encampment, a wartime Anderson shelter, and a derelict bus parked on the edge of a golf course. Nella married at the age of seventeen and had two children, but the relationship broke down and she moved to Abbey Wood, supporting herself by selling rags and later working in a lampshade factory. Later, another relationship produced a second daughter, Gaynor, but this also failed and she moved to Charlton where she started her own house-cleaning business, which ran successfully before ill heath forced her to close in the early 1970s. Aware of her own natural psychic abilities from the age of seven, Nella describes many experiences of premonition, of seeing apparitions, and her ability to work as a successful healer. Following the failure of her cleaning business, Nella Jones became a professional clairvoyant medium. Her reputation as a successful psychic detective began in 1974 when an oil painting, 'The Guitar Player' by the Dutch master Jan Vermeer, was stolen in a £2m art raid on Kenwood House in London. Jones was able to guide police to where the painting's frame, together with a limpet alarm, had been discarded in the estate's grounds by the thieves, who later demanded both a £2m ransom and the release of the IRA terrorist sisters Dolours and Marion Price, for its return. Jones told detectives the painting was being hidden in the catacombs of Highgate Cemetery, which at that time had been closed to the public following vandalism associated with recent incidents of vampire-hunting and sightings of ghostly figures, a controversy fuelled in no small part by two feuding ghost hunters, David Farrant and Sean Manchester. Police searched the cemetery but found nothing and Jones informed them that it had been moved to another London cemetery, where it would soon be found. On 6 May 1974, 'The Guitar Player' was recovered from a churchyard next to St Bartholomew's Hospital. The same year, Jones offered help in finding missing youngster Alison Chadwick and, like psychic detective Robert Cracknell, later attempted to find schoolgirl Genette Tate and track down the Yorkshire Ripper.

Many of the psychic impressions connected with the Yorkshire killings that Nella Jones relayed to journalist Shirley Davenport over a period of several months, beginning in the summer of 1979, proved to be highly accurate. Like Robert Cracknell she felt the killer lived in Bradford, but Jones went further: the murderer's name was Peter and the most significant thing about him were his eyes, which were unsettling and dangerous; he worked as a lorry driver for an engineering firm whose name, written on the cab of his vehicle, began with the letter 'C'; the name Ainsworth was somehow significant with the case, while in the closing months of 1980, she felt the killer would strike again in Leeds on either 17 or 27 November and the victim's initials would be 'JH'. All of this would prove to be chillingly accurate following Peter Sutcliffe's arrest, from T. & H.W. Clark, the haulage company he worked for and in the cab of whose lorry he was photographed for a publicity brochure, to the death of Jacqueline Hill, the thirteenth and final victim; Peter Hainsworth was the name of a local magistrate in the garden of whose house Marguerite Walls was strangled, and several detectives who interviewed Sutcliffe later commented on the soulless quality of his staring black eyes. In her book, published in 1982, Jones notes a comment she made to a reporter from the *Yorkshire Post* in the aftermath of Sutcliffe's trial that, once in prison, the killer would have problems with his eyes. On 10 January 1983, after her book had gone to press, Sutcliffe was attacked in the hospital wing of Parkhurst Prison and sustained four separate wounds to the side of his face. The psychic's prediction came fully true fourteen years later when the Ripper was again attacked, this time in Broadmoor on 10 March 1997, when he was blinded in the left eye by prisoner Ian Kay who stabbed Sutcliffe in the face with a pen; his right eye was also damaged.

During the second week of his trial, on 11 May 1981, Sutcliffe described under cross-examination the first instance of him hearing what he considered to be the voice of God that would later, so he claimed, instruct him to begin his mission of murder. This took place in Bingley cemetery, where he worked as a grave digger during the mid-1960s, and Sutcliffe described hearing 'a voice similar to a human voice – like an echo' coming from the grave of a Polish man named Bronislaw Zapolski. Sutcliffe was alone at the time and in the Catholic section of the cemetery. In 1986, medium and psychic investigator Rita Goold visited Bingley while carrying out research into her family history. Goold's grandmother, a Catholic, had been buried at Cottingley two miles to the south-east, a small village now famous to psychical researchers for the fairy hoax that fooled Sir Arthur Conan Doyle. At some time in the past, Rita Goold's grandmother's coffin, along with a number of others, had been exhumed from Nab Wood cemetery in Cottingley to make way for a new road and had been reinterred at Bingley in the section where Peter Sutcliffe later claimed to have heard disembodied voices. During her visit, Goold spoke with one of the cemetery keepers, who, it turned out, had worked with and knew Sutcliffe twenty years before and who confirmed aspects of his character connected with his employment as a grave digger, notably his morbid fascination with the bones and skulls that they would occasionally unearth during the course of their work. He also claimed that the part of the cemetery where the bodies from Nab Wood had been re-buried had not been consecrated either before or after the burial. Both he and fellow workers had repeatedly heard voices there over the years, often at night, and as such considered it to be a haunted place . . .

NOTES

1. Investigative journalist and film-maker Michael Bilton's definitive *Wicked Beyond Belief: The Hunt for the Yorkshire Ripper* (Harper Collins, London, 2003) contains much background information on all the women mentioned whose lives and tragic circumstances can easily be reduced to mere statistics in a commentary such as the present work.
2. On 21 March 2006, John Humble, an unemployed alcoholic from Sunderland's Ford Estate, was convicted and sentenced to eight years in prison for perverting the course of justice by carrying out the 'Wearside Jack' hoax.

CHAPTER 12

VIEWING A KILLER

SUZANNE PADFIELD AND INESSA TCHURINA, 1980

Now, some twenty years after his death, the English psychical researcher Benson Herbert has become one of the twentieth century's forgotten ghost hunters. Born in County Durham of Irish descent on 16 May 1912, Herbert was a man of many parts whose interests included archaeology, photography, mythology and legends, as well as science and ghosts. An Oxford graduate, he joined the Society for Psychical Research in December 1931 while pursuing a career as a physicist, at the same time undertaking archaeological surveys of historic sites in both Britain and Ireland. Herbert became interested in haunted castles and theorised that the paranormal phenomena that took place there was due to anomalous electrical activity isolated from external radio waves and electromagnetism by the buildings' massive stone walls that performed like ancient 'Faraday cages'. It was a line of thinking from which the discipline of 'paraphysics', the subject with which Herbert is now most closely associated, would grow in the years following the Second World War – that ghosts and hauntings as well as mediumship are due to natural physical phenomena rather than the activities of spirits and discarnate entities.

Herbert later struck up a friendship with fellow SPR member Richard (R.G.) Medhurst (1920-1971), a British mathematician and electrical engineer with an abiding interest in the paranormal, and the two men held séances together at Herbert's Chelsea flat, as well as Medhurst's home in Richmond. Over the course of these experiments, Herbert developed a trance personality and spoke in the voice of a 1,000-year-old Chinese mandarin, although he was disinclined to believe this was a possessing spirit but rather a hidden aspect of his own subconscious mind. Despite believing that mediumship, clairvoyance and healing were subjects based on a hidden and as yet undiscovered faculty of science, Benson Herbert eventually gave up traditional spiritualist-inspired experimentation in favour of a new and radical form of laboratory-based research that drew heavily on his own scientific background as a physicist. In 1966, keen to ensure his experiments were free from the traffic vibration and electrical interference inherent in inner-city environments, Herbert took on the lease of Privett House, a remote farmhouse on a hillside on the edge of the New Forest, near Downton in Wiltshire. There he established the Paraphysical Laboratory, which came to be known informally as the 'Paralab', with himself as Director and Egyptian-born psychical researcher, UFO investigator and SPR member Manfred Cassirer as Honorary Research Officer. With the help of visiting students and other enthusiasts who travelled to Downton at weekends, Herbert began a series of unorthodox and original experiments in order to, as he himself described, 'carry out precise and systematic research into the physics of the paranormal', something that went against the then fashionable statistics and Rhine-inspired trends of contemporary parapsychology.

Despite his shoestring budget and anti-establishment approach, Herbert's Paraphysical Laboratory managed against the odds to establish itself as an international centre of modern paranormal research. The Paralab issued its own publication, the *Journal of Paraphysics* (in reality a photocopied newsletter) that, despite its modest format, included such luminaries as British mathematician Professor John Taylor, Soviet biophysicist Victor Adamenko, and American parapsychologist Stanley Krippner on its editorial board. Herbert courted overseas researchers sympathetic to his style of contemporary psychical research, particularly in the Soviet Union where, in 1972 and 1973, during the course of two visits, he met the remarkable Leningrad housewife Nina Kulagina, who had been filmed moving objects, seemingly by the power of thought alone, and who it was also claimed could see through her own skin.

Back in Britain, Herbert was happy to take part in more conventional ghost busting. In 1963, accompanied by Sybil Leek, a self-professed witch who ran an antique shop by day and a coven at night – both in the New Forest – he was filmed by the BBC at a séance in a haunted house in Southampton and, three years later, also appeared on television investigating Sandford Orcas Manor House in Dorset where the then tenant, Colonel Francis Claridge, whose stirring family motto 'Fear Nought But God' appeared on both his coat of arms and later his gravestone, claimed with his wife to be besieged by a veritable army of phantoms including child poltergeists, a seven foot-tall rapist and an insane sailor, as well as the spectre of a murderous priest. In 1975, Herbert was also seen in the company of sceptical BBC producer and presenter Hugh

Burnett carrying out a planchette experiment at a haunted pub for the highly regarded documentary *The Ghost Hunters*, which also featured Borley Rectory investigators Peter Underwood and Geoffrey Croom-Hollingsworth. This fraternisation with witches and UFOologists, together with his unconventional approach to the paranormal, put Herbert and his work on the fringe of accepted scientific psychical research and to many parapsychologists he was regarded as an enthusiastic oddball who found ghosts at the slightest flick of a dial and appeared to be surrounded by a never-ending supply of young and attractive female assistants. His death, on 21 April 1991, just a few weeks short of his seventy-eighth birthday, seemed to bring to a close an exciting chapter of experimental paranormal research from the 1960s and '70s that included not only Kulagina but also Geller and the 'Raudive voices'.

A number of sensitives and physical mediums took part in experimental work at the Paraphysical Laboratory including psychic healer Josephine Blatch, but the person with whom Herbert had the most success was Suzanne Padfield, a natural young clairvoyant from the West Country who worked as a switchboard operator and wrote poetry and children's stories in her spare time. As we have seen, genuine mediums become aware of their powers at an early age and Suzanne was no exception, her psychic awareness no doubt accentuated by the fact that over the years she spent much time living in a succession of haunted houses. This led to many strange and startling experiences: at the age of three she felt invisible psychic touches and heard the footsteps of an invisible person walking across her bedroom floor; later, at another house in Shepton Mallet she (and her sister) watched coloured lights float around their bedroom and on several occasions she was thrown out of bed by an invisible force and would often wake up to find herself sleeping on the floor. During the late 1960s and early '70s, the time when she was most involved with scientific psychical research, eerie spontaneous phenomena took place almost on a day-to-day basis. This was at an old rectory owned by the Deanery of Wells Cathedral that Padfield leased for a peppercorn rent while acting as a temporary caretaker: furniture moved and doors opened by themselves, water taps and an electric fire turned themselves on and off, a black shape appeared in one of the bedrooms and footsteps followed her around the house.

Suzanne Padfield first visited the Paralab not long after it had been established in the mid-1960s and ultimately went on to spend twelve years on and off being tested by Herbert and his merry band of assistants. In her the physicist felt he had discovered the British equivalent of super-psychics like Uri Gellar and the American Ingo Swann, as well as their Soviet counterpart Nina Kulagina, 'a class of subjects very rare and few in numbers' that Herbert called 'The 5D People', and devised a series of experiments to record her supernormal abilities; these included psychometry, healing, telepathy and psychokinesis. In the Paralab, a table moved around the room by itself and mobiles suspended in sealed jars were rotated simply by her presence. Herbert found that while restrained and isolated she could also induce physical sensations, such as feelings of being touched in other people, and also affect the mechanical workings of clocks and watches. '[S]he exhibits a strange, compelling, "magnetic" radiance, of an almost frightening nature,' he wrote in 1974, describing it as the 'Padfield Effect', a clear comparison with the sensational feats of the young Israeli wunderkind who had burst onto the psychic scene the previous year; and proudly accompanied his star subject to the International Congress of Parapsychology in Genoa organised by Count and Countess Galateri and Gerard Croiset's old mentor, Wilhelm Tenhaeff. The paraphysicist also found Padfield was able to realise a pet project he had nurtured for a number of years and also shared with his Russian counterpart, Professor Dubrov of Moscow. Described as 'biogravitation', this involved a psychic subject with a strong 5D (Dubrov called it a 'psychotronic') ability to bend the trajectory of a beam of light. Herbert devised a piece of experimental apparatus that involved passing a polarised light source through a sealed tube onto a metering device. He found that when Suzanne Padfield placed her hands near the tube and consciously attempted to affect it, she was able to lower the reading on the meter a significant number of times. During one experiment Herbert recorded twenty-four deflections in succession.

In October 1972, Uri Gellar had stopped off in London on his way to the United States and at the Royal Garden Hotel had been introduced to Dr Edward (Ted) Bastin, a quantum physicist from Cambridge University, who went on to carry out a series of experiments with the Israeli psychic at Birkbeck College. During a television programme devoted to the scientific study of Gellar's phenomena, Bastin met Suzanne Padfield and the couple subsequently married in 1975. By this time, Padfield had been involved with the Paralab for nearly ten years but eventually she grew tired of the continuing experimentation and, by the end of the decade, had all but given up her involvement with psychical research.

During the 1970s, the Soviet government gradually became hostile towards the subject of parapsychology. In October 1973, at the height of the Gellar explosion in the West, the Brezhnev regime published a statement that psychic phenomena would be studied collectively by the Soviet Academy of Sciences, with the result that individual researchers began to find it increasingly difficult to continue working in the field. One of these was a correspondent of Benson Herbert, Victor G. Adamenko, a specialist in laser medicine, who had become deeply interested in Kirlian photography and its relationship with acupuncture. As the 1980s developed, Adamenko became disenchanted with authority control and eventually left Russia and moved to Greece, where he took up a position in the psychobiophysics department of Crete University. In 1988, he spent a period in America working at Joseph Rhine's Foundation for Research on the Nature of Man before finally returning to Greece.

Early in 1980, at a time when he was still prominent in Soviet psychical research, Adamenko received a letter from a man named Tchurina who lived in Fryazino on the outskirts of Moscow asking for his help. In December 1979, the man's nine-year-old daughter Inessa Tchurina had gone missing while visiting a local ice rink and several months later the police were no nearer to discovering what had happened to her. In desperation, Tchurina senior requested Adamenko, who he knew had been involved in research with mediums, to get a psychic to try and find out what had become of Inessa. With most of Russia's top psychics under the watchful eye of the Soviet Academy, Adamenko took the decision to write to Benson Herbert in England with the request that he ask Suzanne Padfield if she would effectively come out of retirement and help with the search for Inessa Tchurina. Knowing from practical experience that with clairvoyance his former star subject had a greater success with three-dimensional objects rather than two-dimensional ones such as drawings, Herbert responded with a request that personal items of the missing girl be sent to him in England. Shortly afterwards, an exercise book of Inessa's schoolwork together with a photograph arrived at the Paralab and Herbert sent them on to Padfield, who was having breakfast when the package arrived. Almost immediately as she opened the envelope, vivid and disturbing images seemed to fill her head.

She 'saw' the young Russian girl at the Fryazino ice rink in the company of a stocky man who appeared to be in his early thirties; he had brown hair, bushy eyebrows and a round bearded face. He talked to her in a friendly way and once outside invited her back to his flat to show her some new ice skates he had recently bought. Trustingly, Inessa went with him but back at the man's home she screamed when he made to put an arm around her and, as they struggled, the man hit her a glancing blow and the girl fell to the floor. Brutally, rather than going to her aid, the mystery assailant, seemingly frightened by the implications of what he had done, gripped the girl by the throat and strangled her to death. The image was sickeningly real, as was what followed. Padfield had the impression of the girl's small body being wrapped in blue material and made into a bundle. The killer then took this with him as he left the flat and boarded a bus out of Fryazino. On the outskirts of the town, she had the impression that the blue bundle had been thrown into water; possibly Inessa had been dumped into a river. All these events happened weeks in the past, across the gulf of over 1,700 miles of distance, yet the young British woman was able to view them in real time as if she were watching as a silent and invisible spectator. Suzanne wrote out an account of her vision and sent it to Benson Herbert, who forwarded it to Victor Adamenko in Moscow. The psychical researcher subsequently passed it to the Russian police investigating Inessa Tchurina's disappearance.

A short time afterwards, Adamenko wrote to Benson Herbert with some startling news. The police had made an arrest in the Tchurina case and the suspect had confessed to the Russian schoolgirl's murder. His statement, as well as the killer's description, tallied exactly with the account that Victor Adamenko had given to the Fryazino police: the body had been wrapped in a blue blanket and disposed of exactly as Padfield had seen it happen. The murderer, a labourer, had tried to avert suspicion by shaving off his beard (which the psychic had described) and moving to a neighbouring town, but he had already been interviewed and when detectives following up on Adamenko's information read the description they decided to bring him in for further questioning. Inessa's body, heavily decomposed, had been recovered from the river a short time earlier. The only inaccuracy between real events and those that Suzanne Padfield had remote-viewed concerned the way the killer had left Fryazino – he had caught a commuter train rather than a bus. Soviet justice in the Tchurina case was swift, as the killer was tried and subsequently executed.

We have already discussed the desire for a perfect case of psychic detection; a crime solved by the direct intervention or involvement of a medium or '5D' person – Colin Godman's 'classic work'. The Padfield/Tchurina case is impressive and up until the beginning of the 1980s appeared to be the only documented example of its kind, but some aspects are unfortunately circumspect. Despite researching a number of sources, including previously published accounts, I have been unable to find the killer's name and the actual dates of the crime, details that are needed to defend the case against the robust attack of the sceptics. This information surely does exist, but the fact that it has not become common knowledge reduces the strength of what could be a well-documented case to one of hearsay. It would be twenty-five years before psychical researchers would publish what they considered to be a watertight case for genuine paranormal crime detection involving statements from both a psychic and the police. It would have its foundation, however, in events that were to take place only three years after Suzanne Padfield's disturbing vision of events on the other side of the world.

CHAPTER 13

THE VOICE FROM THE GRAVE

CHRISTINE HOLOHAN AND JACQUELINE POOLE, 1983

On Sunday, 13 February 1983, police called to an end of terrace house in Lakeside Close, a cul-de-sac road in Ruislip, north-west London, not far from the RAF Northolt air base, made a grim discovery. Concerned that his son's girlfriend, twenty-five-year-old Jacqueline Poole (known as Jacqui), had not answered her door or responded to telephone calls for two days, George Lee had put a call through to the local police station and was present when Detective Constable Tony Batters, equally unable to obtain a response, broke down the front door. Inside they found the body of the shop assistant and part-time barmaid lying on the living room floor; she had been sexually assaulted and strangled. Over the course of the next five hours, DC Batters made a detailed examination of the crime scene while a murder enquiry, under the direction of Detective Superintendent Tony Lundy, quickly got underway. It soon transpired that a large amount of jewellery had been stolen from the flat and the police team made an appeal for anyone who had known Jacqueline to come forward and contact them. A post-mortem concluded that she had been murdered around nine o'clock in the evening two days before, on Friday 11 February.

During the first week of the investigation, the incident room at Ruislip police station received a call with an offer of information and on 17 February, four days after the discovery of Jacqueline's body, DC Batters, accompanied by Detective Constable Andy Smith, arrived at an address in Ruislip Gardens, some three miles from Lakeside Close, to interview twenty-two-year-old Christine Holohan, originally from County Laois in Ireland, who at that time was working part-time at RAF Northolt to support herself while she trained to become a professional medium. In her semi-autobiographical book *A Voice from the Grave* (2006), Holohan describes her upbringing in Stradbally in the familiar terms of a young and naturally gifted clairvoyant awakening to her strange and at times unwanted other-worldly abilities: of playing with angels and phantom figures, experiencing premonitions and prophetic dreams of family bereavements, and of seeing apparitions. Over the weekend of 12-13 February, Holohan had felt uncomfortable on a psychic level and had experienced a sensation of sudden coldness when told about the murder of Jacqui Poole in a local shop on the Monday morning. That evening, while trying to get to sleep, she had felt a strong presence in the bedroom with her, which, when challenged, made the room lights flicker on and off. Over the next two days the presence returned and Holohan had a visual impression of a figure – 'a white line like the outline of a person' – standing beside her bed. This personality, alternating between periods of raging and pleading, identified itself as Jacqui Poole and implored the medium to help in bringing her killer to justice. Holohan received such vivid impressions of the murder and details of the victim's house (she neither knew Jacqueline Poole or the road where she lived) that finally, on the Thursday, she contacted Ruislip police.

Frankly sceptical of anything connected with ghosts and mediums, Batters and Smith listened while the young Irishwoman began describing her experiences. At one point during the conversation, Holohan stated that the spirit of Jacqui Poole was close to her and began to relay information in the form of impressions and descriptions of events from her direct to the two policemen. This included a series of names, a description of the interior of Poole's house, as well as the way she had been attacked and murdered. Holohan also spoke about the reasons Poole had been home alone in Lakeside Close on the previous Friday evening, the jewellery that had been stolen, as well as rings that were missing from the murdered woman's hands. Batters then asked if 'Jacqui' could give them either the name of her killer or a clue as to the whereabouts of the missing items. Holohan, still in a semi-trance state, took the policeman's notebook and pen and, attempting to obtain the information through automatic writing, moved her hand across the paper. When Batters took the notebook back he saw that as well as some random squiggles, the medium had written the number '221' as well as the word 'garden' and two names, 'Ickeham' [*sic*] and 'Pokie'. The second of the two names made the policemen exchange glances as they immediately recognised its significance.

Holohan then stated that 'Jacqui' wanted her to give one of the policemen a personal reading to show that the information that was being given out was genuine. This the medium did by psychometrizing DC Smith's keys. Holding the bunch of keys in her hand she spontaneously gave three precise and clear statements that related specifically to Andy Smith, after which Holohan returned to 'normal' and the interview finished. Outside, Smith admitted to his colleague that he was stunned by one of the statements Holohan had given him as it concerned totally accurate private information in extraordinary detail that in no way could have been either guessed or obtained through suggestion or 'cold reading'. The second statement, about a letter he had recently received in connection with a mortgage application on a house that needed rewiring, was also correct, while the third statement, concerning a transfer to another police station (which Smith was aware of but thought unlikely would happen), came through a few days later.

A number of acquaintances of Jacqueline Poole who had come forward had already been interviewed by the Ruislip police and in total the number of potential suspects from this line of enquiry grew to around thirty people. One of these was twenty-two-year-old petty thief Anthony Ruark, a friend of a friend, who went by the nickname of 'Pokie'. He had been picked up in a local pub two days before and interviewed but had since been released, and at the time, was not considered to be a major suspect. Impressed by what they had experienced with Christine Holohan, Batters decided that Ruark should be re-interviewed and officers also visited his home and took away items of clothing for examination. During questioning, DS Lundy noticed scratches on Ruark's hands, which he claimed were due to a minor motorcycle accident; Ruark gave an alibi for his whereabouts on the evening of 11 February and he was later released for lack of evidence. The incident room at Ruislip was kept open for fifteen months but no new leads were forthcoming during that time and eventually it was closed. The Poole murder became a 'cold case' and for several years remained unsolved.

Seventeen years later, in 2000, during which time major breakthroughs in forensic DNA analysis had taken place, the case was reopened following information supplied by a police informant, specifically naming Jacqui Poole's killer. This person was not Anthony Ruark, but during the course of the re-examination, items collected from Ruark's house and kept in storage, including a pullover recovered from a dustbin, were checked against material recovered from the original crime scene using advanced Low Copy Number (LCN) technology that now enable forensic scientists to obtain matches from minute samples. Investigators found forty-six separate matches between the killer of Jacqueline Poole and Anthony Ruark, including clothing fibres, skin cells and body fluids, and he was quickly arrested. On 25 August 2001, an Old Bailey jury found Anthony 'Pokie' Ruark guilty of what Judge Kenneth Machin described as the 'brutal murder of a defenceless woman' and he was sentenced to life imprisonment. It was a conviction that has since been regarded as probably the best example of genuine psychic detection and one which prompted *Psychic News* to proclaim on its front page two months later, on 27 October 2001, 'Medium catches killer and proves life after death'. Had the 'classic work' of psychic detection been found at last?

Following Ruark's successful conviction, the Poole case was investigated by Guy Lyon Playfair and Montague Keen, two long-standing and highly respected members of the Society for Psychical Research. We have already encountered Playfair briefly in connection with the Enfield Poltergeist while Keen, formerly a journalist and farmer, was heavily involved in the late 1990s with what has become known as the 'Scole Experiment', the last great investigation of physical mediumship and its phenomena of the twentieth century[1]. Playfair and Keen collected as much material on the case as was available to them and also carried out tape-recorded interviews with both Tony Batters and Christine Holohan. The policeman had been impressed enough by his experiences to keep a personal file of information, including the notes taken during his original meeting with Holohan; he had also undertaken his own investigation in connection with the missing jewellery and had written an account of the psychic side of the case, which was published two months after the *Psychic News* article in the Police Federation journal, *Police*.

Batters had transcribed his original notes and collated the medium's impressions into a list totalling 125 specific statements about the murdered woman, the crime scene, as well as the name, appearance, method of entry and route taken by the killer that, apart from a handful of impressions which were unverifiable, all but one of which proved to be astonishingly accurate. Holohan had described the inside of Jacqui Poole's house exactly as the policeman had seen it during the extended time he was present at Lakeside Close on 11 February 1983, down to items such as a black address book, a letter and a medical prescription, and two coffee cups, one clean the other a quarter full of cold coffee, on the kitchen draining board. She had given names intimately connected with the life of Jacqueline Poole that could only, it seemed, have come from the dead woman herself: Betty (Poole's mother), Terry (one of her brothers whom she was particularly close to), Barbara Stone (a close friend, killed in a road accident two years before, who was not identified as such until 2001) and Sylvia (her boyfriend's mother); she also gave Poole's maiden name – Hunt – something that had not then been released to the public, and also described someone who lived over a newspaper shop that was later found to be her best friend, Gloria. While Batters was present at the crime scene he answered the telephone three times and the callers proved to be Betty, Gloria and Sylvia. Holohan, through her automatic writing, also gave the names Tony and 'Pokie', which were both connected with Jacqui Poole's killer, and 'Ickeham', a misspelt but almost identical version of Ickenham, the London suburb between Ruislip and Uxbridge where Ruark lived with his girlfriend. Her description of Jacqueline Poole's body including rings missing from her hands, as well as where and how she had been assaulted inside the house were also confirmed by the police investigation as being totally accurate. The one statement that was incorrect concerned the day of the murder: the medium said it had taken place sometime on Saturday rather than the day before.

Although circumstantial, Tony Batters also felt that the word 'garden' and the number '221' from the automatic writing were connected with the route the killer would have taken when making his escape from the murder house back to his own home, and where he may have temporarily hidden the stolen jewellery, which to date has never been recovered. This was Swakeleys Road, the only street on the route Ruark (who admitted in court to visiting Poole's house in Lakeside Close on the evening of the murder) had said he travelled on the way back to Uxbridge, which had house numbers that went up to 221. Interestingly, in the light of the words written down by Christine Holohan while in trance, the plot of what should have been number 221 (between number 219 and some higher numbers) had been replaced with a public garden accessible directly from the road. Batters had found (admittedly in 2001, eighteen years after the event) a hole covered with stones in the shrubbery next to the side wall of number 219 Swakeleys Road that could have been used to store the items while Ruark returned to his house to establish his alibi, later returning to collect the stash and move them to somewhere more secure prior to selling the jewellery on. However, this part of Batter's account is conjecture as the hole the policeman saw and photographed may not have existed in 1983, although it is conceivable that another suitable hiding place did exist in the same garden at that time and this was the impression that the medium was getting during her interview with Batters and Andy Smith.

Playfair and Keen cautiously published their findings in January 2004 as 'A Possibly Unique Case of Psychic Detection' in the *Journal* of the Society for Psychical Research. Unable to totally endorse the sensational claims of the *Psychic News* three years before, they were prepared to qualify the newspaper's original headline and conclude that it could at least be said that 'Medium provides key information that helps lead to the conviction of a murderer and is highly suggestive of discarnate survival'.

In the 1930s, American sociologist and psychical researcher Hornell Norris Hart (1888-1967) carried out extensive research into the phenomenon of apparitions and their relationship to the question of survival after death.

Hart, despite concluding that survival was valid, coined the term 'Super ESP' (sometimes called 'super-psi') as an alternative explanation for evidence obtained from mediums and psychics, that due to its accuracy appears to come from discarnate entities or spirits communicating from beyond the grave. Leaving aside the objections of the sceptics, who by their very nature dismiss out of hand any notion of supernormality where mediums and their phenomena are concerned, it is a counterhypothesis that, like similar non-survival-related concepts such as 'cosmic memory', creates a dilemma in psychical research, as it effectively divides investigators into two camps, survivalists and non-survivalists, by suggesting that all information provided by mediums such as Estelle Roberts, Gerard Croiset, Nella Jones and Christine Holohan, is obtained unconsciously by either tapping into the living memory of a person or people, or telepathically reading documents or records that exist somewhere in the world. Non-survivalists, although sympathetic to the existence of paranormality in the Poole case, would contend that all of the 125 statements provided by Christine Holohan were obtained in this way, either by her reading the minds of the investigating policemen, particularly DC Tony Batters who had spent a large amount of time at the crime scene, as well as Jacqui Poole's relations and friends. Playfair and Keen argue that for the mind reading explanation to be valid, Holohan must have not only been able to read three specific minds (Batters, Ruark and Poole) but, while doing so, select only the information that was relevant from each. 'The strongest argument against a super-psi explanation and in favour of a survivalist one,' they note, 'must surely be that a great deal of the information given by Holohan could only have come from a person who, at the time of communication, was unquestionably dead'.

In assessing the importance of the case as part of the history of paranormal crime investigation, the two researchers also make an important statement when, in the paper's concluding remarks, they note that, 'Common criticisms of cases of psychic detection are that they are self-reported, sometimes long after the event; they are not corroborated by the police; evidence is selected to focus on the hits (or lucky guesses) while suppressing numerous misses; and that sweeping or unspecified statements are made that could apply to anything . . . None of the above criticisms, however, can be justly applied to the Poole case, in which the evidence, much of it highly specific, was recorded within a few days of the murder by the first police officer to visit the crime scene . . . '

Criticisms of the importance of Christine Holohan's involvement in the Jacqui Poole murder and doubts on the genuineness of any paranormality displayed on her part have tended to follow the somewhat well-worn and familiar approach of CSICOP-inspired scepticism that we have encountered elsewhere. In an Internet article published in 2003[2], Tony Youens and Adrian Shaw (then a serving police detective) argue that it was possible for Holohan to have come by her information by normal non-paranormal means, although they acknowledge, somewhat graciously given the hard-line attitude that organised scepticism has taken in recent years, that just because something *is* possible it doesn't automatically mean that it did actually take place in that way. Youens and Shaw use a blanket dismissal of 'cold reading' as an explanation for the information obtained by Tony Batters during his interview with Holohan on 17 February 1983, and suggest that the medium was likely to have became aware of information concerning the crime and Jacqui Poole's background through speaking to people in the local area in the days immediately following police appeals for information, particularly in a number of pubs and shops in the part of Ruislip where she was then living. Youen's initial view of Holohan's involvement with Batters and Smith was that she was being used as a front to pass on information about a suspect (i.e. Anthony Ruark) by a local person who wished to remain anonymous. All of these explanations were robustly dismissed (in a letter to *The Skeptic* magazine) before his sudden death in 2004 by Montague Keen, who passed away only a few days after writing an afterword for Christine Holohan's autobiography.

The case of Jacqueline Poole and Christine Holohan is an important one, not only as perhaps the nearest we have got to date to a British, and perhaps even an international 'classic work' of psychic detection, but also for its farther reaching implications. In his contribution to *A Voice from the Grave*, Keen notes that 'for a world that is still locked within the narrow walls of a philosophy that denies the existence of consciousness, that sees nothing in life beyond mortal flesh and blood, that discerns neither purpose nor plan behind our existence, and looks upon the soul as a figment of man's hopes rather than a demonstrable fact, the traumatic communication which Holohan experienced immediately after the brutal murder of Jacqueline Poole is as profound and important contribution to the repudiation of that philosophy as any piece of evidence of modern times'. For a dedicated and respected psychical researcher, it would also seem a fitting epitaph . . .

NOTES

1. See *The Scole Report* by Montague Keen, Arthur Ellison & David Fontana, published in the *Proceedings* of the Society for Psychical Research, Vol.58, Pt.220, November 1999; also Robin Foy's *Witnessing the Impossible* (Torcal Publications, Diss, Norfolk, 2008) and *The Scole Experiment* (Piatkus, London, 1999) by Grant and Jane Solomon.
2. 'Did a Medium Identify a Murderer?' (Updated 14 October 2006). Retrieved from www.tonyyouens.com on 11 August 2011.

CHAPTER 14

FALL OF THE HOUSE OF DEATH

BRADY AND HINDLEY, 1985

In 1971, American writer Richard Matheson, known for his apocalyptic vampire novel *I Am Legend* (1954), created the archetypal haunted house with the publication of his supernatural thriller *Hell House*, a grim tale of psychics and investigating scientists forming an uneasy alliance in order to uncover the secrets of life after death. Matheson drew on his lifelong interest in the paranormal as well as the literature of psychical research to populate his 'Mount Everest of haunted houses' with chillingly authentic phenomena including apparitions, ectoplasmic materialisations, psychic attacks and telekinesis; and the author also provided the screenplay for director John Hough's special-effects filled cinema version, which was made two years later. Four years after *The Legend of Hell House* appeared in movie theatres, it seemed as though Richard Matheson had somehow been the literary prophet of future events and that his fictional Belasco Mansion had become a terrible reality. In 1977, Jay Anson published *The Amityville Horror*, seemingly a carbon-copy of Matheson's earlier work: the only exception being that Anson's book was presented as non-fiction; everything it contained was said to be true, with the result that it quickly became known as one of 'the most sensational and controversial cases of alleged diabolical presence' ever recorded.

'High Hopes' was a large Dutch-style colonial house at 112 Ocean Avenue in the suburb of Amityville, Long Island, New York. On the night of 13 November 1974, Ronald 'Butch' DeFeo, the twenty-two-year-old son of a wealthy local motor dealer, drugged and shot to death both his parents, Ronald DeFeo Senior and Louise DeFeo, together with his two sisters, eighteen-year-old Dawn and thirteen-year-old Allison, plus his two brothers,

Mark and John, aged twelve and seven respectively. 'Butch' DeFeo initially told police the slaughter was a contract killing, claiming his father had links with the New York underworld, but it soon became clear under intense questioning that DeFeo, an unhappy youth who had taken to drug-addiction, hated his father and had told his family on one occasion that unless he left home he would end up killing them all. DeFeo claimed insanity at his trial, telling the court that when he held the Marlin 35 rifle in his hands he became God and had murdered in self-defence. He was found guilty and given twenty-five years to life on each of the six counts of murder. 'High Hopes' was later refurbished and put up for sale but, unsurprisingly, remained on the market for a year. Eventually, attracted by the low asking price – $80,000 for a substantial six-bedroom house with large grounds, a swimming pool and a boathouse on the water – it was bought by George Lutz, a self-employed construction surveyor and his wife Kathleen. The Lutzes were undaunted by its association with the recent killings and, realising they had picked up a bargain, moved into the house with their three children on 18 December 1975. They stayed a month, and in that time succeeded in laying down the foundations of a modern horror phenomenon that has excited controversy and speculation for over thirty-five years.

In Jay Anson's book, compiled by the author from a series of telephone interviews with both George and Kathy Lutz – Anson, a film and television scriptwriter, never visited the house due to ill health – the Ocean Avenue mansion is portrayed as a literal gateway to Hell populated by an army of violent and terrifying supernatural creatures. The Lutzes claimed to have encountered the apparitions of hooded monk-like figures and a demonic pig with fiery red eyes, fought off unnatural clouds of flies which filled the children's playroom; and experienced rancid smells, debilitating extremes of heat and cold, as well as copious quantities of green slime which cascaded down the main staircase. George Lutz reported seeing his wife levitate into the air on several occasions and at one point transform into the figure of a ninety-year-old woman. Lutz himself felt he was beginning to identify more and more with Ronald DeFeo and imagined he was gradually taking on the killer's physical characteristics.

The Amityville Horror became a best-seller and, like Matheson's *Hell House*, received cinema treatment two years later. This success spawned sequel books and a movie franchise which went a long way to firmly cementing the possessed-house concept in the public consciousness throughout the 1980s and beyond. Unsurprisingly, the allegedly true nature of the case became the target of sceptical criticism almost from the outset. A number of psychical investigators who spent time examining both the Lutzes' testimony and Jay

Anson's presentation of the 'facts' came to the conclusion that there was little if any evidence for genuine paranormal activity at 'High Hopes', findings which were supported by the testimony of Jim and Barbara Cromarty, who had bought the house from George and Kathy Lutz and had reported no strange or unusual happenings while living there. Stephan Kaplan of the Parapsychology Institute of America felt that the story of the haunting was 'mostly fiction' while Karlis Osis, a noted researcher from the American Society for Psychical Research, was also disinclined to credit the happenings as genuine phenomena. A major blow to the case's credibility came from a 1979 local radio interview with Ronald DeFeo's lawyer, William Weber, who claimed that the entire 'horror' was an organised hoax inspired by a drawn-out and wine-fuelled conversation he had had with the Lutzes in the kitchen of their 'haunted house' three years before. Weber eventually sued George and Kathy Lutz for a share of the profits from both Anson's book and *The Amityville Horror* film, claiming that they had reneged on their deal with him to manufacture the haunting and approached the scriptwriter behind his back. This resulted in a countersuit from the Lutzes to reaffirm the reality of their paranormal experiences and, true to the country's rampant litigation culture, Jim and Barbara Cromarty also went to court to sue both the Lutzes and Jay Anson's publisher, Prentice-Hall, for $1.1m damages due to the stress caused by constant streams of sensation seekers and tourists standing outside their house at all hours of the day and night. They were successful and received an unspecified amount, as was Father Ralph Pecararo (known as 'Father Mancuso' in Anson's book and 'Father Delaney' in the film), who sued the Lutzes and received an out-of-court settlement for invasion of privacy and distortion of events – 'Mancuso' was said to have heard a voice commanding him to leave the house while present there alone to bless the building, and later to have suffered sickness and mental trauma due to his violent psychic experiences; Pecararo flatly denied ever entering 'High Hopes' and had only spoken to the Lutzes over the telephone.

Despite the controversy, multiple lawsuits, the hoaxing and sensationalism, the Amityville Horror has become the best-known example of a series of reported paranormal experiences centred around a genuine (and in this case notorious) crime scene; for want of a better description, a 'murder house haunting'. The alleged diabolical nature of the 'possessed' building is the one aspect that sets it apart from many cases, but there are others. In his paranormal gazetteer *Our Haunted Kingdom* (1973), author and psychical researcher Andrew Green (1927-2004) describes his own personal experiences at a house in West London with a ghastly history of suicide and murder. Ellerslie Tower, a three-storey Victorian building constructed in

1883 and located at 16 Montpelier Road in Ealing, was named after the 70 foot-high brick structure incorporated into its design. In 1877, a twelve-year-old girl named Anne Hinchfield became the house's first 'victim' when she threw herself from the top of the tower into the garden below. In the years that followed, if Green's account is to be believed, eighteen more people met their deaths in the same way. In 1934, a nursemaid threw the child she was caring for from the top of the tower and became the final fatality by following the infant to her death.

Andrew Green was born in Ealing in 1927. He later reported that his mother, then a nurse, attended the scene of the double tragedy at Montpelier Road and, while waiting in the garden for a police doctor to finish his examination, witnessed footprints appearing across the lawn in the wet grass in front of her. During wartime in 1944, Green visited Ellerslie Tower with his father, an acting air-raid warden. The house, known locally for its sinister history, had stood empty for the previous ten years, but had recently been the subject of a Government requisition order and was then being used as a store for furniture salvaged from bombed-out buildings. Exploring the house and its grounds, Green was drawn to the tall tower and climbed to the very top. There he was overcome by a force or compulsion that impelled him to step over the edge of the parapet, convinced that the ground was only a few inches away. Luckily for Andrew Green, his father, who unknown to him had followed him up the stairs, appeared and quickly pulled his son back from the edge. The evidence for the haunting of 16 Montpelier Road is made particularly convincing by a photograph that Green took at the time of his visit from a vantage point in the garden at the rear of the house. When the photograph of the back of the building was developed it showed what appears to be the eerie figure of a young woman, possibly one of the many suicides, glancing wistfully out of a first-floor window. Green was adamant that the house was empty and they had met no one inside during the time he and his father were there. Workmen who had previously brought furniture into the house had reported hearing footsteps and experienced doors opening and closing in rooms known to be empty at the time; there was also a strange 'atmosphere' and an unusual smell in one part of the building. Reports of similar phenomena were reported regularly in the post-war years after the house had been split into flats. Several years after his own experience, Green met and talked with a former employee who had worked as a maid at Ellerslie Tower as a young woman. From her reminiscences it seems likely that Black Magic rituals were carried out regularly in the tower, at least during the time that she was living there. The house was demolished in 1971 and a modern block of flats, Elgin Court, now occupies the site.

Number 16 Montpelier Road with its imposing tower clearly looked like the traditional haunted house, but it is often the suburban ordinariness of buildings such as the Enfield home of the Hodgson family and 112 Ocean Avenue, Amityville, that adds to the bizarre unreality of many reported paranormal experiences. This is a point of fact with the building at the centre of another murder house haunting, one that could almost be considered as the British 'Amityville Horror'...

At around twenty to nine on the morning of 7 October 1965, a police superintendant dressed in the overalls of a baker's roundsman knocked on the door of 16 Wardle Brook Avenue in Hattersely, on the outskirts of Manchester. When the door was opened by a blonde-haired woman he pushed his way inside, quickly followed by another officer. The woman identified herself as twenty-four-year-old Myra Hindley; on a divan bed in the living room they found twenty-eight-year-old Ian Brady, dressed only in a vest, writing a sick-note to his employer. The police told the couple there had been reports of a disturbance at the house the night before and that they intended to carry out a search of the premises. Upstairs, one of the bedroom doors was found to be locked and, when asked to open it, Hindley stonewalled by saying she had left the key at work. When one of the officers said he would drive her there to get it she relented and unlocked the door. Inside they found the body of a young man – seventeen-year-old Edward Evans – trussed up with rope and wrapped in a polythene sheet; he had been repeatedly battered about the head and strangled with a length of flex. Brady was arrested, after which the police carried out an intensive search of the house. Inside the spine of a prayer book – Hindley was a convert to Catholicism – were found two tickets which were traced to a pair of suitcases at the left luggage office at Manchester Central Station. Inside, the police recovered an assortment of items that included wigs, coshes, paperwork, pornographic photographs and two reel-to-reel tape recordings. A week after Brady's arrest, Myra Hindley was also taken into custody. It was the beginning of a grim unravelling of past events that, the following year, would stun the country and send shock waves around the world. Even today, during which time an intervening forty-plus years of seemingly perpetually increasing violence has made the reporting of shocking acts of murder commonplace, the Moors Murders remain one of the darkest and most despised chapters in British criminal history.

Ian Brady, born Ian Duncan Stewart in pre-war Glasgow in 1938, was the bastard son of a Scottish waitress who never knew his father. He grew up in the Gorbals, a rough slum district. In 1950, his mother moved to Manchester, where she remarried, but Brady remained in Scotland, eventually joining her after a period of four years, during which time he was put on probation several times for a range of offences including burglary and stealing. A court order had forced the reunion with his mother but he continued to offend and, shortly after his eighteenth birthday, was sent to Borstal for two years for theft. Although Brady was a thug, he was also clever and throughout his teenage years and on into his early twenties exhibited an intellectual quest that was designed to support and reinforce both his penchant for violence and lawlessness, as well as a hatred for the people around him who, he collectively considered, were totally worthless when compared to himself. He formed a cult-worship for Nazism and collected books on Hitler, Heinrich Himmler and the Nuremberg war crimes. Brady also immersed himself in the literature of the Marquis de Sade, compiling a library of his writings, as well as books on sex crime, torture and perversions. By early 1961, when he was working as an office clerk for Millwards, a chemical supply company based in West Gorton, Manchester, he had taught himself German in order to read *Mein Kampf* in the original edition, something he did at his desk during lunch breaks. It was at Millwards that Brady met a new typist, Myra Hindley, then aged nineteen. They eventually went out on a date (to the cinema to see the documentary film *Trial at Nuremberg*) after which Brady accompanied Hindley back to her grandmother's house where, with the old lady asleep upstairs, he took her virginity on the front room sofa. Brady quickly began an 'education' into his world of sadism, Nazism and pornography, to which Hindley proved a willing disciple. Like an English 'Bonnie and Clyde', they planned bank robberies and talked of murder, all of which were justified as part of their anti-establishment existence. The armed raids never took place but the killings did, with, as Donald Seaman and Colin Wilson have described, 'the young and unsuspecting as their prey'.

By the time of their arrest in October 1965, Brady and Hindley had carried out five murders. On 12 July 1963, Hindley enticed sixteen-year-old Pauline Reade of Wiles Street, Gorton, whom she lived close to and knew by sight, into her car on the pretence of looking for a lost glove on nearby Saddleworth Moor. Brady was waiting at a pre-arranged location, where the teenager was killed and buried in a shallow grave; this would not be found until twenty-four years later, in August 1987. On 23 November 1963, four months after their first killing, cruising in Hindley's car in Ashton-under-Lyne, they offered a lift to twelve-year-old John Kilbride, who was waiting to catch a bus, in return for helping them to move some boxes. Like Pauline Reade, he was taken to Saddleworth Moor, where he was sexually abused by Brady before being murdered. Soon after Brady photographed Hindley, holding her pet dog, kneeling on Kilbride's grave. The following year, just after eight o'clock on the evening of 16 June 1964, Keith Bennett disappeared in the Longsight district of Manchester while walking alone to his grandmother's house. As with

Pauline Reade, it would not be until 1986 that Myra Hindley would admit to killing the twelve-year-old schoolboy, whose grave has never been found.

Three months after the abduction and murder of Keith Bennett, in September 1964, Brady and Hindley moved into Hindley's grandmother's newly-built council house at Wardle Brook Avenue in Hattersley. Number sixteen, a two-storey two-bedroomed end of terrace property, occupied an elevated site and was overlooked by surrounding houses. It was there that ten-year-old Lesley Ann Downey was taken on Boxing Day the same year. The brutal sexual assault she underwent was documented in the photographs later recovered from the suitcases at Manchester Central Station and Hindley made the tape recordings found at the same time of the child begging for her life before Brady strangled her to death. The horror felt by those present at the Assize Court in Chester when the recording was played at Brady and Hindley's trial in April 1966 reverberated across the country and is easily the most shocking piece of evidence to be presented in a British courtroom.

The second murder to take place at the house in Wardle Brook Avenue – the killing of Edward Evans the day before Brady's arrest – was another planned attack, a display of power that formed the culmination of the couple's grooming of Hindley's seventeen-year-old brother-in-law, David Smith, into their anarchic and deadly lifestyle. Brady had taken Smith to Saddleworth Moor where, as they practiced pistol shooting as a precursor for armed robbery, he had boasted about having killed several times before. Early in October 1965, Brady had visited a gay club in Manchester, where he had struck up a friendship with teenage homosexual Edward Evans. Evans was lured back to Wardle Brook Avenue while Hindley went and fetched her sister's husband on the pretence that her boyfriend wanted to give him some miniature wine bottles as a present. When Smith walked into the front room he witnessed Brady reigning blows on the screaming and defenceless youth with an axe. Evans fought for his life and Brady was forced to complete his 'demonstration murder' by smothering him with a cushion and, when that proved ineffective, using strangulation. While Hindley placated her grandmother, who had been woken up by Evans' screams, Brady and Smith concealed the body in Hindley's bedroom, after which all three cleaned up the living room. Smith, promising to return the next day with a pram that they could use to move Evans' body into Hindley's car, left the house in the early hours of the morning and went home. There he blurted out the entire episode to Hindley's sister and the terrified couple went to a public telephone box to call the police. Seven months later, on 6 May 1966, Ian Brady and Myra Hindley were found guilty of the murders of Lesley Ann Downey, John Kilbride and Edward Evans and sentenced to life imprisonment.

By 1987, thirty years after the Moors Murders had come to an end, 16 Wardle Brook Avenue was an empty boarded-up shell. Shunned and locally reviled, it was demolished the same year, the bricks and rubble being carted away and crushed to deter souvenir hunters. In the preceding decades, a succession of residents had claimed, both privately and publicly, that the former home of Ian Brady and Myra Hindley was a haunted house in which the horror of the notorious couple's shocking crimes lived on. There were stories of an exorcism being carried out by a local priest at the request of one tenant, while another petitioned the local authority to have the house demolished, several years before it was actually pulled down. In March 1985, the experiences of the last occupant of number 16, forty-year-old Brian Dunne and his family, were reported in the national press, and gave an insight into the phenomena alleged to have taken place there, all of which were inextricably linked with the brutal killings of the 1960s[1]. Dunne, together with his thirty-one-year-old wife Margaret and their three children, three-year-old Joseph, Ann Marie aged two and eight-month-old Brian, all originally from Dublin, moved into Wardle Brook Avenue unaware of its unenviable association. They later claimed to have all experienced a number of strange and inexplicable happenings: loud banging noises and the sound of smashing furniture; the unnerving sound of children's screams and crying, as well as the outline of a human body impressed on the counterpane of a newly-made bed. The house, unlike the adjoining properties in the same terrace, was mysteriously plagued with damp that representatives from the local housing department could not explain. 'Damp just runs down the walls. The council have been round but can't stop it,' Dunne told newspapermen. 'The adjoining houses aren't like it. It is as if this one is crying.'

Claims for ghosts and paranormal activity at Wardle Brook Avenue were always dismissed or sidestepped by Manchester City Council, who felt it was not in the interests of their tenants to discuss such matters. To my knowledge no investigation by psychical researchers was ever undertaken in the house, with the result that practically all of the claims for a haunting cannot be substantiated. During the time that Brian Dunne was living there, he entered into a brief correspondence with Richard Lee-Van den Daele, a paranormal researcher from Shipley in Yorkshire, who also carried out an examination of the Borley haunting in the 1980s. Dunne confirmed a number of his experiences but later declined to talk about the haunting. Not long after, the Dunnes were re-housed and the 'house of death' was reduced to rubble. Today nothing remains except a grassed area that is easily overlooked.

Sceptics would argue that the haunting of Wardle Brook Avenue owes much to the familiar 'possessed house' blueprint of the Amityville case, which by the early 1980s was extremely well known, and tenants unhappy with living at an address with such a grim and unpleasant past would be likely to exploit stories of ghostly experiences, real or otherwise, as leverage in a case for being assigned accommodation elsewhere. It was a fact that Brian and Margaret Dunne with their three children plus a fourth on the horizon – Mrs Dunne was expecting at the time her husband was interviewed by the press – were all living in a cramped two-bedroom house clearly too small for their needs. However, it would be subjective and too casual to dismiss the Dunnes' claims out of hand without a fuller examination of the facts, which now is not possible.

Writing in his *The Haunted House Handbook* (1978), American psychical researcher D. Scott Rogo reinforces what is still the current state of knowledge regarding haunted buildings – that despite years of study we do not know what makes a house haunted. 'There are so many types of hauntings – human ghosts, animal hauntings, evil presences, and so on – that no one working in parapsychology has of yet ever come up with . . . what underlying force causes a house to become haunted', but he goes on to note: 'To be sure, there *are* [Rogo's italics] cases on record in which houses have become haunted after having been the scene of some violence or tragedy. And the ghosts which appear in these places very often resemble the unfortunate victims of these melodramas.' Rogo, a respected and prolific writer and researcher on paranormal subjects, himself was the victim of such an incident – on 14 August 1990 he was found stabbed to death in his Los Angeles home after a robbery.

If, then, the 'mental imprint'-type haunting mentioned before *can* be created by an outburst of psychic or electrical energy resulting from a powerful outburst of emotion, to become locked inside either the physical structure or enclosed environment of a building, and is then able to either replay or manifest itself in some way at future times, it would seem that no more suitable building in England could possibly be found than the house that once stood on the former plot of number 16 Wardle Brook Avenue . . .

NOTE

1. 'Terror in the house of death', *Daily Express*, 9 March 1985.

CHAPTER 15

THE EVIL WITHIN

MUHAMMAD BASHIR, 1991

In the first part of his monumental two-volume history of mankind *The Curse of Ignorance* (1947), written during the dark days of the Second World War in the imposing setting of Rockingham Castle, Scottish businessman, writer and philosopher J. Arthur Findlay (1883-1964) makes a sweeping but at the same time intuitive statement when he says that 'All religions are based on psychic phenomena, but are encrusted with theological error, which sooner or later must be dismissed as the drapings of an age of ignorance'. Findlay became convinced as to the reality of life after death after attending séances in Glasgow with the direct-voice medium John Campbell Sloan (1869-1951) in the years immediately following the Great War, experiences which were later reinforced in February 1936 when, at the headquarters of the London Spiritualist Alliance, he sat with clairvoyant and trumpet medium Agnes Abbott (1885-1942), who brought him convincing proof of the survival of his mother. Findlay ultimately bequeathed his estate, Stanstead Hall, to the Spiritualists' National Union as a teaching college for mediumship and psychic subjects on the understanding that his extensive series of books on Spiritualism and survival, including the movement's first real bestseller *On the Edge of the Etheric* (1931), remained in print for perpetuity.

Other Spiritualist writers and thinkers have followed Arthur Findlay's reasoning behind the origins of organised religious beliefs and practices. Maurice Barbanell, who we have already met in connection with the mediumship of Estelle Roberts, writing in *This is Spiritualism* in 1959, described the story of revealed religion as 'one that shows the interaction of spirit and matter'. 'The power of the spirit has always been at work,'

Barbanell notes, 'adapting itself, through the centuries, to the needs, understanding and capacity of its recipients.' He continues:

> The Bible, like many other sacred books, is a testament to spirit activity. Whether many of its characters are called prophets, seers or mediums makes no difference. They were all the instruments of a higher power which, as it flowed through human channels, produced signs and wonders which were wrongly regarded as miracles.

Aspects of the ministry of Jesus have been described in recent times in terms of the paranormal phenomena familiar to and investigated by, as Professor Archie Roy has described them, 'hard-headed, initially sceptical but brilliant scientists, psychologists and others', for over 100 years since the founding of organised paranormal study: these include materialisation, psychic healing, telepathy, precognition and psychokinesis, while American parapsychologist Arthur S. Berger has described Jesus of Nazareth as 'an extraordinary noted witness [i.e. an outstanding and reliable historical figure] whose testimony in support of the paranormal should be considered'. In her book *Séances With God* (2002), an historical exploration of the eschatological (i.e. after-death) information provided by global mediumship over the course of thousands of years and its relationship with international religions and cultures, Dr Jacqueline Jones-Hunt follows in exhaustive detail in Findlay's footsteps, examining from the standpoint of the findings of psychical research (a discipline that Hungarian-born writer Paul Tabori described, when writing about the life and work of Sir Oliver Lodge, as 'the most important (and perhaps the only possible) way to reconcile science and faith') world faiths including Shamanism, Hinduism, Buddhism, Judaism, Christianity and Islam.

It is with the last of these great religions that we are briefly concerned with here. The psychic world of Islam represents a fascinating and compelling area of study as yet little explored by Western psychical researchers. As with the ministry of Jesus of Nazareth, many aspects of the life of Muhammad, who founded the religion of Islam in the seventh century AD, can be considered in the language of modern parapsychology, i.e. prophethood as mediumship, channelling, automatic writing, out-of-body experiences and altered states of consciousness, while a study of the lives of the Sufi shaykhs and mystics reveals a wealth of paranormal phenomena that encompasses remote viewing, bilocation (the ability to be in two places at once), mind over matter and psychic healing. The revelation of the Qur'an to Muhammad can be looked upon as spirit communication through automatic writing (the favoured interpretation of commentators such as Arthur Findlay and

Dr Jones-Hunt) and other noted Muslims have demonstrated unique and seemingly inexplicable paranormal abilities. Hazrat Ibn al-'Arabi (d.1240), the noted Sufi theologian and metaphysician (often called the 'Shaykh Al-Akbar' or 'greatest teacher') of some eight centuries ago, claimed to have visited the moon and compiled written accounts of his experiences, while as a six-year-old child another Islamic saint, the Persian mystic Hazrat Mawlānā Rūmī (d.1273), is said to have jumped into the air and dematerialised, his spectacular vanishing, apparently in front of his playmates, lasting a whole afternoon. Nearer to our own times, the American Shaykh Moinuddin Chishti, a former Fulbright scholar, writing in his *The Book of Sufi Healing* (1991) describes an incident that took place in his presence while visiting a Sufi order in northern Afghanistan. During a ceremony of dhikr (described as 'the touchstone of all mystical practices' in Islam), which had been carried out every Thursday evening on the same site for an unbroken period of 1,200 years, Chishti heard 'a loud grinding and whooshing sound' that filled the entire room and saw a cleft appear in the far wall which almost instantly sealed itself, a collective hallucination witnessed by over forty people and which, according to the shaykh who was leading the meeting, had allowed 'pious souls' to enter the building to take part in the dhikr. In the West, other phenomena with its origins in devout religious belief and practice include the levitations of the seventeenth-century Franciscan monk St Joseph of Copertino and the twentieth-century stigmata of Teresa Neumann.

One aspect of Muslim belief for which the Qur'an gives examples and explanations is the existence of *jinn*, described as invisible beings created from 'smokeless flame' which, together with angels, inhabit the earth with mankind; what appears at first glance to be an interpretation in religious language of forces, both for good and evil, in the universe. Western Sufi teacher Shaykh Fadhlalla Haeri has commented (in his *The Elements of Islam* (1993)) that, 'Made of light, angels have no choice but to follow their prescribed patterning, whereas *jinn*, who are made of fire and air, reflect their elemental volatility in virtuous or evil behaviour'. For those Muslim persons brought up on a literal or simplistic interpretation of the Qur'an and Islamic traditions (known as hadiths), with its concept of a final Day of Judgement and a Balance of souls for the dead, the *jinn* have become a blanket explanation for most types of reported paranormal phenomena, including ghosts and apparitions, poltergeists, hauntings and, most importantly, for the subject which concerns us here: diabolical human possession. This view is supported by the fact that practically the only book to appear in the English language in recent years that addresses the subject, Hasan Moiz Ansari's *Islam and the Paranormal* (2006), despite the author's admission of a lifelong interest in the occult and psychical subjects, applies a literal Qur'anic approach, and as such does not look beyond assigning the origins of all reported supernormal phenomena to the workings of the *jinn*.

As noted by Haeri and most other Islamic commentators, *jinn* are regarded in most cases to be mischievous, evil and threatening entities against which the Qur'an provides remedies and suitable protection. However, a closer examination of reports from haunted houses and experiences of apparitions shows that one single explanation does not fit all of the facts and provide, for want of a better description, a general theory of the paranormal. We have already briefly discussed the 'atmospheric photograph' or 'stone tape' theory as applied to reported encounters with apparitions and phantom figures. To this can be added other forms or 'types' of ghost, each of which appear to suggest different explanations for their origins: apparitions of the living (hallucinations of persons known to be alive and well at the time of the experience), death bed visions, crisis ghosts (visions of persons either at the point or moment of death or involved in some tremendous emotional or physical upheaval), cyclical hauntings (a recurring form of the mental imprint ghost), as well as apparitions that impart information in such a way that is highly suggestive of some form of survival after death, i.e. an after-life apparition. In this respect, with such a clear diversity of reported phenomena, the Islamic or Qur'anic *jinn* appears to be more closely related to the concept of an elemental spirit or discarnate non-human intelligence as concluded by researchers such as Guy Playfair and Colin Wilson to be behind such modern poltergeist hauntings as Enfield, Pontefract and Cardiff. The evil side noted by Shaykh Haeri is amply demonstrated in all three of these well attested cases.

Writing about the use of exorcism on victims of poltergeist activity in *The Unexplained* magazine in the early 1980s, Andrew Green, who we have already briefly encountered in connection with the Ealing murder house haunting, commented that only around two per cent of poltergeist cases involved genuine inexplicable phenomena, and he questioned the need for any kind of organised exorcism ceremony to take place 'even in cases where the effects themselves [i.e. poltergeist phenomena] may be explicable in emotional terms, and even regardless of the individual's religious commitment'. 'For some atheists,' Green notes, 'the rite may be comforting and effective; for some believers, who have unwittingly engaged fanatics or incompetents to perform the rite, the results can be as terrifying as the work of the "demon" itself'. Few cases of Islamic exorcism involving the alleged 'possession' of men and women by *jinn* and evil spirits in Muslim countries such as Malaysia, Egypt and rural Pakistan are reported in the Western media, although they undoubtedly take place on a regular basis and have done so for countless years, in the same way that 'casting out the devils' has been a cornerstone since the earliest days of Christianity. However, a case from the north of England in the early 1990s that made newspaper headlines goes a long way to proving that Green's viewpoint is correct.

During the spring of 1991, Muhammad Bashir, a machine operator in his mid-thirties from Coppice in Oldham, Lancashire, together with his wife, both originally from Pakistan, became increasingly concerned about the well-being of their daughter, twenty-year-old Kousar Bashir. An attractive young woman, over a period of months she had become increasingly withdrawn and depressive, a condition for which initially her parents, both devout Muslims, were unable to offer any explanation. When Kousar failed a driving test for which she had been working for some length of time, her depression grew to the point that her parents considered her behaviour as totally unnatural and turned to their local religious community for help. The cleric or imam from the Bashir's nearby mosque, sixty-three-year-old Muhammad Nurani Sayeed, quickly diagnosed that Kousar Bashir had become possessed by a *jinn* which was revealing its presence through the twenty-year-old's strange and unnatural behaviour. The Bashirs took recourse initially to the Qur'an but when the regular recitation of prescribed passages had little or no effect, they again consulted Imam Sayeed, who felt that there was little choice but to perform an exorcism ceremony to rid Kousar of the unwanted presence. Unable to carry out the ritual himself, Nurani Sayeed advised Mr and Mrs Bashir that an experienced exorcist was needed and recommended them to hire Muhammad Bashir (no family relation), an experienced Islamic teacher in his early sixties. Warned that the exorcism could be a long, drawn-out process, the Bashirs paid a fee of £200 and in June 1991, Imam Muhammad Bashir, together with Nurani Sayeed acting as his assistant, arrived at the family home in Oldham to drive out the possessing *jinn*. It was to prove the beginning of what was later described as a week-long 'orgy of violence' with ultimately tragic consequences.

The exorcist expertly drew a chalk circle on the floor of the Bashir's house in which, for the next eight days, Kousar Bashir was imprisoned, deprived of both food and sleep. Bashir's initial approach was to literally smoke out the *jinn* using burning mustard oil, the fumes from which the young woman was made to inhale, as well as being regularly force fed with a cocktail of chilli powder. When it became plain to the two men that the invading entity was not giving up its hold, the screaming and crying woman was systematically beaten with a walking stick, a glass ashtray and Bashir's fists. All the time her distraught parents were assured that it was the *jinn* which was protesting and crying, not their daughter, and that in order to defeat the supernatural creature, extreme measures were necessary. When police and an ambulance team were eventually called to the house they found Kousar Bashir's bruised and bloody body lying within the same chalk circle – she had been beaten to death. A post-mortem revealed a horrific catalogue of violent physical abuse including cuts and extensive bruising to the young woman's head, arms and legs, slashes between her breasts, a fractured sternum and sixteen broken ribs, one of which had penetrated through into a lung and resulted in fatal internal haemorrhaging. Nurani Sayeed and Muhammad Bashir were quickly arrested and charged with murder. At Manchester Crown Court in April 1992, Imam Bashir was found guilty and sentenced to life imprisonment; Sayeed was given five years for plotting to cause grievous bodily harm. The Manchester jury were unimpressed with the defence case citing the two cleric's genuine belief in the existence of supernatural forces inhabiting the body of the young and troubled twenty-year-old Asian woman, against which the two 'holy men' had resorted to such outrageous violence. That the two priests had continually addressed the *jinn* as 'John Wayne' during the course of the week-long ritual and under this name had repeatedly demanded the 'entity' to leave the body of Kousar Bashir, no doubt exemplified and reinforced a grotesque and medieval thinking that belonged to the pages of history rather than the modern world of fax machines, computing and international communication.

The grim events of 1991 were to cast long shadows over the Bashir family and provide a tragic postscript to an already unhappy story. In the years following his daughter's death, Muhammad Bashir lived what would seem a haunted life plagued with depression, heavy drinking and mobility problems. In March 2005, his wife was admitted to the Royal Oldham Hospital suffering from leukaemia, where she died the following month. A few days later, Bashir invited some female relatives, including his younger sister, to his St Thomas Street North home, where they read traditional prayers for the dead woman and recited passages from the Qur'an. Unbeknown to the family, earlier in the morning Bashir had asked some children to fill up a nine-litre jerry can of petrol. Around half past three in the afternoon of 28 April, emergency services attending a call to the house found Muhammad Bashir with almost 100 per cent burns to his body in the back garden, as well as the half-empty petrol can and a cigarette lighter. He was taken to Oldham hospital and died later the same day, admitting to dousing himself with the fuel and lighting it. At an inquest the following year it was ruled that Bashir had taken his own life while in a state of depression, a tragedy that had its routes in the events that had taken place fourteen years before.

In modern times the Bashir case is not without precedent where other religious faiths are concerned. In 1966, a young Swiss girl who claimed to be possessed by a devil was beaten to death during an exorcism ceremony, while ten years later, in July 1976, the parents of Annaliese Michel, together with two local priests, were all found guilty of causing 'death by negligence' after the German girl's emaciated body was discovered dead from a circulatory disease after she had been entrusted into the priests' care to rid her of an evil spirit. In 1991, the same year that Kousar Bashir was confined within the chalk circle in Oldham, the American ABC television network broadcast a live exorcism of a young Catholic girl who had been receiving medical treatment for a psychiatric condition. An audience expecting to see *Exorcist*-style effects were disappointed and, after the ceremony had been concluded, the girl continued to receive medical counselling, the exorcism having proved ineffective. It would seem that in this respect she was one of the lucky ones. The case of Kousar Bashir perhaps defines more aptly than anything that we have looked at during the course of this book the reality of true crime and the paranormal.

CHAPTER 16

THE HAUNTING MURDERERS

1910-PRESENT

A glance through the published literature of hauntings and haunted places, such as London newspaperman Jack Hallam's 1977 paranormal dictionary *The Ghosts' Who's Who*, quickly shows that where crime-related legends and stories – as well as well-documented cases involving eyewitness accounts and reliable testimony – that feature some form of supernormal phenomena or haunting are concerned, it is most often the ghost of the unfortunate victim rather than the perpetrator that predominates. As the ghostly or psychic phenomena described in the featured cases in this book follow this trend and have mostly concerned the victims of murder, I felt our survey might end with a brief discussion of some reported ghosts and hauntings associated specifically with the murderers themselves. For this I have limited the selection to four noted, and for the criminologist as well as the psychical researcher, interesting cases from the twentieth century.

Before it was reduced to rubble by enemy bombing during the Second World War, number 39 Hilldrop Crescent in London's Kentish Town was the most noted murder house in the capital. It was there at the beginning of February 1910 that American-born Hawley Harvey 'Peter' Crippen, a graduate of the Hospital College of Cleveland, Ohio, committed the wife murder that has made him one of the most infamous names in the annals of British crime. His story is well known but remains a fascinating one. Crippen had arrived in England in 1900 but, when his qualifications were not recognised for him to practice medicine; he was forced to take a lesser career working for the Munyon Patent Medicine Company, while his wife took in paying guests. Mrs Crippen, whose real name was Kunigunde Mackamotzki, an aspiring but unsuccessful stage artist, went under a number of aliases including Cora Turner and Belle Elmore. She was a forceful, dominant woman who ruled the Crippens' home at Hilldrop Crescent with a firm hand. Her seemingly mild-mannered husband did much of the housework and, perhaps unsurprisingly, eventually elevated his secretary, twenty-seven-year-old Ethel Le Neve, to the status of mistress.

Mrs Crippen, who was treasurer of the Music Hall Ladies Guild, was last seen alive on 31 January 1910, when she and her husband invited two retired stage performers, Mr and Mrs Martinetti, to dinner. Two days later, the Ladies Guild received Cora Crippen's resignation – due to her need to return to American to nurse a sick relative – and Dr Crippen quickly moved Ethel Le Neve into 39 Hilldrop Crescent, where she was soon openly wearing Mrs Crippen's jewellery. Not long after, Crippen was breaking the news to friends and relatives that his wife had died of pneumonia in California. Most were convinced by the little doctor's story, but a friend of his late wife was unhappy enough to take her suspicions to the police, with the result that Chief Inspector Walter Dew of Scotland Yard paid Crippen a visit. Dew found nothing untoward at Hilldrop Crescent and seemed satisfied with the doctor's explanations, but the experience was enough to convince Crippen and his lover that it was too dangerous to remain in London. Crippen shaved off his moustache, dressed Ethel Le Neve as a boy, and the couple fled the country to Antwerp, where they boarded the SS *Montrose* bound for Quebec. News of Crippen's flight reached Walter Dew at Scotland Yard and he returned to Hilldrop Cresent. In the cellar, officers unearthed parts of a human body wrapped in a woman's underclothes and part of a pyjama jacket. Dr Bernard Spilsbury, on his first major case, found traces of hyoscine, a narcotic poison, in the remains as well as scar tissue that corresponded with an abdominal operation Mrs Crippen was known to have undergone. This, together with the fact that the underwear and pyjamas belonged to Cora Crippen and her husband respectively, made the identity of the body obvious, despite the fact that the head, limbs and entire skeleton were missing. All ports were notified and an arrest warrant was issued for the 'London cellar murderer' and his mistress. On board the SS *Montrose* just over a week later, the suspicions of the ship's Captain Kendall that the fugitives appeared to be on board his vessel famously resulted in the wireless telegraph being used for the first time in a murder investigation. Walter Dew was alerted and boarded a faster ship for Quebec. On 31 July, six months after the disappearance of Mrs Cora Crippen, her husband, who had written a suicide note during the voyage, was promptly arrested as he and his disguised mistress disembarked at Father Port. Dr Crippen's trial for murder began at the Old Bailey on 18 October and lasted four days. Found guilty he was hanged at Pentonville Prison at six o'clock on the morning of 23 November 1910; he was fifty years of age. Ethel Le Neve, who was tried separately as an accessory after the fact, was acquitted and later moved to Australia.

A traditional cyclical haunting is associated with the Crippen case, although it may in fact stem from a single incident that is said to have taken place in the immediate aftermath of the trial and execution. The Hilldrop Crescent that the Crippens knew has undergone extensive changes in the hundred years since that time and the Victorian villa where Cora Crippen lived and died, together with the houses either side, were demolished by post-war developers and subsequently replaced by the Margaret Bondfield House, a modern block of flats. Close by number 32 was a plot of wasteground and a pond which have now also disappeared. It was here that the troubled doctor was known to have spent time walking at night in the weeks leading up to the dramatic events of 1910, and it is this particular location that developed a reputation as the place where his ghost returned on the night of 31 January, the anniversary of the likely date of the murder. The haunting, which comprises a re-enactment of the disposal of the missing parts of Cora Crippen's body, is said to have been witnessed by an unnamed psychical researcher during the week following Crippen's execution. During the course of several night-time vigils, the first just before midnight on the day that Crippen walked to the gallows, a vague shadowy form accompanied by a sensation of intense coldness was seen moving across the wasteground adjoining Hilldrop Crescent. This developed into an apparition with staring eyes and a drooping moustache that resembled the cellar murderer and which carried a large, bulky paper parcel under one arm. The figure, surrounded by a palpable aura of sadness, moved into the shadows in the direction of the pond for a short time, after which it was seen returning, having seemingly left the parcel somewhere in the darkness. It passed on and was observed for a few more seconds before suddenly vanishing. With the name of the witness lost to history, the ghost of Hilldrop Crescent is sadly rather unsatisfactory, like the similar appearance of the apparition of William Corder at Polstead. The haunting was first brought to light many years after the alleged event by Peter Underwood in his *Haunted London* (1973); Underwood, a crime buff as well as a paranormalist, knew Fred Cavill, Crippen's jailor at Bow Street Police Court, who described him as 'a quiet, monkey-faced little man who never spoke except to ask the time, which he did twenty times a day'. Whether Crippen did dispose of the missing parts of his wife's body in this way will never be known. That nothing has come to light over the years, during which time extensive building work has transformed the original Hilldrop Crescent, makes it unlikely, but not impossible: in 2010, a human skull discovered in Richmond, Surrey by contractor's digging foundations for an extension to the house of the well-known naturalist Sir David Attenborough, was identified as being that of Mrs Julia Thomas, who was murdered in 1879 by her servant, thirty-year-old Irishwoman Kate Webster. Webster had disposed of parts of the body in the River Thames and it was alleged she had also sold jars of human dripping in a local public house, but her victim's head was never recovered. It was long believed she had kept it for a time in a black bag that she carried around with her.

If the haunting associated with such a noted case as that of Dr Crippen is unsatisfactory, then another slightly better, but nonetheless anecdotal, account is that of another poisoner, forty-three-year-old Ethel Lillie Major, who was tried at Lincoln Assizes in November 1934 for the murder of her husband. When Arthur Major, a lorry driver, married Ethel in 1918, he was unaware that his wife's two-year-old sister Auriel was in fact her illegitimate daughter, who was being raised by Ethel's parents as their own; Ethel had had an affair and fallen pregnant when she was twenty-four. In 1929, by which time the couple were living at Kirkby-on-Bain and had a child of their own, Arthur learnt through local gossip the truth about his real relationship to his young sister-in-law. When Ethel refused to name Auriel's father he became violent and she suffered for several years, until 1934, from his increasingly quarrelsome and abusive behaviour. The Majors' problems became well known in the local area, as did the fact that Arthur Major himself had taken a mistress, something that his wife found out about when love letters from the other woman started arriving at their house. On 22 May 1934, Arthur Major became violently ill with food poisoning after his wife made him a meal of corned beef; he died two days later. A local doctor certified the death as being due to 'status epilepticus' and Ethel Major began arranging the funeral, unaware that leftovers from her husband's fatal meal had been given to a neighbour's dog, which had also died. Soon the police received an anonymous letter that the animal's death was due to strychnine poisoning and the police intervened, halting the funeral in order to carry out a full post-mortem. When it was found that Arthur Major's body also contained strychnine his wife was questioned, and made the deadly mistake of implicating herself by denying any knowledge of strychnine as a cause of death before the subject was mentioned. The police found that her father, a gamekeeper, owned a box of the poison to which his daughter had access, and Mrs Major was arrested. The jury found her guilty of murder but their recommendation for clemency was ignored and a sentence of death was passed. When Ethel Major, a tragic figure, stepped onto the gallows on 19 December 1934, despite a last hour appeal by telegram to the King by the Lord Mayor, she became the last person to be executed at Hull Prison, as well as the first woman that the well-known executioner Albert Pierrepoint had the experience of hanging – on this occasion he was assisting his uncle, Thomas Pierrepoint.

Perhaps some aspect of the unhappiness of Mrs Major's last years, as well as the final days she spent in the condemned cell, have resulted in her ghost being seen in Hull Prison on a number of occasions in the years following her execution. The haunting is well known and despite there being no documented evidence, it was confirmed to me by Rob Nicholson, the prison historian at HMP Hull, that various prisoners have claimed to have seen Ethel Major in their cell at various times and had subsequently requested a transfer to another part of the prison. As well as prison inmates, a former Prison Officer at one time reported sick after allegedly seeing her apparition.

Another woman, also a poisoner, who is said to haunt the prison where she was hanged is the former Blackpool housekeeper Louisa May Merrifield, who was executed at Manchester's Strangeways Prison in 1953 for the murder of her elderly employer, seventy-nine-year-old Sarah Ann Ricketts, an eccentric widow whose two previous husbands had both gassed themselves to death. Louisa, in her mid-forties, was a scheming woman of dubious character. Recently married to her third husband, Alfred Merrifield, who was nearly thirty years her senior, she had already served a prison sentence for ration book fraud when, on 12 March 1953, the couple were taken on by Mrs Ricketts as live-in housekeepers and companions at her bungalow in Devonshire Road, Blackpool. A month later, Mrs Merrifield met a friend, a Mrs Brewer, and told her that they had moved in with an old lady who had since died and left them her property, worth £3,000. Sarah Ricketts had indeed altered her will in the Merrifields' favour, but at that particular point in time she was very much alive. She obliged the couple by passing away three days later, on 14 April. Louisa attempted to get an undertaker to organise an immediate cremation but she was unsuccessful as Mrs Brewer had seen the notice – and the date – of Mrs Ricketts' death in a local newspaper and, remembering the housekeeper's boastful conversation, contacted the police. A post-mortem showed that the old lady had died from poisoning by yellow phosphorous, a substance contained in a type of rat poison that Louisa Merrifield was known to have recently purchased. The couple were arrested and appeared at the Manchester Assizes in July 1953 charged with murder. Despite the police being unable to find traces of poison at Mrs Rickett's bungalow, as well as the evidence of one of the defence's expert witnesses, Professor (formerly Dr) James Webster, who carried out the post-mortem on the body of Mona

Tinsley in 1937, that Mrs Ricketts had died from natural causes, Louisa was found guilty. The jury was, however, unable to reach a verdict concerning her husband and the judge ordered a retrial at the next session of Assizes. When the Attorney-General issued a fiat of *nolle prosequi* (unwilling to prosecute) he was released to inherit his half-share in Mrs Ricketts' bungalow. He died in 1962 aged eighty, while his wife was hanged by Albert Pierrepoint and Robert 'Jock' Stewart on 18 September 1953.

Louisa Merrifield was one of only two women to be executed at Strangeways Prison during the twentieth century; the other, forty-three-year-old Margaret Allen, went to her death four years before, in January 1949. No doubt the notoriety that the 'Blackpool Poisoner' obtained during her eleven-day trial has meant that the female apparition alleged to have been seen in the prison on occasions over the years has been identified as her rather than that of her predecessor to the gallows, Mrs Allen. Reports of a short woman dressed in black walking on the landing near to the former condemned cell (later used as part of the clinic attached to the prison hospital) apparently reached a peak during the early 1980s, and in 1981 she was reportedly seen by two people – a prisoner and a hospital officer – collectively, accompanied by a sudden drop in temperature. Today the official line from HMP Manchester, given to me in a letter from the Governor in response to an enquiry made during the course of researching for this book, is that no hauntings are currently known from the prison, which would also rule out the other ghost associated with Strangeways, that of the apparition of a man carrying a briefcase and thought to be former hangman John Ellis, a troubled man who committed suicide in 1932 after carrying out several executions at Manchester in the preceding two decades.

The tragedy of humankind's ceaseless violence towards itself is apparent in the many cases that have formed the subject matter of this book, but our final case is perhaps the most tragic of all: that of the young delinquent Derek Bentley, hanged in January 1953 for his part in the shooting of a London policeman, Sidney Miles, at a warehouse in Croydon on 2 November the previous year. Bentley, aged nineteen and described as being 'illiterate and educationally sub-normal', had accompanied another teenage youth, sixteen-year-old Christopher Craig, who modelled himself on American gangster figures like Al Capone and John Dillinger and hated the police; three days before their arrest at Croydon, Craig's brother, twenty-six-year-old Niven Craig, an armed robber, had been given a sentence of imprisonment at the Old Bailey. Craig and Bentley's attempted robbery went wrong when they were seen climbing over the factory gates and the police were called. During a scuffle, Derek Bentley was arrested but Craig climbed onto the roof of the building, where he fired several shots, one of which hit PC Miles in the head, killing him instantly. The teenagers were tried at the Old Bailey in December 1952. Bentley performed poorly in the witness box and together with his companion was found guilty of murder, despite it being Craig who had fired the fatal shot. The real impetus behind Bentley's notorious exclamation 'Let him have it, Chris', that he shouted while under arrest by officers and which featured prominently in the trial, has become one of the most debated sentences in British crime. Due to his age, Christopher Craig was imprisoned while Bentley was sentenced to death, although the jury gave a recommendation for clemency. This was dismissed by the Court of Appeal and Bentley, amidst much public protest, kept a deadly appointment with Albert Pierrepoint and Harry Allen at Wandsworth Prison on 28 January 1953. Craig served ten years' imprisonment and was released in 1963.

In the years that followed their son's death, Bentley's family lead a persistent campaign to clear his name. It was not until 1993 that Derek Bentley received a posthumous Royal Pardon for the death sentence passed forty years before; the Court of Appeal finally quashed his murder conviction in 1998. Before then his parents were reported to have left his bedroom at their house in Colliers Wood untouched and exactly as it was during the time that Bentley lived there. It was also reported that the same room was haunted regularly by his presence: bedclothes were disturbed, the family heard footsteps, and his dog seemed to acknowledge his former owner, howling on occasion as if announcing his arrival. Following the death of Bentley's father William in 1974, it was alleged that their parish priest had in one instance fallen into a mediumistic trance and had channelled his dead son and spoken in his voice.

At the beginning of this book, the analogy between criminal detective work and scientific psychical research – both exact and demanding disciplines – was highlighted, and the cases in this book have given some indication of the continuing British fascination with eerie stories of ghosts and gallows. A growing increase in the credibility of psychic detection and the continuing involvement of mediums in police work, particularly cases of murder, may result at some future time in a solution to more than individual crimes, but also to the mysteries of the paranormal world that continue to intrigue and fascinate us all. At that point, it will be possible to look at the cases we have discussed here in an entirely different light, as they will form a body of compelling evidence for the reality of an unseen world, as well as hidden faculties of man, that cannot be summarily dismissed out of hand. In Britain the gallows may have gone, but the ghosts, it seems, will always be with us . . .

BIBLIOGRAPHY AND FURTHER READING

Ansari, Hasan Moiz, *Islam and the Paranormal* (iUniverse, Lincoln, NE, 2006)

Archer, Fred, *Ghost Detectives: Crime and the Psychic World* (W.H. Allen, London, 1970)

Baker, Phil, *The Devil is a Gentleman: The Life & Times of Dennis Wheatley* (Dedalus Ltd, Sawtry, 2009)

Barbanell, Maurice, *This is Spiritualism* (Herbert Jenkins, London, 1959)

Begg, Paul, *Jack the Ripper: The Definitive History* (Pearson Education Ltd, Harlow, 2005)

Bilton, Michael, *Wicked Beyond Belief* (Harper Collins, London, 2003)

Burn, Gordon, *'. . . somebody's husband, somebody's son': The Story of Peter Sutcliffe* (Heinemann, London, 1984)

Carlin, Francis, *Reminiscences of an Ex-Detective* (Hutchinson & Co., London, 1927)

Cohen, David, *Price and his Spirit Child 'Rosalie'* (Regency Press, London, 1965)

Connell, Nicholas & Stratton, Ruth, *Hertfordshire Murders* (Sutton Publishing, Stroud, 2003)

Dahl, Ludwig, *We Are Here: Psychic Experiences* (Rider & Co., London, 1931)

Duke, Winifred (Ed.), *The Trials of Frederick Nodder – The Mona Tinsley Case* (William Hodge & Co. Ltd, London, 1950)

Eddleston, John J., *Jack the Ripper: An Encyclopaedia* (Metro Publishing, London, 2002)

Evans, Stewart & Skinner, Keith, *Jack the Ripper: Letters From Hell* (Sutton Publishing, Gloucestershire, 2001)

Fielding, Steve, *The Executioner's Bible* (John Blake, London, 2008)

Fletcher, Tony, *Memories of Murder: The Great Cases of a Fingerprint Expert* (Weidenfeld & Nicholson, London, 1986)

Fortune, Dion, *Psychic Self-Defence: A Study in Occult Pathology and Criminality* (Rider & Co., London, 1930)

Gaute, J.H.H. & Odell, Robin, *The Murderers' Who's Who* (George G. Harrap & Co. Ltd, London, 1979)

Gaute, J.H.H. & Odell, Robin, *Murder Whereabouts* (Harrap Ltd, London, 1986)

Gibbs, Dorothy & Maltby, Herbert, *The True Story of Maria Marten* (East Anglian Magazine, Ipswich, 1949)

Goodman, Jonathan (Ed.), *The Supernatural Murders: Classic True-Crime Stories* (BCA, London, 1992)

Haeri, Shaykh Fadhlalla, *The Elements of Islam* (Element Books Ltd, Shaftesbury, Dorset, 1993)
Haining, Peter, *Maria Marten – The Murder in the Red Barn* (Richard Castell Publishing Ltd, Plymouth, 1992)
Hallam, Jack, *The Ghosts' Who's Who* (David & Charles, Newton Abbot, 1977)
Harris, Melvin, *Jack the Ripper: The Bloody Truth* (Columbus Books, London, 1987)
Holohan, Christine & McHugh, Vera, *A Voice from the Grave: The Unseen Witness in the Jacqui Poole Murder Case* (Maverick House, Dunshaughlin, 2006)
Jackson, Robert, *Francis Camps: Famous Case Histories of the Most Celebrated Pathologist of our Time* (Hart-Davis MacGibbon Ltd, London, 1975)
Jones, Nella & Davenport, Shirley, *Ghost of a Chance: The Life Story of a Psychic Detective* (Pan Books Ltd, London, 1982)
Jones, Nella & Bruce, Mandy, *Nella: A Psychic Eye* (Ebury Press, London, 1992)
Lane, Brian, *The Encyclopedia of Occult and Supernatural Murder* (Headline Book Publishing, London, 1995)
Lindley, Charles, *Lord Halifax's Ghost Book* (Geoffrey Bles Ltd, London, 1936)
Lucas, Norman, *The Child Killers* (Arthur Barker Ltd, London, 1970)
McCormick, Donald, *The Red Barn Mystery: Some New Evidence on an Old Murder* (John Long, London, 1967)
Newton, Toyne, *The Demonic Connection* (Blandford Press, Poole, 1987)
Pollack, Jack Harrison, *The Amazing Story of Croiset the Clairvoyant* (W.H. Allen, London, 1965)
Price, Harry, *Fifty Years of Psychical Research* (Longmans, Green & Co. Ltd, London, 1939)
Roberts, Estelle, *Forty Years a Medium* (Herbert Jenkins, London, 1959)
Rogo, D. Scott, *The Haunted House Handbook* (Tempo Books, New York, 1978)
Roughead, William, *Twelve Scots Trials* (William Green & Sons, Edinburgh, 1913)
Scott, Sir Walter, *Letters on Demonology and Witchcraft* (J. Murray, London, 1830)
Stemman, Roy, *Spirit Communication* (Piatkus Books Ltd, London, 2005)
Symonds, John, *The Great Beast* (Rider & Co., London, 1951)
Tabori, Cornelius, *My Occult Diary* (Rider & Co., London, 1951)
Underwood, Peter, *Haunted London* (George G. Harrap & Co. Ltd, London, 1973)
Ibid., *The Ghost Hunters: Who They Are & What They Do* (Robert Hale Ltd, London, 1985)
Wheatley, Dennis, *The Time Has Come . . . The Memoirs of Dennis Wheatley: Officer and Temporary Gentleman 1914-1919* (Hutchinson, London, 1978)
Ibid., *The Time Has Come . . . The Memoirs of Dennis Wheatley: Drink and Ink 1919-1977* (Hutchinson, London, 1979)
Wilson, Colin & Pitman, Patricia, *Encyclopaedia of Murder* (Arthur Barker Ltd, London, 1961)
Wilson, Colin & Seaman, Donald, *Encyclopaedia of Modern Murder* (Arthur Barker Ltd, London, 1983)
Wilson, Colin, *The Psychic Detectives* (Pan Books, London, 1984)
Ibid., *A Criminal History of Mankind* (Granada Publishing, London, 1985)
Ibid., *The Mammoth Book of Murder* (Robinson, London, 2000)
Wilson, David, *A History of British Serial Killing* (Sphere, London, 2009)
Wilson, Ian, *The After Death Experience* (Sidgwick & Jackson, London, 1987)
Wilson, Richard, *Scotland's Unsolved Mysteries of the Twentieth Century* (Robert Hale, London, 1995)

INDEX OF NAMES

INDEX OF PHENOMENA

Levitations & Psychic Forces

Mediumship & Spiritualism

Poltergeists

Psychic Detection

Prophetic Dreams

About the Author

PAUL ADAMS was born in Epsom, Surrey in 1966 and has been interested in the paranormal since the mid-1970s. Employed as a draughtsman in the UK construction industry for nearly thirty years, he has worked in three haunted buildings but has yet to see a true ghost. As well as the history of psychical research, his main interests at present are in materialisation mediumship, and the physical phenomena of Spiritualism. He has contributed articles to several specialist paranormal periodicals and acted as editor and publisher for *Two Haunted Counties* (2010), the memoirs of Luton ghost-hunter Tony Broughall. He is also co-author of *The Borley Rectory Companion* (2009) and *Shadows in the Nave* (2011) along with Peter Underwood and Eddie Brazil, and has recently completed *Haunted Luton*, where he has lived since 2006. Paul is also an amateur mycologist and viola player.